Longman
Advanced
English

Coursebook

Roy Kingsbury and Guy Wellman

Longman Group UK Limited
Longman House, Burnt Mill, Harlow,
Essex CM20 2JE, England
and Associated Companies throughout
the world.

First published 1986
Eleventh impression 1991

ISBN 0-582-74355-9

Set in Univers 689 9/11pt

Produced by Longman Singapore Publishers Pte Ltd
Printed in Singapore

Authors' acknowledgements

We would like to express our sincere thanks to
– members of staff at the B.E.E.T. Language Centre,
  Bournemouth, for trialling the materials, and to Pat Hughes
  and Paul Newman for trialling and reporting on the materials.
– all those agreed to have their voices and opinions
  recorded on tape: Roger Scott, Alan Tankard, Terry, Anna
  Karsay, Yvonne Weston, Sally Wellman and Jill Kingsbury.
– Heather Daldry, Eddie Edmundson, Sidney Phipps and
  others who, through their constructive criticism, helped us
  constantly to question and improve what we were writing.
– our publisher, Howard Middle, for his encouragement and
  patience throughout.

Roy Kingsbury and Guy Wellman, Dorset, 1985

Introduction to the student

Who *Longman Advanced English* is for

The course is designed as a general advanced English course, and more specifically a course to 'bridge that gap' between the two Cambridge examinations – the First Certificate and Proficiency. Since you do not have to worry about training for exam skills and techniques at this stage, the course allows you to concentrate on developing all-round ability in the language.

The broad aims of *Longman Advanced English*

The most important aim of this course is to help you expand or broaden your knowledge of and proficiency in general English. Within this general aim, therefore, and through a variety of topics of general adult interest, the course provides:

- practice and development of the four language skills equally, including listening to and reading authentic English
- revision, consolidation and extension of major structural or grammatical areas of English
- constant and progressive vocabulary building
- practice in 'functioning' in English (in speech and writing) through a wide range of situations
- help in the acquisition of an appreciation of style, register and appropriateness for your own (active) use and for (passive) recognition of style and register in writers' and speakers' choice of language
- progressive development of summary and extended writing skills.

The organisation and content of the course

The course contains 20 Units preceded by what we have called an Introductory Unit (see below). Following on from *Longman First Certificate*, this course covers ten major structural areas in English. They are dealt with in the following Units:

Units 1 and 11:   tenses (Present, Present Perfect and Future)
Units 2 and 12:   gerund, infinitive and participle constructions
Units 3 and 13:   mass and unit
Units 4 and 14:   adjectives and adverbs
Units 5 and 15:   relative (and other) clauses
Units 6 and 16:   tenses (Past and Past Perfect)
Units 7 and 17:   modal verbs and concepts
Units 8 and 18:   passive constructions
Units 9 and 19:   reported speech
Units 10 and 20: conditional constructions

The form and content of a Unit

While all Units differ in some respects, most of them follow a form which you will become familiar with as the course progresses. Instead of describing a typical Unit here, we have designed the Introductory Unit specifically to help you get used to the material while already beginning to learn more English.

A few words of advice

This course is designed to help you broaden your English, to use the language confidently and accurately, to build up your vocabulary and to develop a sense of appropriacy. To do this, you must participate fully in lessons, and particularly in pair, group and discussion work. And outside the class, you should not only do homework set, but also read and listen to as much English as you can.

Contents

Contents

Introductory Unit

English:varieties and register

To the student

The aim of this Introductory Unit is to help you become familiar with the format of the other Units in this course. While you will learn some English from the Unit, you will be involved in some of the activities that you will be expected to take part in throughout the course.

Most Units of the course begin with a 'warm-up' phase (**A1**). This is designed to start you thinking and talking about the topic of the Unit.

Then follows (usually **A2**) a 'presentation' text which introduces the subject or topic and which generally contains examples of the language to be practised.

Some Units, like this one, begin with a reading text, some with a listening text. Sometimes you will read or listen on your own, sometimes in pairs or small groups.

A1 Discuss these questions in small groups:
How long have you been learning English? What courses have you done? What textbooks have you used? Did you enjoy learning from them? Why?/Why not?
Have you taken any exams in English? If so, which and when?
What are some of the main differences between English and your own language?

A2 Read this passage to find answers to these questions:
1 Why is the English language, in a sense, many languages?
2 What does the term 'common core' mean when applied to a language?
3 In what ways are written and spoken English different?
4 What is 'formal language' and what is 'informal language'?

To use a language properly, we of course have to know the grammatical structures of the language and their meanings. But we also have to know what forms of language are appropriate for given situations . . . The English language is, in a sense, not a single language, but many languages, each of which belongs to a particular geographical area or to a particular kind of situation. The English used in the United States is somewhat different from the English used in Great Britain; the English used in formal written communications is in some ways different from the English used in informal conversation . . .
Luckily for the learner, many of the features of English are found in all, or nearly all varieties. We say that general features of this kind belong to the 'common core' of the language. Take, for instance, the three words *children, offspring* and *kids. Children* is a 'common core' term; *offspring* is rather formal (and used of animals as well as human beings); *kids* is informal and familiar. It is safest, when in doubt, to use the 'common core' term; thus *children* is the word you would want to use most often. But part of 'knowing English' is knowing in what circumstances it would be possible to use *offspring* or *kids* instead of *children.* Let us take another illustration, this time from grammar:

    Feeling tired, John went to bed early.   (1)
    John went to bed early because he felt tired. (2)
    John felt tired, so he went to bed early.   (3)

Sentence (2) is a 'common core' construction. It could (for example) be used in both speech and writing. (1) is rather formal in construction, typical of written exposition; (3) is informal, and is likely to occur in a relaxed conversation.

Written and spoken English

The English of speech tends to be different from the English of writing in some fairly obvious ways. For example, in writing we usually have time to plan our message, to think about it carefully while writing, and to revise it afterwards if necessary. In speech (unless it is, say, a lecture prepared in advance), we have no time to do this, but must shape our message as we go . . . Often we use in speech words and phrases like *well, you see,* and *kind of* which add little information, but tell us something of the speaker's attitude to his audience and to what he is saying. We also often hesitate, or fill in gaps with 'hesitation fillers' like *er* and *um* while we think of what next to say. We may fail to complete a sentence, or lose track of our sentence and mix up one grammatical construction with another. All these features do not normally occur in writing.

Formal and informal English

Formal language is the type of language we use publicly for some serious purpose, for example, in official reports, business letters and regulations. Formal English is nearly always written. Exceptionally it is used in speech, for example in public speeches.

Informal language (i.e. colloquial language) is the language of private conversation, of personal letters, etc. It is the first type of language that a native-speaking child becomes familiar with.

Because it is generally easier to understand than formal English, it is often used nowadays in public communication of a popular kind: for example, advertisements and popular newspapers mainly employ a colloquial or informal style.

To the student

Whatever form the 'presentation' text may take (reading or listening), it will always be accompanied by exercises of various kinds. The exercises here, which include group discussion and reporting back to the rest of the class (**A4**), are typical of exercises you will be engaged in.

A3 From what you have read in the text, which of the following would probably be written and which spoken, which are informal in register and which formal? Tick the columns.

		written	spoken	informal	formal
1	Well, you see, the kids are um outside.				
2	The female tends to return to her offspring at regular hourly intervals.				
3	When we got home, we went to bed straightaway.				
4	Then, you know, I er kind of apologised.				
5	What I wish to tell you is that I shall unfortunately have to resign.				

A4 In groups of four, discuss the following for about five minutes each. Write brief notes during your discussions and appoint a spokesperson to report to the rest of the class.

1 There are probably places or situations in which you might find it difficult to understand people who speak your own language. Tell each other about some of the places and situations, and say what the problems are.

2 If an English speaker wanted to come to your country to learn your language, where would you recommend him or her to go, and why?

To the student

This Communicative Grammar section nearly always follows the presentation (reading or listening) text and exercises. It will concentrate on aspects of a particular grammatical area of English, and will give you practice in the language needed to communicate in given situations.

The section in this Introductory Unit takes two grammatical points from the presentation text on pages 6–7 in order to demonstrate some of the kinds of exercises and activities you will be engaged in.

B Communicative grammar

B1 Adverbs of frequency with Present Simple to express how often or rarely someone does something

1 With the Present Simple tense, adverbs of frequency (*often, usually, generally, mainly, (nearly) always*, etc.) usually precede the main verb. Here are examples from the text on pages 6–7:

> . . . in writing we **usually** have time to plan . . .
> We also **often** hesitate, or fill in gaps . . .
> All these features do not **normally** occur in writing.
> . . . popular newspapers **mainly** employ . . .

2 Adverbs of frequency generally follow the verb *be*, as in these examples from the text on pages 6–7:

> Formal English is **nearly always** written.
> . . . it is **generally** easier to understand . . .
> . . . it is **often** used nowadays . . .

However, they can precede the verb *be* when expressing emphatic agreement or contradiction, for example:

> You're right. It **generally** *is* easier to understand.
> No, he **never** *is* on time.
> Yes, they **nearly always** *are* right.

3 The adverbs *often, sometimes, occasionally* and *usually* can begin a sentence for the sake of emphasis or to make a contrast with a previous or following statement:

> **Often** we use in speech words and phrases like . . .

Now add the adverb in italics to these sentences. If you think the adverb can appear in one of two or three positions, explain why.

a He finishes a sentence. (*never*)
b We are first in class. (*always*)
c He writes in a very formal style. (*usually*)
d Foreigners use the wrong word in a particular situation. (*often*)
e I meet people from another part of the country whom I can't understand at all. (*occasionally*)

B2 Deleted relative pronoun *which*

A clause like *The English used in the United States* . . . means 'The English *which is* used in the United States . . .'. The relative pronoun *which* + auxiliary verb *be* has been deleted. Deletion is a common feature of English and different examples of it will often occur in this course. Look at these examples, and then do the exercise:

> The English (which is) used in the United States is somewhat different from the English (which is) used in Great Britain.
> The Spanish (which is) spoken in Chile is in some ways different from the Spanish (which is) spoken in Spain.

Now make similar statements about these:

1 Portuguese in Brazil and Portugal.
2 German in North Germany, Austria and Switzerland.
3 French in Quebec (Canada) and France.
4 Arabic in Libya and Saudi Arabia.

Finally discuss or tell each other about some of the differences a) between your own language spoken in the capital and in other regions of the country, or b) between your own language spoken in your own country and your own language spoken in another country.

C Vocabulary

To the student

In the Vocabulary section, which occurs in most Units, you will study a specific area of vocabulary. It might concentrate on nouns formed from phrasal verbs (e.g. a breakdown – to break down), a group of words similar in meaning (e.g. leave, give up, quit, retire, vacate), a word family (e.g. to tolerate, tolerant, tolerance, intolerant, intolerable, etc.), and so on. Whatever the area of vocabulary under study, you will find it necessary from now on to use an English-English dictionary.

In this particular section we concentrate on a further aspect of register as seen in vocabulary.

Read this short passage, then study the words below and do the exercise.

> *Polite and familiar language*
> Our language tends to be more polite when we are talking to a person we do not know well, or a person senior to ourselves in terms of age or social position.
> The opposite of 'polite' (in this context) is 'familiar'. When we know someone well or intimately, we tend to drop polite forms of language. For example, instead of using the polite form *Mr Brown*, we use a first name (*Peter*) or a short name (*Pete*) or even a nickname (*Shortie*).

formal; polite; technical, literary, etc.; impersonal; (written)	'common core' (written and spoken)	informal; familiar; colloquial; personal; sometimes slang*; (spoken)
offspring	children	kids, brats*
gentlemen	men	guys, chaps, blokes
impecunious	short of money	broke
convenience	toilet	lavatory, loo*

Rephrase these sentences so that they would be acceptable to anyone in almost any situation (i.e. 'common core'):

1 Could you tell me where the loo is, please?
2 Those two blokes used to work in our office.
3 I'm broke – at least until I get my next pay.
4 How are your three brats today, Mrs Jones?
5 I think you should pen a card to John's offspring.

Introductory Unit

D   Listening

You are going to hear part of a talk about varieties of English and register. It deals with an aspect of the subject not mentioned so far in this Unit.

D1   Listen once and then answer this one question:
Which aspect of English did the speaker talk about?

D2   In pairs, listen again more closely and make notes.

Student A listens for answers to these questions:
1   What is politeness closely tied to (in language)?
2   Why do foreigners sometimes offend native English speakers?
3   What extreme case did the speaker quote of a person being tactful?
4   How can the request 'Post this letter for me on your way home, will you?' be made more tactful and tentative?

Student B listens for answers to these questions:
1   Why do we tend to use a lot of tactful language in British English?
2   What examples did the speaker give of 'euphemism'?
3   Why do we tend to make requests and so on tentatively?
4   Why should we learn to use tactful, tentative forms of English?

Now ask each other the questions.

D3   Discuss and list (or tell other students about) euphemistic forms or words that you use in your native language.

E   Register and socialising: interpreting or explaining written public notices in polite but informal speech

One distinct variety or register of English which you will often see and have to understand is the English used in written public notices, warnings, etc. You may well have to explain such notices, so look what happens to the English. Then, in pairs, explain the others.

A: What does that notice/sign mean? It says 'No Parking'.
B: That? Oh, that (simply) means you can't park your car there.

F Functions

F1 Making requests

Politeness or familiarity is shown in English through the vocabulary we use (e.g. *gentlemen* or *blokes*), but it is also shown in the structure we choose. Study ways of making a request, and then do the exercise:

familiar	Shut the door,	will you? / would you?
polite	Will you / Would you	please shut the door?
more polite	I wonder if you would mind shutting the door?	

How would you ask these people to do these things?
1 Ask your English boss to come to your office.
2 Ask a good friend to post some letters for you.
3 Ask a stranger to pass you a menu in a restaurant.
4 Ask a very good friend to get you a newspaper in town.
5 Ask your teacher to explain something to you again.

F2 Introducing examples as illustrations

When explaining something in speech or in writing we often use an illustration or an example. Look at the ways we do this, and then do the exercise:

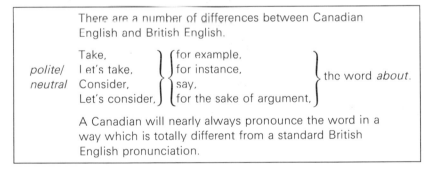

There are a number of differences between Canadian English and British English.

polite/ neutral	Take, / Let's take, / Consider, / Let's consider,	for example, / for instance, / say, / for the sake of argument,	the word *about*.

A Canadian will nearly always pronounce the word in a way which is totally different from a standard British English pronunciation.

Note that *e.g.* is found in writing and is usually read as 'for example'. Note, too, that the phrase 'Let me give you a for-instance' is used in informal British English speech.

Now make statements of opinion about each of the following subjects and give an example with each, e.g.:

I think television is getting better. Take, for instance, that new programme on Monday nights . . .

1 The standard of newspaper reporting nowadays   2 New pop music   3 Trade unions   4 New films   5 The present world economic situation

Introductory Unit

<table>
</table>

To the student

Each Unit ends with exercises for homework. These will include both reading and writing as well as an exercise specifically designed to help you practise the skills needed in writing summaries and compositions.

G Exercises for homework

G1 Look at this picture and then choose which you think the young man is saying – A, B, C or D.

A Hey, guv! How about some more money then?

B Sir, I would appreciate it immensely if you could bring yourself to consider granting me a higher remuneration at some unspecified time in the future.

C Mr Smith, I'd like to ask you if I could possibly have a wage rise.

D Since the other gentlemen in the establishment have received an increase in wages, I wonder if I could have one, too.

Write brief reasons for your choice of the most appropriate (A, B, C or D), and why you think the other statements or questions would be inappropriate here.

G2 Finish each of the following sentences in such a way that it means the same as the sentence printed before it.

1 There is a tendency for them to grow quite quickly.
They ....

2 Would you please repeat what you said?
Would you mind ....

3 All the articles sold in the auction were very good.
The articles which ....

4 Let's stay behind and get the job finished.
I suggest ....

5 Why don't we, for instance, look at a camping holiday?
Let's ....

G3 Read this passage and then answer the two multiple-choice questions:

It is apparent that no member of a speech community can say anything he wants to, in any form he cares to use, on any occasion, even though he may be fluent in the sound system and the grammar of the particular language he is speaking. And no visitor to a foreign speech community – regardless of the amount of instruction he has received in the grammar of its language – is ever prepared for the countless subtleties he will find in the way the language is used by its native speakers. Even a child born into that foreign speech community, and who thereby acquires his native tongue effortlessly, nevertheless still has not learned the appropriate use of his language in all situations. By the age of five, the child can utter a wide repertory of grammatical sentences, but he is still learning which of these sentences to use at a given time. Only as he matures within his speech community does he acquire the ability to make statements appropriate for any situation and to judge the appropriateness of statements made by others.

1 According to the writer, when you know the grammar of a language perfectly,
  A you will sound like a native speaker.
  B you still have a lot to learn.
  C you can be subtle in the language.
  D you can speak it in any situation.

2 The most difficult thing for a child to acquire in his native language is
  A the sound system.
  B the use of vocabulary.
  C the grammatical system.
  D the rules of use.

G4 Write, as part of a letter to an English-speaking friend, a brief description of some of the main varieties of your own native language, giving examples (with translations and/or explanations in English) wherever you can. Remember that you should use 'common core' or polite informal language, since you are writing to a friend; you should certainly not use very formal language. (You should aim to write 150–200 words.)

Here is a suggested plan with some ideas in the form of questions. Answering these questions will help you write part of the letter.

Introduction **1** What is your (first) native language?
  2 Where is that language spoken? i.e. in which parts of the world, in which countries, or in which areas of the continent in which you live?

Paragraph 2 **3** What are some of the main differences a foreign learner might notice between varieties of your language spoken in different geographical (national or regional) areas?
  4 Are such differences important for any reason?

Paragraph 3 **5** What differences might a foreign learner notice between the way your language is written and spoken, or the way it is spoken by different social groups?

Finally, don't forget to try to use language you have practised in this Unit.

Unit 1

Oh, to see ourselves as others see us!

A1   Read this situation and discuss the questions.

Four strangers, an Englishman, a Japanese, an American and a Greek, all of whom speak English, have to spend a four-hour train journey in the same railway compartment.
Who do you think would start speaking first? Why?
Who do you think would give the most/the least information about himself? Why?
What do you think each would do if a young lady came into the compartment with two large heavy suitcases?
How do you think each would react if they found they could not open the door of the compartment at the end of the journey?

A2   You have probably been describing national stereotypes through your answers. We all do it.
The following passage is adapted from *Fodor's Guide to Great Britain 1983* and is therefore a foreigner's view of Britain and the British.
Read these questions and then study the passage to find answers to them. You might work in pairs to compare and discuss your answers.

1   Which words does the writer use to describe 'the typical Englishman'? Do you agree with them? Why?/Why not?

2   According to the writer, what is the Englishman's attitude towards **a** foreigners, and **b** his immediate neighbours (the Scots and the Welsh)?

3   According to the writer, what, on first impressions, are the following like: the typical Englishman, the typical Welshman, the typical Scot?

4   What do the following people have in common: a Briton working abroad, a Briton living in Britain, and many foreign residents in Britain?

5   How is the typical Briton described?

First impressions
'You were born an Englishman,' wrote a 19th-century Empire-builder, 'and therefore you have been awarded first prize in the lottery of life.' No amount of dissatisfaction with the state of the weather, the national football team or the demonstrations of the jobless will shake the natives' belief in the truth of that statement.

The typical Englishman is too polite and too inarticulate to say so. But he can't avoid a slightly patronising attitude to foreigners, which foreigners sometimes find hard to accept. He's not aware of it himself. He's not aware that he looks down on his immediate neighbours. He likes the Scots and the Welsh – they're the sort of people he would like to be if he couldn't be English. He even pays them the compliment of *calling* them English, and is puzzled to find they resent it.

First-time visitors meet a number of British stereotypes – tongue-tied Englishmen, unreliable Welshmen, bad-tempered Scots. After a while these cartoon characters disappear and the truth emerges that people all over the world are pretty much alike when you get to know them.

The British character
Britons working abroad long for the day when they can retire home and Britons at home rarely consider retirement abroad. Yet you meet many foreign residents in Britain who are determined to extend their tours of duty or settle down for good somewhere in Britain. If the natives are not all that sociable, if since the early seventies the economic prospects have been getting steadily worse, and if some deprived inner-city areas have become subject to a kind of violence unknown in Britain before . . ., what's the attraction?

The attraction has something to do with Britain's stable society, her insular position and freedom from foreign invasions down the ages. 'You're so relaxed, you're really civilised,' is the comment of foreign residents in Britain; to which they add something about the 'quality of life' and 'wonderful policemen'. These days the police are coming in for criticism, but the foreign visitor still finds them wonderfully helpful and courteous.

The laws and customs are respected by the vast majority of people. There is not the violent commitment to political, religious or social ideas that you sometimes find in other lands; though football, the winter game, can rouse passions. On the whole, the typical Briton is patient and docile, and polite to strangers. He hates to make a fuss and would rather live with his problem and grumble about it than look for a dramatic solution to it.

A3 Discussion

1 First, write some brief notes about your own national character as you think foreigners see you. For example, do foreigners regard you as a nation as excitable? reserved? hard-working? polite? noisy? talkative? patient? helpful, etc.? Then, in small groups, describe to each other this 'foreign' view of your nation and say why you agree or disagree with it.

2 How far do factors like climate, the geography of a country, its history, religion(s), system of government, distribution of wealth, etc. affect national character? Give examples.

3 And now about YOU personally! How do you think other people describe you? Write down adjectives which you think the following people use (or might use) to describe you: other members of your family, your best friend, your teacher or employer, your neighbours, school or college friends or workmates or colleagues. Are any or all of them right in their assessment of your character?

1

B Communicative grammar

B1 Expressing permanent and temporary habits and trends
(with *does/do* or *is/are doing*)

1 You will remember that we use the Present Simple to express
permanent habits and routines e.g. *He gets up at 6 every
morning*, and that we use the Present Continuous to say what is
happening at this moment e.g. *He's getting up (right now)*.
You also know that we use the two to express future ideas, the
Present Simple for a 'timetable' future e.g. *The train leaves at six
tomorrow*, and the Present Continuous to express a future
arrangement e.g. *We are staying home tomorrow evening*.

2 But now look at these sentences where the speaker is expressing

a) permanent known habits   b) activities becoming habits

*A lot of people still **drive** big cars, but more people **are buying** small cars (nowadays).*
*Most people still **eat** meat (generally), but quite a lot **are becoming** vegetarians (these days).*
*I **live** in London (most of the time), but I'**m living** in Brighton (for this summer).*

Now practise this exchange with the prompts, for example:
engaged before married/married without engaged first
A: Most people get engaged before they get married, don't they?
B: Well, I don't know. I think a lot of people are getting married
nowadays without getting engaged first.

a   retire at 65 / retire earlier
b   spend holidays at home / go abroad
c   have a reasonable standard of living / find it
more difficult to make ends meet

d   respect the police / begin to criticise them
e   pay cash for things / use credit cards
f   young people – pop music / go back to
classical music

3 Now listen to a conversation between two people who meet on
holiday. Listen carefully, noting the verb forms they use.
Listen again and make brief notes on where each lives, what he/
she is doing now, etc. Then in pairs, re-enact the conversation as
far as you can from the notes you have made.

B2 Expressing the regularity of past-present habits (with
has/have been doing)

1 You will know that the Present Perfect Simple can be used to
express completed 'no time' or recent past actions e.g. *I have had
some bad news. / We have just come back from France. / She
has already done the job. / I've written three reports today.*
And you also know that the Present Perfect Continuous is used
to describe actions which began in the past and which are still
going on now e.g. *I've been sitting here for half an hour. / She's
been watching television since 6 o'clock.*

2 But now look at these sentences where the speaker is describing
a routine or habit which is not literally as continuous as 'sitting'
or 'watching', but which uses the continuous form to reinforce
the regularity or continuity of the action:
*I'**ve been visiting** France regularly since I was twelve years old.*
(Contrast with: *I'**ve visited** France 50 times since I was twelve.*)
*He'**s been going** on climbing expeditions for years.*
*She'**s been operating** the computer at work for about a month now.*

Now practise this exchange with the prompts below:
A: Have you ever been to Italy?
B: Yes, we've been going there regularly for years!

a garlic cheese? / six months!
b a Japanese car? / past ten years!
c any music by Elgar? / his music – I was ten!
d one of these newfangled bottle openers? / they first came out!
e abroad? / on and off – a number of years!

C Vocabulary: nationalities, and personal and national characteristics

C1 Study the names we give to some nationalities (apologies to those not mentioned). NOTE: *the Chinese* = all the people who are Chinese.

the Americans	the Egyptians	the Danish	the Swiss	the Scots
the Argentinians	the Germans	(*or* the Danes)	the Finns	the Turks
the Australians	the Italians	the English	the Greeks	the Chinese
the Austrians	the Mexicans	the Dutch	the Poles	the Japanese
the Brazilians	the Norwegians	the French	the Swedes	the Maltese

Game: 'Getting from A to B' (see Teacher's Guide Unit 1)

C2 Study some of the common adjectives we use to describe personal and national characteristics.

friendly	courteous	unfriendly	aloof	discourteous
sociable	reliable	insular	impolite	bad-tempered
thoughtful	patient	difficult	rude	sullen
considerate	charming	quarrelsome	excitable	lazy
polite	even-tempered	reserved	patronising	impatient
hard-working	easy-going	cool/cold	unreliable	unsociable

In small groups, discuss as many nationalities as you can using sentences like this:

I think the English (generally) tend to be /charming/.
The English always strike me/ have always struck me as being /very reserved/.
Whenever anyone mentions the English, I always think of someone who is /friendly but reserved/

The English are often { *thought of as / regarded as* / *considered / thought to be* } *rather /aloof/, (but I'm not so sure).*
I've always been under the impression that the English are /very insular/.

C3 The adjectives above can also be used to describe individuals of course. Note how the verb *be* is in the Continuous form to stress the idea of 'right now' e.g.
She's usually very friendly, but right now she's being very unfriendly.
Now do the same with these:
1 he/generally hard-working/lazy
2 they/usually easy-going/difficult
3 you/normally polite/very rude
4 he/normally quite considerate/very selfish
5 you/generally sensible/very silly

D Listening and socialising

D1 You are considering opening a bank account, and are therefore very interested in a conversation you overhear in which a man and a woman discuss their banks and the people who work in them.

1 Study this list of adjectives:

unfriendly	suspicious
efficient	unreliable
cheerful	chatty
disrespectful	businesslike
impersonal	officious
informal	slapdash
unprofessional	patronising
careless	security-conscious

2 Now listen to the conversation. Write 'Man's bank' and 'Woman's bank' on a piece of paper and, as you listen, write down appropriate adjectives from the list to describe the employees. Add under each column the name of the bank.

3 Which bank will you open an account at? Why? Why not the other one?

D2 An English-speaking visitor is asking for advice and opinions regarding certain services in your town. In pairs, using this brief 'starter' exchange as a model, ask for and give the advice, using the kind of language you heard above.

A: Do you know/Do you happen to know a good dentist?
B: Yes, I'd advise you to go to X.
    or No, I don't. But whatever you do, don't go to X.
A: Why?
B: Well, he's/she's/they're/the people there are . . .

1 dentist   2 garage   3 travel agent's   4 hairdresser   5 drycleaner's

E Functions: complaining, criticising and expressing annoyance

E1 This is part of a letter to a magazine. (The writer is letting off steam about everything he/she can think of!) Read it carefully and then ask and answer the questions.

Sir,
This country really is getting me down!

Take politicians. One lot is always telling us that things couldn't be better: the others are continually telling us that things couldn't be worse. And the media are always telling us that they're *all* wrong!

And while on the subject of television, why *will* they insist on putting on all the best films very late at night?! I've been meaning to write to the television people for ages, but never seem to get round to it.

Anyway, I can't stand the way they obviously edit all the letters they publish. (Please don't edit this!)

And still on the subject of television, it amazes me the way programmes have been moved around in the past weeks to accommodate Party Political Broadcasts. (In case you hadn't noticed, Election Time is here!) The politicians come on our screens and tell us they've done this and that, and then promise to do this, that and the other . . . Anybody would think they *owned* the television companies!

1 What annoys the writer about politicians?
2 What does he say about the media?
3 Why does he complain about television films?
4 What can't he stand about published letters?
5 What is he amazed at?
6 What does he say politicians do?

E2 Study the ways we complain about, express annoyance at or criticise other people:

a He's *always* smoking!
They're *continually* moving house!
She's *forever* talking about her son!

> NOTE this use of the Present Continuous with *always, continually, forever, constantly* and *perpetually* to express criticism and annoyance.

b She *will* leave the front door unlocked (whenever she goes out)!
They *will* keep repeating programmes on TV!

> NOTE the use of *will* (stressed when spoken) also to express criticism and annoyance.

c They've been promising to do that job for ages (and they still haven't done it)!

d I hate/can't stand/don't like the way she looks down her nose at everyone!

e He just walks in whenever he feels like it, sits down and watches TV as if he owned the place! And he doesn't even live here!

Now complain about or criticise these people. Finish the sentences.

1 He's a real scrounger! I hate people like that! They're always ....
2 She's a real know-all! I can't stand people like that! They *will* ....
3 They're both gluttons! They're constantly ....
4 He's a real lazy-bones! He just *won't* ....
5 He's a real bully! He's continually   ....

E3 In pairs, talk about neighbours, relatives, colleagues and other students you know. Student A criticises or complains about the person, student B asks for reasons, for example:

A: My nextdoor neighbour's terrible!
B: Why? What's wrong with him/her? / Why do you say that? / What makes you say that?
A: Well, she's *constantly* screaming at her children, and she *will* have the radio on all day at full blast!

(Further, student B might defend the person with expressions like: *Well, you must remember/you've got to bear in mind that she's got five children . . .*)

F Exercises for homework

F1 Write out this conversation again, putting in the most suitable form of the verbs: *does/do, is/are doing, has/have done* or *has/have been doing.*

TOM: Hello, Chris! What (*you/do*) for the past few weeks? Why (*I/not/see*) you?

CHRIS: Well, I (*not/feel*) very well lately. I (*get*) a lot of rather bad headaches.

TOM: Oh, dear. (*you/see*) a doctor about it?

CHRIS: Not yet. I (*see*) one later this evening.

TOM: I (*expect*) you (*overdo*) it.

CHRIS: I must say I (*begin*) to feel my age in the office now. (*you/realise*) I (*work*) over fifty hours this week – and it's only Thursday? You know, every night now, while I (*sit*) on the bus on the way home, I (*stare*) out of the window and (*wonder*) what I (*do*) with my life. It seems I (*constantly work*). Where (*my youth/go*), Tom?

TOM: Hey, steady on. (*you/not/be*) a bit melodramatic? You (*be*) only twenty-three!

F2 Read this passage carefully, answer the multiple-choice questions, and then write the letter (**F3**). (The passage is an extract from *Boomerang: Australia Rediscovered*, a somewhat ironic and humorous picture of Australia and its people by George Mikes, the well-known Hungarian-born English writer.)

Australians are proud of their egalitarian society and boast about it. They are right: their society is more egalitarian than any other and this is a trait to be proud of. But when informality is a cult, you have to learn how to be informal. Its rules are just as strict as those of formality. You must never forget to be truly and boisterously informal. You have to be on the lookout not to break the rules in this world of strict and formal informality; you cannot relax any more than you could a hundred years ago at the court of some German princeling.

This, however, may be the unjust assessment of one used to the stuffier atmosphere of London. Australian egalitarianism and informality are genuine and not affected; the Australians are not pompous and pretentious. The Australian air in this respect – as in many others – is clear, refreshing and transparent.

If you want to see somebody, even a high official or a business tycoon, you ring him up, you ask for him and he – as likely as not – will come to the telephone. No fussy and protective secretaries with their 'I'll see if he's in' line will bar your way. Should you appear in person you'll be led to the great man's presence, without the 'Have you got an appointment?' and 'May I ask you what it is about?' inquisition. A friend of mine rang a gentleman who occupies a high position in the political hierarchy and asked him when he could see me. 'Tell him to come along right now,' was the answer – the customary, straightforward, no-nonsense answer of Australia. We had a long chat in his room in Parliament building, then he took me to the Parliament restaurant and while we were giving our order, one of his secretaries appeared with a query. She was told to sit down and have dinner with us. Later, walking along the corridor towards the exit, my host noticed that the light in one of the Ministers' rooms was on, so we dropped in and had a chat with the Minister. I called the Rt. Hon. Gentleman by his Christian name and even when we left I did not have the faintest idea what his surname was – a situation unlikely to arise for someone meeting say, Lord Salisbury or even Mr Dean Rusk. Afterwards my host walked back with me to my hotel and accepted my invitation for a night-cap. In the lounge we met another member of the Government drinking with an Australian ambassador, home on a visit, and we joined them. The conversation was, I daresay, better than it would have been with chance acquaintances in a pub, but it was just as easy-going, informal and friendly.

I had similar prompt ('Well, just come along!') appointments with, and even invitations to luncheon from, Vice-Chancellors of universities (or their equivalents), busy professors and administrators. Occasionally, those who worked in offices far out of town volunteered to come in and meet me.

In Australia you are on Christian-name terms with almost everybody, immediately after the introduction. It is regarded as unfriendly and stand-offish to address the president of a vast industrial combine as 'Mr Brown' instead of 'Joe'.

1 According to the writer, a foreigner might find Australian informality a little difficult to cope with because
  A Australians are very proud.
  B you have to learn to assess every situation carefully.
  C Australians are so pretentious.
  D the rules are just as strict as those for formal behaviour.

2 Which of these statements or questions (according to the writer) typifies the Australian way?
  A 'I'll see if he's in.'
  B 'Have you got an appointment?'
  C 'Tell him to come along right now.'
  D 'May I ask what it is about?'

3 From what he says in the third paragraph, the writer implies that Ministers in other countries
  A always invite their secretaries to lunch.
  B expect to be addressed by their surname.
  C never work late at night in Parliament.
  D rarely go to a pub for a night-cap.

4 What do the last two short paragraphs do?
  A They give further examples of Australian informality.
  B They introduce important new information.
  C They contradict what the writer said earlier.
  D They lead to a new aspect of Australian society.

F3 You are writing a letter to an acquaintance in which you tell him or her about George Mikes' *Boomerang: Australia Rediscovered*. Write a paragraph of about 150 words summarising what Mikes says about Australian informality. Begin like this:

I don't know if you've read George Mikes' book Boomerang: Australia Rediscovered, *but I've just read some of it and enjoyed it very much. In one place he describes Australian informality.*

Then continue, referring to the passage and answering the questions below to form a complete paragraph:

— How does he describe Australian society? And what does he say about being informal?
— Does he think Australian egalitarianism and informality are a good thing or a bad thing?
— How easy or difficult is it to meet a high official or a business tycoon in Australia? What examples does he give?
— What other people did Mikes meet in the same way? And how are formal introductions and so on regarded?

Finally, conclude your paragraph with an appropriate version of this sentence:

Mikes' description of the Australians is slightly ironic, of course,
but { *since I've never been to Australia/I don't know any Australians, I don't know . . .*
      since I've been to Australia/I know some Australians, I can tell you . . .

Unit 2

Attitudes and interests

A1 Below is the title, sub-title and first paragraph of an article which appeared in a British weekend magazine in summer 1982. Read it carefully to find answers to these questions:

1 What has the image of the 'average student' been for the past few years?

2 What virtues seem to be fashionable among students now?

Are students still revolting?
A DEGREE OF CONFORMITY

'When the LSE students put on a Christmas pantomime, I knew it was the beginning of the end of the revolt.' That was how a Cambridge tutor marked the return of relative tranquility to university life. For years, the average student – if such a thing exists – had seemed to breathe a mixture of CS gas and marijuana, wore flowers in his (long) hair and took his religion from the Himalayas and his politics from Peking.

There has been a change. God, hard work and short hair are not universal, but they are fashionable.

A2 What other changes have taken place, do you think? For example, what jobs do you think students might now intend to do which they wouldn't have taken a few years ago? Why do you think there has been a change of attitude among students? Is it easy or difficult to get into university in your country now?

A3 The article (above) went on to describe changing attitudes among university students in different countries. Read the extract below about Manchester University, England, to find out

1 what students at Manchester are interested in and what their ambitions are.

2 who Phil Woolas is and what he thinks of the new attitudes (and why).

Manchester

'The place has changed since I came up in '78,' says Phil Woolas, leader of the 11,500-strong student union at Manchester University. 'People work much harder. They are far more interested in a good degree than in being radical. A first or a two-one is really important now and that's what they work for, that's what they talk about.'

Woolas does not wholly approve of this: 'I've slept in the Bursar's office myself,' he says. 'But students are fed up with demos now. You've got to be politically realistic to survive in student politics. The hippies and extremists and anarchists who got the University in the news, they've gone.'

That is reflected in the candidates for student offices. 'Hobbies squash, badminton and parachuting, reading economics and accountancy,' reads one election address on the Union noticeboard.

Ambitions are similarly modified. 'The high status jobs are in accountancy and the big insurance companies,' says Woolas. 'People scramble for the civil service, marketing, managerial sciences. I suppose they always did, but now they don't mind admitting it. You can dream of something smart like the telly but you know you're not going to get it. And a lot of graduates are joining the police. That is new.'

A4 In pairs, read one of these further extracts from the article and complete the relevant part of this table.

Students at	Kyoto, Japan	the Sorbonne, (Paris), France	Berkeley, USA
like, or are interested in	*reading cartoon magazines;*		
don't like, or show no interest in			
(in general) want to			

Kyoto

It is difficult to get into a top Japanese university, from which most of the big companies recruit their staffs. Pre-university examinations, throughout school life, are horrifically competitive. Nine-year-olds have been treated for ulcers after going to evening classes five nights a week. In one year, 335 schoolchildren killed themselves through the pressure to succeed.

But once at university, life is a doddle. Exams are easy and can be sat again. More than 95 per cent of students graduate successfully, often with a minimum of work. A survey this year showed that 98 per cent of students own television sets and refrigerators – and more of them have washing machines and electric footwarmers than have bookcases. The survey found that 'reading cartoon magazines is the favourite pastime'.

Attitudes were tested in the same survey – and it is clear that ideas of revolt are out. The words that Japanese students like include *hometown, femininity, fidelity to parents, virginal purity* and *duty*. The concepts they most dislike include *women's lib, punk fashion* and *datsu-sara*. Disapproval of *datsu-sara* is significant, for the term means to quit a salaried job in a large corporation, with guaranteed employment for life, to branch out on one's own.

While they wait to join the big company, Japanese students have a good time.

Paris

'Philosophers and psychiatrists are no longer the kings of the Sorbonne,' says Fréderique Feron, a 22-year-old history student. 'It's not clever to rebel any more. Student movements have no impact whatever on the scene. The pressure on students to succeed is enormous.

'We just write until our fingers bleed.'

Sorbonne students, and a fair number of staff, tried their best to bring down the French state in 1968. 'That was light years ago,' says Feron. 'Now you've got youth unemployment, you've got 55,000 who didn't get into university last year.

'There has been a swing away from arts subjects to natural sciences, mathematics and economics, and business courses are over-subscribed.

'Business, that's the smart thing to do. Or accountancy or medicine or the media,' says Feron, 'not being a genius in a garret or a revolutionary with a paving stone. Maybe that's a little sad, but that's the way it is.'

Berkeley

'There's been a change in the mentality of people,' says Liz Rivera, the vice-president of the Associated Students of Universities of California. 'You notice it particularly with the young ones. It's become very important for them to get As, to work, to get the results and to get into graduate school.

'Getting to law school or medical school, that's the tops. That, and the money studies, where the jobs are: business studies, engineering, information systems, computer science, that's what people go for.

'It's only in the past year that things have really accelerated,' she says. 'Before, you still felt in touch with the old days, the flower power, the demos, the fights with the cops. Not any more. To the young kids, that's history and they don't believe history repeats itself.

'I can't get them interested in student politics,' complains Miss Rivera. 'They won't take time off studying.'

A5 Report and discuss

1 Report on the attitudes of students at 'your' university (e.g. The Sorbonne) for the rest of the class to complete the table and to ask questions.

2 What is the situation in universities in your own country? In other words, are the interests, attitudes and ambitions of university/college students in your own country similar to those in the universities in the extracts you have read?

2

B Communicative grammar

B1 The gerund or -*ing* form to express general likes and dislikes

You will remember that we often use the gerund as the subject of a sentence, e.g.: *Reading cartoon magazines is a favourite pastime, Getting to law school is the best thing you can do, Parachuting is a new hobby among students*, etc. Practise this brief conversation:

A: Do you enjoy working as a barman?
B: Well, mixing cocktails is fun, and serving the regular customers is nice, but I don't like having to throw the noisy ones out. That's quite tricky sometimes.

Now in pairs talk about the pros and cons of the following activities in the same way. Ask the questions and think of as many pros and cons as you can.

1 Do you like gardening?
2 Do you really enjoy shopping?
3 How do you feel about throwing parties?
4 Do you enjoy driving?
5 Do you like doing housework?

B2 Likes, dislikes, boredom, objections, etc. in varying degrees

Study the different ways we can express these, noting which expressions are followed by a gerund and which by an infinitive (with or without *to*). Then express your own feelings about the topics below.

strong	weak
I can't bear (doing) . . .	I'm not too keen on (doing) . . .
I can't stand (doing) . . .	I'm not particularly fond of (doing) . . .
I hate/loathe (doing) . . .	I'm not mad about (doing) . . .
I couldn't bear to (do) . . .	I'd rather not (do) . . .
I object to (doing/having to do) . . .	I don't much like the idea of (doing) . . .
I love/adore (doing) . . .	I quite/rather like/enjoy (doing) . . .
I'd love to (do) . . .	I quite fancy (doing) . . .
I'm dying to (do) . . .	I wouldn't mind (doing) . . .
I just can't wait to (do) . . .	I'm quite looking forward to (doing) . . .
I'm fed up with/sick to death of (doing) . . .	I'm getting a bit tired of (doing) . . .

1 In pairs, tell each other how you feel about
  a leaving school.
  b learning a new language.
  c reading through old letters.
  d getting up early at weekends.
  e starting a new job.
  f meeting new people.
  g taking examinations.
  h writing letters.

Use exchanges like this to express your feelings:
A: (You know,) I can't stand listening to classical music.
B: Well, to be honest/No, I'm not too keen on it/ listening to it either.

24

2 How did you feel about these things when you were very young?

Examples: *When I was very young, I used to hate having a bath.*
Strangely enough, when I was young, I didn't mind going to bed early.

a going to the dentist
b having your hair done
c going to bed early
d meeting uncles and aunts
e going on holiday
f washing
g going to school
h having parties

Tell another student about more things you used to love or hate, things you objected to or didn't object to, things you couldn't wait to do, etc.

B3 Two constructions to express how difficult, enjoyable, exciting, etc. something is: gerund as subject, or *It's* + adjective + *to do*

On page 24 you practised using the gerund as subject e.g. *Mixing cocktails is fun.* Study these pairs of sentences and notice what happens when we begin a sentence not with the gerund, but with *It*.

Getting into a top Japanese university is difficult.	↔	*It's difficult to get into a top Japanese university.*
Reading books in a foreign language is fun.	↔	*It's fun to read books in a foreign language.*
Getting good grades has become very important for them.	↔	*It has become very important for them to get good grades.*

Practise these exchanges and then adapt them to the prompts below:
A: It's difficult to write accurately in English, isn't it?
B: Well, yes. But writing accurately in any foreign language is difficult, isn't it?

A: It was rather disappointing to see that filmstar in the flesh, wasn't it?
B: Yes, I suppose it was. But meeting any famous person face-to-face can be a bit of a letdown, can't it?

1 enjoyable – meet old schoolfriends/ any faces from the past
2 boring – sit through that film again/ any film for a second time
3 fun – go to a different disco/ any new place
4 hard work – listen to that symphony/ any new electronic music
5 exciting – watch the end of the marathon/ any great sporting event
6 difficult – get young people interested in politics/ anything serious

B4 The *-ing* form after prepositions

Certain prepositions (+ gerund) often occur in compound sentences, for example *after, before, on* (= when), *by* (= by means of), *from* (= as a result of), etc. Study these examples then join the sentences with the preposition given.

*Nine-year-olds have been treated for ulcers **after going** to evening classes.*
***Instead of rebelling**, students are beginning to study a lot harder now.*
***On getting** to university, Mary began to waste a lot of her time.*

1 Don't sit around complaining. Why don't you do something about it? (*instead of*)
2 He lost five kilos. All he did was cut bread out of his diet. (*by*)
3 Now touch your toes. Don't bend your knees. (*without*)
4 He reached his thirtieth birthday. He decided to change his job. (*on*)
5 My eyes are sore. I've been swimming underwater. (*from*)

2

C Listening and socialising

C1 You are going to hear a radio interview with Sheila, an 18-year-old schoolgirl, about her plans for the future, in particular the next three years. Listen carefully and complete these sentences:

1 Before she left school, Sheila objected to ....
2 In September, Sheila intends to ....
3 At university, she is planning ....
4 She didn't feel like going on with .... because ....
5 When she leaves university, she is hoping ....
6 First of all, she wants to get ....
7 At university, she will not be taking part in ....
8 She is looking forward to ....

C2 Now in pairs, and using the expressions on the right, ask and tell each other about your plans or intentions regarding

1 this evening.	I'm going to . . . / I intend to . . .
2 next weekend.	I'm hoping to . . .
3 your further education.	I'm thinking of . . . /I'm planning to . . .
4 marriage and family.	I don't really feel like . . . / I'm not planning to . . .
5 your career and ambitions.	I'm not going to . . . / I don't intend to . . .

D Vocabulary: nouns related to adjectives and verbs

Nouns are formed from verbs and adjectives in many ways. The problem, however, is that a verb which is normally followed by an infinitive, for example, may have a corresponding noun which is followed by a preposition + gerund e.g. *I hope to be there tomorrow* v. *We have no hope of getting there today.* Note in the following exercises the forms of the nouns and the constructions in which they are used.

D1 It was a bad year at the Comprehensive School. First, . . .

A few of the pupils were enthusiastic about studying certain subjects, but the majority of them showed little or no enthusiasm for any subjects whatsoever.

Make similar comments, matching prompts from the left and right columns.

1	were proud of their school	had great difficulty in
2	didn't find it difficult to concentrate	had no expectations of
3	wanted to make progress	took no pleasure in
4	were interested in some of the lessons	had no plans to
5	planned to take some examinations	took no pride in
6	intended to look for a job	had no intention of
7	expected to get somewhere in life	displayed no interest in
8	were afraid of being unemployed	showed no affection for
9	were quite fond of their teachers	seemed to have no fear of
10	were pleased to be at a 'good school'	showed no desire to

Now try the exercise again, covering the right-hand column.

D2 Then things began to get worse . . .

Study the nouns on the right, then cover them and combine these pairs of sentences as in this example.

The pupils threatened to strike. This angered the staff. (*threat*)
You write: *The pupils' threat to strike angered the staff.*

1 The pupils decided to 'sit in'. This made things worse. (*decision*)
2 The Headmaster failed to impose order. This was the real problem. (*failure*)
3 The pupils refused to move. This brought the police in. (*refusal*)
4 The Headmaster was unable to keep control. This was frightening. (*inability*)
5 The local authority wished to avoid publicity. This was in vain. (*wish*)
6 The press tended to exaggerate everything. This didn't help. (*tendency*)
7 The Head was still reluctant to act. This added to the chaos. (*reluctance*)
8 The authorities tried to put pressure on the Head. This succeeded. (*attempt*)
9 He agreed to an amnesty. This was a step in the right direction. (*agreement*)
10 The parents insisted on an enquiry. This had the desired effect. (*insistence*)

E Register

One register of English which is particularly recognisable is that often employed in formal English letters. Features to note are:

a the use of verb phrase to replace the more informal or 'ritual' common spoken form: compare *I must apologise for not sending . . .* and *(I'm) sorry I haven't sent . . .*

b the use of nouns to replace verbs or adjectives: compare:
You are under no obligation to accept . . . and *You are not obliged/don't have to accept . . .*
He showed considerable interest in our proposals . . . and *He was very interested in what we (had) proposed . . .*

Read these snippets from formal letters and then in pairs ask and tell each other what the writer says, using informal everyday speech, as on the right.

I feel I must apologise for not communicating with you earlier on the subject of

I had every intention of informing you of the Committee's decision some days ago,

After careful consideration of the problems involved, we have taken the decision to proceed

We have made arrangements for you to meet the other members of the team next week

We regret to inform you, however, that your refusal to agree to the conditions of the contract would mean that

The Committee expressed a preference for the first suggestion

A: What does he mean when he says 'I feel I must apologise for not communicating with you earlier on the subject of . . .'?
B: (I think he means) he's sorry he didn't write to you earlier about . . . (whatever it is).
A: Oh, is that all?/Well, why didn't he say so?

F Exercises for homework

F1 For each of the sentences below, write a new sentence as similar as possible in meaning to the original sentence, but using the words given: these words must not be altered in any way.

Example: I'm not planning to do anything special tonight.
  (*intend*)
You write: I don't intend to do anything special tonight.

  1 They were very proud of winning the football trophy. *(pride)*
  2 I just can't wait to leave school and start work. *(dying)*
  3 She never intended to go to university. *(intention)*
  4 It's easier to learn a foreign language if you live in the country. *(learning)*
  5 She never studied much, but she always passed her exams easily. *(without)*
  6 You don't have to take the job if you don't want to. *(obligation)*
  7 You will have to go to court if you refuse to pay the full amount. *(refusal)*
  8 We considered the proposal carefully before we accepted it. *(consideration)*
  9 I won't let myself be treated like this. *(object)*
  10 The fact that he couldn't remember names was a constant source of embarrassment. *(inability)*

F2 Fill each of the numbered blanks in the following passage with *one* suitable word.

It would seem from recent reports that university students in most countries are once again _____(1) more serious about their studies. One reason for this, it has been _____(2), is that _____(3) into university nowadays is very much tougher _____(4) it was ten or twenty years _____(5). In Britain, for example, _____(6) of being able to walk into a university place with a number of O levels and perhaps two or three A levels _____(7) a reasonable level, any prospective student must now obtain three A levels with good passes. And there _____(8) to be a certain _____(9) on the part of students to obtain such good grades in order to obtain a good job when they _____(10) university. Further, students in the 80s seem to be fed up _____(11) the 'long hair, drugs and demo' image that students _____(12) in the 60s and 70s. True, hard work, short hair and lack of interest _____(13) politics are not universal, but these and other virtues like duty, _____(14) to parents and reading are more fashionable. There is a clear _____(15) for students to take their studies a lot more seriously. And yet another

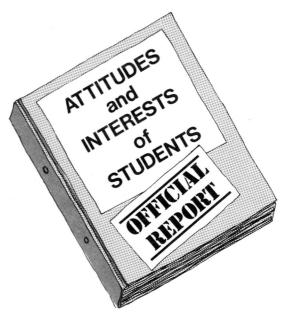

reason for this may be that _____(16) to pass mid-course examinations can _____(17) in their being asked to leave. University places are in short _____(18) and students generally have no _____(19) to lose the place they have studied so hard to obtain _____(20) failing grades halfway through their course.

F3 Complete this letter to a friend, in which you comment on changing attitudes towards certain aspects of life in your country. Answering the questions will help you to write your composition. They are the kind you should ask yourself when planning a composition.

Dear Marilyn,

Thank you very much for your last letter. I was very interested to read your comments on how attitudes seem to have changed in Britain over the past few decades. I thought you might like to know what has been happening here in ..

In terms of work and jobs, . . .

(Are people more willing to work hard now than before? Are they more fussy about the job they choose? What sort of jobs are many people keen on getting? What sort of jobs do they hope to get, or dream of getting? How important are salary, status and working conditions nowadays?)

As regards home life, . . .

(Is the family unit as strong as it used to be? How are parents' attitudes different today (if at all)? What things didn't parents approve of before (or even forbid) which they allow or don't mind now? And what are teenagers most interested in these days?)

On the question of trends and current fashions, . . .

(What sort of music are people keen on (listening to/buying) now? What sort of films do they like? What clothes? How do most people spend their leisure time – evenings/weekends/holidays? Is there a tendency for people to go out more? – or less?)

And when it comes to politics and social questions, . . .

(Has there been a swing recently away from one political party towards another? What are the main 'issues' that people are taking an interest in? Animal rights? Nuclear weapons? Jobs for all? Social equality? Human rights? Is there hope of people changing their attitudes on some of these issues?)

I hope that this has given you some idea of what things are like here nowadays. Please write again soon. I always look forward to and enjoy reading your interesting letters.

Yours,

Unit 3

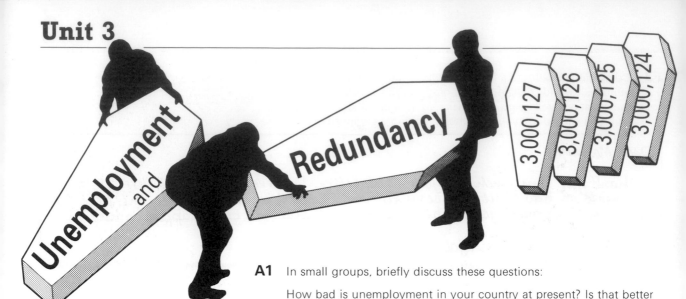

Unemployment and **Redundancy**

3,000,127 3,000,126 3,000,125 3,000,124

A1   In small groups, briefly discuss these questions:

How bad is unemployment in your country at present? Is that better or worse than it has been in recent years?
Why do you think unemployment has risen so dramatically in many countries since the mid-seventies? What are some of the problems created by high unemployment? What solutions have been suggested to counter its effects? How effective do you think some of these solutions have been or will be?

A2   You are going to hear two people talking about being unemployed or redundant. First, listen to Anne, aged 18, interviewed on the same radio programme as Sheila (Unit 2). She tries to put into words her feelings about employment, or rather, lack of it.

📼 **1**   Listen and try to remember what she says about:
   a   job opportunities schemes.
   b   her dream job.
   c   her last year at school.
   d   her source(s) of income.
   e   her relationship with her parents.
   f   her innermost feelings.
   g   marriage.

📼 **2**   Listen again, then see if you can place these comments that Anne makes. When does she make them, what do they refer to?
   a   that's it, in a nutshell   **g**   in circumstances like that
   b   that's a laugh   **h**   It's not very pleasant.
   c   A start!   **i**   I don't know what against.
   d   the day of the secretary   **j**   Or doesn't come.
   e   Out of the question!   **k**   As a last resort.
   f   A nightmare!

A3   In your country, what could a person like Anne do – in your town or elsewhere? Discuss in pairs what advice you should give her as her two best friends. Further training? A change of direction in her job-hunting? A revised approach, more positive attitudes? A move away from home? To or away from the capital? The seeking of expert advice? The possibilities of self-employment?
Then form groups of three and see how the third person, 'Anne', reacts to your advice.

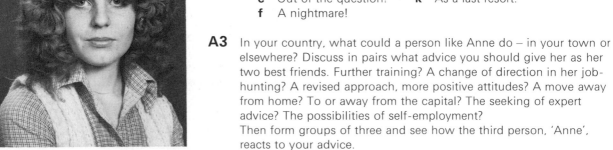

A4 In a moment you are going to hear an interview with Terry, an electronics man (as opposed to an electronic man), who was recently made redundant after many years' working for a company. Consider together first how his situation now will probably differ from Anne's – socially, financially, psychologically. (See later if you are right.) Which of them do you expect to sympathise with more?

1 Now listen to Terry talking. Half the class should concentrate on finding the answers to the first set of questions, the other half the second.

What do we learn from what Terry says about:
a his academic qualifications?
b his initial reaction to losing his job?
c his position in the company?
d his philosophy of work?

What does Terry tell us about:
a the reasons for his redundancy?
b the months prior to his dismissal?
c his feelings now about being out of work?
d his thoughts about the future?

Now exchange the information you have obtained. You may also want to ask members of the other group supplementary questions for clarification.

2 Look at the half-sentences below about Terry and what he has to say. Listen again to the interview, then see if you can complete them, briefly or at length.
a I sympathised with him when he talked about how . . .
b I thought he was remarkably objective when he spoke of . . .
c I agreed with him when he described . . .
d There was perhaps a trace of bitterness when he commented on . . .
e The interviewer seemed rather tentative when he asked . . .
f I felt the interviewer's most interesting question was when he . . .
Comment in the same sort of way about other remarks which caught your attention.

A5 In small groups, make a list of twelve jobs or professions of today which you think will survive the next 25 years, a further list of five which you think will actually increase in popularity, and a third column of notes on five 'new' jobs that you think will appear in that period. Then discuss your lists with those of other groups. Be ready to explain the reasons for your choices.

THE TIMES FRIDAY AUGUST 5 1983

Yet ANOTHER dinosaur

B Communicative grammar

B1 Study these four advertisements, noting especially the use of nouns in them. Write down what you think the ads are for; then compare your ideas with others'.

1
Do you suffer from:
nerves? shyness?
an inferiority complex?
feelings of insecurity,
frustration and despair?
the feeling that
everyone can do everything better than you?
Then you need:

3
Have you got ambition? Drive?
An outgoing personality?
The will to succeed? Sound
judgement? Leadership qualities?
An awareness of your own potential?
If so, why not give us a ring on

2
Are these qualities old-fashioned?
Obedience? Bravery?
A sense of discipline?
The courage of your convictions?
Of course they aren't!
If you combine them with:
physical strength, mental agility,
natural aptitude and a mature outlook on life,
then you could be the person we are

4
Want to work for us? Maybe?
Well, have you got the three D's?
DEDICATION
DETERMINATION
DEVOTION
Experience is desirable
Patience is vital
A love of people is essential
A lively, open mind is indispensib
If you don't need the comfort
of a regular salary, the security

B2 Among the many principles guiding the use and omission of articles in English, consider these features:

1 No article with a general concept, **but** the use of *a/an* with a particular example of it:
> *We need someone with: personality / a lively personality . . .*
> *Are you looking for: work? / a job? . . .*
> *We offer: good money / a high salary . . .*
> *We provide: accommodation / a hotel room . . .*
> *You'll have: good prospects of promotion / the chance of a higher position*

2 Similarly, no article with abstract nouns used in a general sense:
> *We need people who have: experience / strength of character / respect for others / compassion*

but the use of *the* with a defined aspect of that quality:
> *the right experience / the patience of a saint / the strength of an ox / the enthusiasm of youth*

3 Nouns like *maths*, *physics* and *economics* operate as singular nouns:
> *Electronics is one of the most popular subjects in our college.*

4 Many idiomatic phrases with nouns do not take an article:
> *in danger / at risk / on loan / out of work*

but, of course, many do:
> *in a flash / at the moment / on the brain / out of the blue*

Unfortunately, these have to be learnt *by heart* (no article!).

B3 Now in pairs write advertisements similar to those above for the following:
1 for a holiday in the Himalayas
2 for a fourth person to share a flat
3 to sell a new kind of dental treatment
4 for the job of teacher at your school
5 for a teacher of the deaf and dumb
6 for a newly-opened discotheque

C Vocabulary: phrases with *in*, *on* and *at*

C1 Read the opinions on employment and unemployment below.
Choose the *one* which is closest to your own feelings and be
prepared to convey the sentiments expressed to the rest of the class
and to explain why you chose that particular view. (As you read,
also note the phrases with *in*, *on* and *at*. Make three lists of your
own and add to them in the days to come.)

1 'In principle, there's nothing noble about work;
on the contrary, in most cases, it's rather
degrading. In essence, for most people work is a
pay-packet – at any rate, as far as most manual
work is concerned. In short, a necessary evil.'

2 'In one sense, being unemployed is like having
one long holiday; in another way, it's like a hefty
prison sentence. On the one hand, you've got
freedom; on the other, you've got no freedom at
all. On balance, I'd rather have a job.'

3 'At first sight, being idle all day might seem
attractive; in reality, it's horrific – at least, it is for
me. In some respects, I feel the Government are
in the wrong. But in general, I think it's just a
phenomenon of the age we're living in.'

4 'In my view, it's unfair. In theory, unemployment
benefit is for those who can't get a job. In
practice, though, a lot of people choose the dole
in preference to a job – in particular the lower-
paid – because, in effect, they can take home
nearly as much in benefit as they would in
wages; in fact, some can claim more. In other
words, people like me are paying tax on their
behalf.'

5 'In the main, it's the uneducated who are losing
their jobs; often at short notice – too short, in my
opinion. And at the same time new jobs are
being created which in the long run will only be
done by highly qualified and super-intelligent
people. In the end, only the clever will work. I'm
against that on principle.'

C2 Now invent a similarly phrased opinion on each of these topics:

1 Equality of the sexes
2 The fairness of your education system
3 The wisdom of the law
Hand your papers to your teacher, who will read out
some of them. Guess whose opinion it is each time.

C3 You are going to hear part of a sketch in which a man describes how
his addiction to television grew. Study these time phrases, which he
uses, before you listen.

at first	at the beginning	in a matter of weeks
all at once	in no time at all	in time
in next to no time	in due course	at the moment
in the past	in the future	at present
in the short term	in the long run	in the end

Divide into three groups; Group A concentrate on the left-hand column,
Group B on the middle column and Group C on the right-hand one.
After listening, recall for each other in what context 'your' phrases were used.

C4 Using these and similar phrases of time, tell your partner about one or two of these:

1 your highly successful career, with its rapid rise to fame.
2 a 'rogue' car which, from the day you bought it, never stopped going wrong.
3 a surprisingly swift recovery from a serious illness or accident.
4 (if you're feeling sentimental) the way a romantic relationship went sour.

D Register: declining (formally and informally)

D1 Read this short article, then comment on the suitability of the headline.

SWEET WORDS DON'T EASE REJECTION

Why not be honest?

WHAT really brings home the pain of being unemployed is not the indignity of the dole queue or the tedium of endless hours in the local library but the inevitability of the sight of another rejection letter, after the envelope is furtively opened on the doorstep.

Nothing is so depressing as to be told that you are not worth employing – and then have the

message reinforced by an avalanche of rejection letters. But such is the employment situation that personnel officers in their efforts to sweeten the pill have had to refine to new heights the art of saying no.

Flicking through the 150 letters of 'personal research' one is struck by the indirectness of the message. Circumlocutions and tortuous passive constructions are used with a skill worthy of a Ministry of Defence spokesman.

D2 Here are extracts from some of the many 'rejection letters' that Terry (see page 31) has received. What do you notice about the style of them? Which seem to you particularly diplomatic or tactless, encouraging or discouraging, cool or flattering?

'I am afraid I have decided not to invite you for interview on this occasion.'
'I regret that on this occasion we will be unable to proceed with your application.'
'We regret to inform you that we will not be processing your application to the short-list stage.'
'I regret to advise you that having now carefully considered all the applications received, we have not been able to include your name amongst those selected for interview.'

'First of all, let me say how impressive your qualifications are and a person of your calibre would indeed be a great asset to any company. Much to our regret, however, I have to inform you that at present we do not a have a suitable vacancy.'
'There has been a large response and we have heard from a number of applicants whose backgrounds more closely match our particular requirements.'
'I would like to take this opportunity to wish you every success in . . .'

D3 You see above many examples of an exceptionally formal tone:

'I regret to inform you that we are not in a position to . . .'
'Much to my regret, I am obliged to advise you that we find ourselves unable to . . .'

Much written English falls into a rather less formal (but still 'correct') register:

'I regret that I shall be unable to . . .'
'Regretfully I have to inform you that I shall not be able to . . .'

These two styles contrast dramatically with the much more informal tone of:

'I'm sorry, but I can't . . .' or *'I'm afraid it won't be possible for me to . . .'*

Write the key sentences for these three letters:
1 a very formal one declining the offer of a job, owing to . . .
2 a formal one excusing yourself from the boss's anniversary celebrations, as . . .
3 an informal one saying 'no' to a friend's invitation to a beach party, because . . .

E Functions: argument strategies

E1 Read this headline and excerpts from an article in *The Times* on the case for a new kind of 'national service' for young people. (Until now this name has only been applied in Britain to 'military service' for men.) What do you think the rest of the article might say? What further points can you think of, for and against the scheme?

A new national service: the way to find a million jobs

Recent opinion polls suggest that a nationwide community service scheme for young people commands the support of a clear majority of the population. Serious doubts persist, however, about how such a scheme could be implemented.

Where the young would work

In care of the elderly	250,000
In hospitals & health care	35,000
In education	250,000
In environmental conservation	52,000
In conservation in urban areas	203,000
Skills development	37,100
Total jobs	827,100

Can enough jobs be found in the community for young people to do? How would such a scheme be organised and what would it cost? In short, is it really a practical proposition rather than an idealistic dream?

At a time of high unemployment and cutbacks in public spending it is not surprising that public sector unions in particular might regard such a scheme, particularly if introduced by the present Government, as a way of getting labour on the cheap.

It is a great pity that the argument in favour of nationwide community service has been put forward at a time of very high unemployment. The justification for the one is not the existence of the other. However appealing it may be to politicians, the temporary removal of large numbers of young people from the labour market, and therefore from the unemployment statistics, would be essentially only a by-product of national community service and not its main purpose or benefit.

E2 Before you continue this argument in **E4**, look through the list of phrases below. You already know many ways of prefacing a simple opinion: *In my view, . . .; To my mind, . . .; As I see it, . . .; In my opinion. . . .*, etc. Here are other strategies you may wish to employ as discussion continues.

persuading	Don't you see . . .? / Surely . . .! / You must know that . . . / Wouldn't you agree/accept that . . .? / But isn't it a fact (that) . . .?
contradicting gently	You seem to be forgetting . . . / But you're missing the whole point, which is . . . / Surely you're not saying . . . / Aren't you overlooking the fact that . . .? / Are you telling me (that) . . .? Who says (that) . . .?
contradicting bluntly	That's absurd! / That's ridiculous! / Nonsense! / Rubbish! / Come off it! / You know that's not true! / Come on!
conceding half a point	That's true, I suppose. / That may be true, but . . . / Yes, I can see that, but on the other hand . . . / Well, to a certain extent, yes, but . . . / Yes, that's all very well, but . . . / Yes, of course, there is that, but . . .
dismissing a point	That makes no difference! / That's irrelevant! / That's beside the point! / But that (just) doesn't make sense! / That has nothing to do with it!
playing hard to convince	What point are you making? / What exactly are you getting at? / I can't quite see your point? / What do you really mean by . . .? / It depends on what you mean/understand by . . .
building up an argument stage by stage	For a start, . . . / First of all, . . . / And what's more, . . . / And that's not all! / And don't forget, either, that . . . / Of course, another consideration must be . . . / And finally you've got to bear in mind (that) . . .

E3 Before you practise these yourselves, listen to four colleagues arguing about the scheme in **E1**. As you listen, tick the phrases you hear them use.

E4 Now you continue the argument. Here are some notes for and against the community service scheme. Study them carefully, add to them, then see if in groups you can enact an exchange of views similar to the one you have just heard.

FOR
- it works in other countries
- gives young people sense of usefulness, independence, pocket money
- more relevant than academic training
- helpful to community, sick, old, young
- good for environment, conservation of nature, rebuilding of inner cities etc.
- save on state payments to unemployed

AGAINST
- massive cost of setting-up
- impossible to organise, would increase bureaucracy, etc.
- cheap labour, unethical
- training more useful in long term
- not all young people suitable for work in primary schools, hospitals etc.
- guaranteed job = no competition, no drive

F Exercises for homework

F1 Fill each of the spaces in the narrative below with *a/an* or *the*, or leave it blank, as would be most appropriate.

It was in the spring of ...... year 1982, when ...... unemployment situation was constantly in the news. ...... good job was like ...... gold dust, and yet I felt full of ...... confidence as I edged the car out of the garage. I drove in ...... third gear all ...... way, both ...... hands on ...... steering wheel, not once exceeding ...... speed limit of thirty miles ...... hour. ...... last thing I wanted was a confrontation with ...... police.

The office was on ...... first floor of ...... four-storey building at the end of ...... street called More Avenue. ...... reception area was ...... smallish room with ...... chairs all around ...... walls. I sat down, recalling the advertisement I had seen in ...... copy of ...... previous Tuesday's *Daily Telegraph*: 'Wanted – a man of ...... initiative and ...... ideas, with ...... experience of ...... buying and selling'. Yes, yes, yes, and the qualifications I had gained at ...... university – ...... degree in ...... economics and ...... diploma in ...... business management – were a bonus.

Suddenly, the only other man in ...... room moved from ...... chair he was sitting on to ...... one directly to ...... left of mine.

'Do you mind if I ask you a question in ...... confidence?' he asked in a whisper.

'Not in ...... least,' I said in ...... reply.

'Are you after ...... position of Chief Buyer in the company?' There was ...... note of ...... panic in the voice. 'As ...... matter of ...... fact, I am,' I said.

...... expression of ...... horror came over his face.

'Please!' he began. 'I've been out of ...... work for the last three years. I have ...... family commitments. The children are all at ...... school. I'm over a thousand pounds in ...... debt. My wife had ...... nervous breakdown in December. She's been in and out of ...... hospital. Now the doctors say she may have ...... cancer. She says if I don't find ...... work soon, she'll commit ...... suicide.'

I stared at the man in ...... amazement, in ...... search of a clue as to whether this was ...... awful truth or ...... cunning lie. All of ...... sudden, the door of ...... Personnel Manager's office opened and ...... voice called my name.

F2 Look carefully at the graph on the right, which shows the number of jobless people in the UK from the beginning of 1979 to the end of 1982. Then consider the questions below, which are designed to help you build up an article based on the figures.

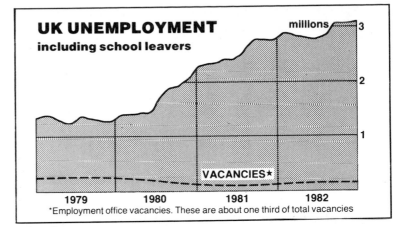

UK UNEMPLOYMENT
including school leavers

millions

VACANCIES★

1979   1980   1981   1982

*Employment office vacancies. These are about one third of total vacancies

1 During which period was there:
a a dramatic increase
b a slight fall
c little variation } in the numbers?
d a steady rise
e a slight fluctuation

Consider these phrases to help you answer accurately:

in (1979); during the course of (1980); throughout (1981); early in (1980); in the second half of (1981); towards the end of (1982); in the first three months of (1979); in the autumn of (1980)

2 True or false? Read the following statements carefully – taking note of the language used – and decide which of them are true, on the basis of the graph.
a The figure rose by almost a million during 1980.
b By the end of 1981, the total had reached three million.
c The figure had topped two million by the end of 1980.
d The figure had gone up to three million by the autumn of 1982.
e Numbers remained reasonably constant through 1979.
f The number fell to below two and a half million during 1982.
g There was an overall increase of several hundred thousand in 1979.
h The total doubled between early '79 and the latter half of '81.
i There were far more job vacancies in 1982 than in '79.

3 Incorporating as much of the language above as you need, compose your own summary of what the figures tell us. These few further phrases might help:

the following year
the previous autumn
which went on into (1980)
which continued until (mid-1982)
which was not halted until (late in the year)
which was only reversed (a year later)
meanwhile
at the same time

Your article might begin:
At the start of 1979, the number of unemployed people in the United Kingdom stood at . . .

Quality *before* **Quantity**

Austria

Magnificent mountains, crystal-clear lakes, deep valleys, tree-clad slopes, rushing rivers, rolling meadows and snow-capped peaks . . . this variety and contrast of scenery make Austria a marvellous place for a holiday.

The area is picture postcard Austria with its river valleys, fairy-tale castles, sparkling lakes and sleepy villages. There is an old-world charm about the country with its warm-hearted, fun-loving people who will do all they can to help you enjoy your holiday. There are many interesting walks where you can enjoy the crisp, mountain air, or take a cable car up to the high peaks and enjoy spectacular panoramic views of the Alpine-dominated scenery. For those who enjoy bathing, the cool invigorating lakes are very inviting.

Set in its own spacious grounds, this impressive, well-established hotel is ideally positioned in the town centre, close to the enchanting shops. The dining room is particularly attractive with traditional wood-panelled walls and ceiling, and polished wooden floor covered with handwoven rugs. The hotel serves candle-lit meals on Wednesdays in addition to the excellent cuisine, of which trout and venison are specialities. The open plan reception and lounge, with easy chairs and decorated with lush plants, is a lovely place to relax after dinner, or try an exotic cocktail in the friendly atmosphere of the original Tyrolean bar.

All rooms are comfortably furnished in traditional style. The hotel has an indoor swimming pool where you may also enjoy a sauna or massage. From here, you can admire the splendid panoramic views of the beautiful landscape.

France

Below the towering peak of Mont Blanc lies Chamonix, famous for skiing and mountaineering alike. Besides its quaint charm and interesting architecture, it has some of the best skiing in Europe, including the world-famous Vallée Blanche run.

Delightfully furnished in traditional French style with wood-panelled corridors, this simple but clean hotel offers a friendly welcome and is conveniently located near Chamonix's apres-ski centre. This friendly hotel retains much of the typical French atmosphere found in this part of the Alps and its homely restaurant, decorated in natural wood, provides good, traditional meals.

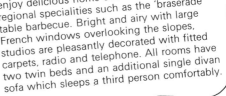

Besides a comfortable lounge and dining room the hotel boasts one of the most popular apres-ski bars in the town. The bar, noted for its exotic cocktails, is often the scene of lively and spontaneous entertainment around the big, open stone fireplace. In the pleasant restaurant with its excellent views of the mountains and forests our guests can enjoy delicious home cooking including two regional specialities such as the 'braserade' table barbecue. Bright and airy with large French windows overlooking the slopes, studios are pleasantly decorated with fitted carpets, radio and telephone. All rooms have two twin beds and an additional single divan sofa which sleeps a third person comfortably.

A1 What do you look for in a hotel? Peace and quiet? Comfort? First-class service? Or do you prefer to spend your holidays in a self-catering establishment?

Switzerland

Situated on a picturesque, sunny plateau surrounded by pine forests and spectacular Alpine views, Anzere combines the atmosphere of an unspoilt village with the facilities of a well-organised, modern ski resort. With its lively traffic-free centre Anzere offers exhilarating skiing in a relaxed and friendly setting.

Recently renovated and offering fabulous views of the mountains, this excellent hotel lies some 500m from the resort's gondola lift and 12 minutes' walk from the town. Three sun terraces ensure there's plenty of room for sunbathing or relaxing and the hotel's indoor heated swimming pool opposite with its own bar, sauna and solarium facilities all add to that feeling of luxury. The pleasantly furnished reception area leads into a spacious wood-beamed lounge and adjacent cosy informal bar with open fire. A generous buffet breakfast is offered each morning and once a week a special regional dinner is arranged by our representative at no extra charge. The modern bedrooms are comfortable and well-appointed, all with radio and telephone.

The friendly, informal mood inspires jovial gatherings in the lounge or around the bar, where live piano music and dancing are a nightly occurrence.

A2 On the left you see three examples of tour operators trying to attract the winter holiday-maker through carefully composed brochure English. Form groups of three and each of you study one of the advertisements. Then close your books and tell each other about the brochure extract you read. Try to persuade the other two that yours is the holiday you should all be going on next year.

A3 The result of **A2** was probably inconclusive. What you need is more detailed information about each of the offers, helping you to get underneath the glossy image to some real facts. In pairs, and referring to the extracts, improvise conversations for each in which one of you, the agent, answers a multitude of questions on every conceivable point from the prospective client: *What does 'spacious' really mean?*, *What exactly is a 'generous breakfast'?* etc.

A4 You made your choice, you paid your money, you got what you paid for. Or did you? Study the exchanges below, as two of you compare notes after the holiday.

> A: Well, according to the brochure, the facilities were supposed to be superb, but in (actual) fact they were dreadful, weren't they?
> B: Well, they weren't all that impressive, I must admit.
> A: Not that impressive? They were absolutely diabolical!
> B: Oh, I wouldn't go so far as to say that. One or two of the things they had were quite tolerable, I thought.

> A: We were led to believe that the whole thing would be out of this world. It turned out to be ghastly in every way, didn't it?
> B: Well, it wasn't that marvellous, it's true.
> A: Not that marvellous? It was nothing less than/nothing short of frightful.
> B: Oh, I wouldn't have said that/called it frightful. One or two of the days were pleasant enough, weren't they?

Practise these exchanges in groups of four, each couple taking turns to grumble to the other pair. Then continue in similar mood with the help of these prompts and keeping the basic framework of the dialogues above.
1 food/meals: *delicious/absolutely tasteless – tasty – virtually inedible – passable*
2 service/waiters: *excellent/terribly sub-standard – good – appalling – fairly quick*
3 hotel/rooms: *spotless/very dirty – hygienic – filthy – reasonably clean*
4 scenery/views: *fantastic/terrible – great – downright awful – reasonable*
5 excursions/trips: *thrilling/downright boring – exciting – tedious – quite interesting*
Now use claims made in the extracts on the left to generate similar conversations of your own, still in groups of two pairs.

A5 In small groups, write a brochure entry advertising your own region and local accommodation. See which group makes a holiday there sound most attractive.

4

B Communicative grammar

B1 You probably 'know' three or four thousand English adjectives, but do you use more than one of them confidently with any given noun?

A £200	B	C	D
a magnificent 19th-century hand-carved mahogany easy chair	a pair of superb 13-inch French solid brass candlesticks	a set of 6 fine amber cut-glass German champagne glasses	a Victorian rosewood chiming grandfather clock

Here is a summary of principles (not rules) governing the ordering of adjectives:

that	my	(*determiner*)
fantastic	nasty	(*subjective comment*)
large	little	(*size*)
Edwardian	modern	(*age*)
round	triangular	(*shape*)
dark brown	white	(*colour*)
English	Korean	(*nationality/origin*)
oak	plastic	(*material*)
kitchen	dining-	(*compound element*)
table	table	(*noun*)

(Though, of course, only two or three would normally be used at one time.)

The 'compound element' includes many nouns and verbs acting adjectivally – *car door, Christmas present, running shoes, frozen food* – and a few adjectives which are so close to their noun that in many languages they produce a single word: *old woman, young man, double bed.*
Another principle is that general descriptive adjectives precede more specific or more powerful ones – leaving the best till last, as it were. For example: *a loud, piercing, ear-splitting scream.*

B2 On the basis of the above, how would you move the adjectives below to find a home in front of their respective noun?
1 I want some apples. (*green / nice / eating / big*)
2 She was wearing a scarf. (*beautiful / Japanese / silk / red*)
3 I met a lady. (*old / little / good-natured*)
4 We need a pot. (*iron / cooking / large / round*)
5 I had an experience last night. (*frightening / almost supernatural / strange*)
6 He bought a pair of boots. (*riding / size 9 / Spanish / brown / leather*)
7 We saw a film. (*sentimental / deeply moving / sad*)
8 We stayed in a cottage. (*200-year-old / picturesque / lovely / thatched*)

B3 Game: 'Add a word' (see Teacher's Guide Unit 4)

B4 Look again at the four 'lots' on page 40. First, write down the amount of money (in pounds) that you think three of them fetched in a recent auction. (The first one may act as a price-guide.) In a moment you are going to hear the sale of lots B, C and D. After each sale, comment on the accuracy of your guesses using one of these sentences.

> It's far more/much less valuable than I anticipated.
>
> It's worth rather less/slightly more than I guessed it was.
>
> It's not quite/nearly as valuable as I thought it would be.
>
> It's nothing like/nowhere near as valuable as I imagined.
>
> I had no idea it was worth $\left\{ \begin{array}{l} \text{anything like} \\ \text{anywhere near} \end{array} \right\}$ as much as that.
>
> It was about $\left\{ \begin{array}{l} \text{the same value as I expected it to be.} \\ \text{as valuable as I thought it might be.} \end{array} \right.$

B5 Incorporating similar sentences into your conversation, but varying the adjectives, tell your partner about how the following shocked, astonished or mildy surprised you:

1 a hotel you stayed at a little while ago
2 a recent sporting event you've seen
3 a town you recently visited for the first time
4 a party you were at not long ago
5 a film you saw the other day
6 a book you've read lately

C Vocabulary: more adjectives

C1 Study how adjectives are 'weighted' in the following exchanges.

> A: Don't you think that actress is beautiful?
> B: I wouldn't call her beautiful. Pretty, perhaps.
> A: Oh, come on. She's more than pretty. I find her really stunning.

> A: Hasn't that chap got a massive physique?
> B: I don't know about massive. I suppose he is on the large side.
> A: On the large side? Look at his shoulders! He's absolutely colossal!

> A: Is it me, or is this wine vinegary?
> B: I wouldn't say it was vinegary. It is a bit sharp though, I admit.
> A: It may seem sharp to you. It tastes terribly sour to me.

In pairs, take part in similar exchanges with the prompts below, finding a suitable (and truthful) phrase or clause to follow *of* each time.

1 the smell of . . . (*horrible / rather unpleasant / disgusting*)
2 the cost of . . . (*astronomical / rather high / staggering*)
3 the prospect of . . . (*frightening / a little daunting / absolutely terrifying*)
4 the sight of . . . (*moving / quite sweet / very touching*)
5 the sound of . . . (*exquisite / quite pleasant / enchanting*)
6 the problem . . . (*enormous / pretty big / huge*)
7 the idea of . . . (*idiotic / a bit silly / lunatic*)
8 the news of . . . (*astonishing / somewhat unexpected / incredible*)
9 the chances of . . . (*remote / rather slim / virtually non-existent*)
10 the thought of . . . (*really depressing / slightly disturbing / horrifying*)

C2 Still considering the 'weight' of adjectives, which in each group below do you feel is the most complimentary and which the least so? Order the ones in between accordingly, then compare notes with other students, giving reasons for your ordering. Group A words refer to your latest effort as film director; B to your piano-playing; C to that political speech you made; D to your recent contribution to modern art.

A	B	C	D
professional	embarrassing	tedious	sophisticated
mediocre	breathtaking	magnificent	nondescript
enjoyable	heavy-handed	tremendous	grotesque
powerful	workmanlike	stimulating	appealing
efficient	respectable	fascinating	inventive
effective	spectacular	boring	revolting
gripping	delightful	repetitive	hideous
patchy	adequate	interesting	chaotic
corny	uneven	original	naive

C3 Adjectives with an -ed ending are among the most interesting in English. With *well-established, tree-clad* and *Alpine-dominated*, we can see an underlying passive structure operating; not so with *warm-hearted* (=with a warm heart) and the examples below. In each box, match the adjectives with the nouns to make the most appropriate pairs. Use these in short sentences for example:

Acrobats are often double-jointed.

I want a long-sleeved sweater.

hypocrites	light-fingered
professors	dark-skinned
tennis stars	silver-tongued
acrobats	absent-minded
sun-worshippers	bow-legged
cowboys and cellists	bad-tempered
kleptomaniacs	broad-shouldered
bodyguards	two-faced
beer drinkers	double-jointed
travelling salesmen	pot-bellied

	wide-brimmed	saucepan
	twin-bedded	spectacles
a	double-breasted	room
	two-roomed	shoes
a pair of	short-haired	jacket
	gold-rimmed	flat
	long-sleeved	stool
some	high-heeled	hat
	copper-bottomed	sweater
	three-legged	terrier

You might also look out for yet another family of -ed adjectives: *much-travelled, badly-behaved, well-read* and so on.

D Register: expressing enthusiasm and disappointment

D1 Listen first to an enthusiastic theatre-goer, and then a professional reviewer on the phone to her editor, giving their opinions on a play they have just seen. Comment on all the linguistic differences between the two styles of expression, giving examples each time.

D2 Imitating as far as you can the style of the first speaker, talk in pairs about:
1 a concert that disappointed both of you.

2 a film you both agree was fantastic.
3 a politician's speech on which you have different opinions.
4 an exhibition of modern art on which neither of you can make up your mind.

D3 Dictation

Listen again, and write out the article the theatre critic wants printed.

E Functions: describing and identifying, being explicit

E1 You are going to hear someone describing to a friend the shop in which he intends to buy things he needs for his holiday. Notice how the description is largely based on points of comparison with shops they both know.

1 Listen, and then say which shop in the neighbourhood of the school you are in most closely fits the description you heard.

2 In pairs, incorporate elements of that conversation, describing to your partner:
   a a shop that is something between a supermarket and a delicatessen.
   b a club that is half disco and half a sports club.
   c a restaurant that is a cross between a pub, a bistro and a pizzeria.

E2 Now listen to the same man in that particular shop, having a little trouble in the shirt department. Again notice the elements of comparison.

1 Listen, then say what you now know about the shirt he finally buys.

2 In pairs, improvise a similar conversation with one of you in search of:
   a a long-sleeved, plain red, pure-wool sweater.
   b a relatively inexpensive, steel-framed tennis racket.
   c a Japanese digital watch with a pale blue leather strap.

E3 Soon after arriving at his exclusive holiday resort, the man had all his luggage stolen. Here he is describing his case and bag to the local police sergeant.

1 Listen, then draw a sketch of the baggage that disappeared.

2 In pairs, describe in as much detail as possible:
   a the bicycle you've lost.
   b the baby and pram that have gone missing.
   c the briefcase containing all your papers, which is nowhere to be found.

E4 The man in our story saw a suspicious-looking individual near his hotel room at about the time his luggage vanished. The police sergeant is now taking notes on the description.

1 Listen, make notes too, then say in what ways the individual described is different from the one in the picture (right).

2 In pairs, improvise a similar conversation, in which one of you describes someone in this room (without naming names of course). Use the comparing techniques you heard, and make sure the 'sergeant' does his fair share of prompting.

F   Language practice game: 'Call my bluff' (see Teacher's Guide Unit 4)

Read the following notes and example of the game. Then play it in teams in class.

'Call my bluff' is the title of a very successful panel game on English television. It is played by two opposing teams and a chairman. A word is put up on a board and the three members of one team give a definition of the word. Only one of these definitions is true; the other two are 'bluffs'. (Team members have to try and bluff their opponents into thinking that their definition is correct.) The opposing team has to work out which is the true definition. There is a simple points scoring system.

Here is an example of a word (which very few English people know!) with definitions.

a   You all have a picture of the typical brave Wild West sheriff in America. He's the tall, handsome, clean-shaven one with shiny silver guns and clean leather jacket, clean black trousers and shiny black leather riding boots – even when there's a dust-storm all around him! He's as tough as nails and as strong as an ox. You know him, of course. What you probably don't know is that he was not always called a sheriff. There is one small part of the Wild West where the man was originally called an eriff. Eriff – another name for a Wild West sheriff.
(It's a bluff – all lies!)

b   There are lots of expressions in the English language which show how much the English think of birds, for example: as proud as a peacock, as happy as a lark, as free as a bird, cocksure, and so on. And indeed many English people keep a small caged bird at home – often a budgerigar or a canary. And one way you can tell if a canary is two years old is by the maturity of its plumage: it will be an eriff, with its final flight feathers. Believe it or not, an eriff is a two-year-old canary.
(True! – but you don't have to learn the word!)

c   The word 'errif', pronounced *er'if*, with the stress on the second syllable, is an adjective which used to mean 'ugly and awkward' and was used in the eighteenth century in Scotland to describe an animal which no one would buy. A passage in a novel by Sir Walter Scott reads: 'There was indeed little point in taking the horse to market for it was too eriff to sell.' The word isn't used now and although you may find it hard to believe, that's what it used to mean: ugly and awkward.
(It's a bluff – a pack of lies!)

Now play the game yourselves.
Here are some expressions you may like to use in your definitions:

You may not believe this, but . . .
You may find this hard/difficult to believe, but . . .
Strange as it may seem, . . ./Believe it or not, . . .
This is as true as I'm sitting here!

Odd as it may sound, . . .
Oddly enough, . . ./Surprisingly enough, . . .
This is absolutely true!
This is the gospel truth!

G Exercises for homework

G1 Read carefully these claims made by advertisers on behalf of their products, then write down what you think each of them is trying to sell.
Example: 'pure, natural, concentrated goodness'
You write: *fruit juice*

1 'washable, durable, easy to hang'
2 'tasty and nourishing, top breeders recommend it'
3 'mild and satisfying, made from three different kinds of beans'
4 'it's tough on dirt, but kind to your hands'
5 'guaranteed non-stick, with a stainless copper bottom'
6 'gentle and caressing, powerful and effective, unwanted dandruff a thing of the past'
7 'crispy and light but chewy too, delicious with cheese or by itself, an essential part of your calorie-controlled diet'
8 'as easy as falling off a log to apply, it gives a perfect, long-lasting satin finish'
9 'its revolutionary twin-blade action gets closer than you ever thought possible'
10 'completely safe and lifelike, it will cry and wet itself'

G2 This was the advertisement which led you to book a two-week stay at the Sunshine Luxury Camp Site:

And this is part of the miserable card you sent home mid-holiday:

SUNSHINE LUXURY
CAMP SITE

Large, well-appointed site within easy reach of beach and shops:
- clean, hygienic washing and toilet facilities
- free use of showers
- well-stocked shop
- tight security
- friendly service

Rates per Week:

We're in the middle of a nightmare! We tried to leave after one night, but the idiot in charge told us point-blank we wouldn't get a penny back. The site is a swamp in the middle of nowhere. Added to that, the place is a complete mess – the toilets look as if they've never been cleaned. One shower costs a fortune, you wouldn't believe it. And to cap it all, we've had nearly all our equipment stolen. I'm going to be writing to the owner as soon as we get back. Talking of which, I can't wait to be back there.

Now write that letter to the owner.
Comment on the unacceptable conditions at his site and demand a full refund. Choose your adjectives especially carefully.
- Were the toilets dirty, unsanitary, foul or scandalous?
- Were those extra charges high, disgraceful, nonsensical or exorbitant?
- Was the site itself unsightly, disgusting or uninhabitable?
- Was that manager casual, offhand, unhelpful or downright rude?
- Was the advert misleading, inaccurate, flagrantly dishonest or illegal?

Try to keep a formal tone throughout the letter. Refer to page 27 before you begin, then consider linking your attacks with two or three of these expressions:

What is more, . . .
Moreover, . . .
Furthermore, . . .
In addition to this, . . .
As if this were not enough, . . .

Activity 1 (see Teacher's Guide Unit 4)

One man's vision of the future

BIG BROTHER
IS WATCHING YOU

A1 In 1949, just four years after the end of World War II, the English writer George Orwell published his now famous novel *Nineteen Eighty-Four*, a vision of the future in which the world is divided into three great powers, Oceania, Eurasia and Eastasia. This is the opening of that novel.
Read it first to find answers to these general questions. (As you read, note down any words or phrases you do not understand, but do not look them up in a dictionary.)

1 What did you learn about Winston's physical appearance, character and attitudes?

2 How good or bad were Winston's living conditions?

3 How would you describe the kind of State that Winston was living in? Why?

4 What features of life in 1984, as described by the author, impressed or horrified you most? Why?

IT was a bright cold day in April, and the clocks were striking thirteen. Winston Smith, his chin nuzzled into his breast in an effort to escape the vile wind, slipped quickly through the glass doors of Victory Mansions, though not quickly enough to prevent a swirl of gritty dust from entering along with him.

The hallway smelt of boiled cabbage and old rag mats. At one end of it a coloured poster, too large for indoor display, had been tacked to the wall. It depicted simply an enormous face, more than a metre wide: the face of a man of about forty-five, with a heavy black moustache and ruggedly handsome features. Winston made for the stairs. It was no use trying the lift. Even at the best of times it was seldom working, and at present the electric current was cut off during daylight hours. It was part of the economy drive in preparation for Hate Week. The flat was seven flights up, and Winston, who was thirty-nine and had a varicose ulcer above his right ankle, went slowly, resting several times on the way. On each landing, opposite the lift-shaft, the poster with the enormous face gazed from the wall. It was one of those pictures which are so contrived that the eyes follow you about when you move. BIG BROTHER IS WATCHING YOU, the caption beneath it ran.

Inside the flat a fruity voice was reading out a list of figures which had something to do with the production of pig-iron. The voice came from an oblong metal plaque like a dulled mirror which formed part of the surface of the right-hand wall. Winston turned a switch and the voice sank somewhat, though the words were still distinguishable. The instrument (the telescreen, it was called) could be dimmed, but there was no way of shutting it off completely. He moved over to the window: a smallish, frail figure, the meagreness of his body merely emphasised by the blue overalls which were the uniform of the Party. His hair was very fair, his face naturally sanguine, his skin roughened by coarse soap and blunt razor blades and the cold of the winter that had just ended.

Outside, even through the shut window-pane, the world looked cold. Down in the street little eddies of wind were whirling dust and torn paper into spirals, and though the sun was shining and the sky a harsh blue, there seemed to be no colour in anything, except the posters that were plastered everywhere. The black-moustachio'd face gazed down from every commanding corner. There was one on the house-front immediately opposite. BIG BROTHER IS WATCHING YOU, the caption said, while the dark eyes looked deep into Winston's own. Down at street level another poster, torn at one corner, flapped fitfully in the wind, alternately covering and uncovering the single word INGSOC. In the far distance a helicopter skimmed down between the roofs, hovered for an instant like a bluebottle, and darted away again with a curving flight. It was the police patrol, snooping into people's windows. The patrols did not matter, however. Only the Thought Police mattered.

Behind Winston's back the voice from the telescreen was still babbling away about pig-iron and the overfulfilment of the Ninth Three-Year Plan. The telescreen received and transmitted simultaneously. Any sound that Winston made, above the level of a very low whisper, would be picked up by it; moreover, so long as he remained within the field of vision which the metal plaque commanded, he could be seen as well as heard. There was of course no way of knowing whether you were being watched at any given moment. How often, or on what system, the Thought Police plugged in on any individual wire was guesswork. It was even conceivable that they watched everybody all the time. But at any rate they could plug in your wire whenever they wanted to. You had to live – did live, from habit that became instinct – in the assumption that every sound you made was overheard, and, except in darkness, every movement scrutinised.

Winston kept his back turned to the telescreen. It was safer; though, as he well knew, even a back can be revealing. A kilometre away the Ministry of Truth, his place of work, towered vast and white above the grimy landscape. This, he thought with a sort of vague distaste – this was London, chief city of Airstrip One, itself the third most populous of the provinces of Oceania. He tried to squeeze out some childhood memory that should tell him whether London had always been quite like this. Were there always these vistas of rotting nineteenth-century houses, their sides shored up with baulks of timber, their windows patched with cardboard and their roofs with corrugated iron, their crazy garden walls sagging in all directions? And the bombed sites where the plaster dust swirled in the air and the willow-herb straggled over the heaps of rubble; and the places where the bombs had cleared a larger patch and there had sprung up sordid colonies of wooden dwellings like chicken-houses? But it was no use, he could not remember: nothing remained of his childhood except a series of bright-lit tableaux, occurring against no background and mostly unintelligible.

A2 Now read the text again and, in pairs or groups of three, help each other to understand the vocabulary. Here is an example: *From the context, the word 'nuzzled' must mean something like 'pressed close' because Winston was trying to keep his face protected from the cold wind.*

Now do the same with other words and phrases you don't understand (e.g. *slipped, swirl, tacked, depicted,* etc.), only referring to a dictionary when you can't deduce meanings.

A3 Now in pairs, without looking at the text, ask and tell each other
   1 what the weather was like.
   2 where Winston lived.
   3 what the block of flats was like that Winston lived in.
   4 what the poster was which was tacked to the wall.
   5 why Winston couldn't use the lift.
   6 why he had to go up the stairs slowly.
   7 what the *oblong metal plaque* was that was on the wall of his flat.
   8 why Winston couldn't shut it off.
   9 what Winston wore (and why).
   10 why the skin on his face was rough.
Write down and then ask each other more questions like this about the rest of the text.

A4 Discussion

When 1st January, 1984, dawned, was the world really like this? Were there (or are there) any similarities between life now and that described by George Orwell? If you think so, what were (or are) they? If you don't think so, what about the future?

B Communicative grammar

B1 Defining, describing or specifying more closely who or
what you are referring to using relative pronouns

1 Defining (or restrictive) clauses

subject   *People **who/that** live in glass houses shouldn't throw stones.*
*The poster **which/that** faced you when you went in had been tacked to the wall.*

object   *The man **(who(m)/that)** you met yesterday is staying with us.*
*The house **(which/that)** your friends bought is the oldest in the village.*

Note that

a *where* and *when* will often replace *in which* and *on which* in sentences like
That's the house *where (= in which)* I was born.
That was the day *when (= on which)* we went swimming.

b prepositions can occur at the beginning or end of a clause, depending on formality:
The room *in which* Winston lived was very small. (formal)
The room *(that)* Winston lived *in* was very small. (informal)

Now practise these two dialogues and adapt them to talk about the
things or people below. Express your likes and dislikes as you think.

A: That house is very nice, isn't it?	A: I don't like that woman. Do you?
B: I don't know. Which do you mean?	B: I don't know. Who are you talking about?
A: The house (that/which) your friends have just moved into.	A: The woman (who(m)/that) we were introduced to yesterday.
or The house that's/which has got those big windows in the front.	*or* The woman who's/that's just moved into the flat upstairs.

1 car – Fiat have just produced it *or* . . .
2 secretary – she's just joined the firm *or* . . .
3 video game – it's a bit like *Star Wars or* . . .

4 newsreader – we saw her on TV last night *or* . . .
5 shop – they've just opened it near the church *or* . . .

2 Non-defining (or non-restrictive) clauses

subject	Harry Smith, who	is a friend of mine	, lives near you.
	This house, which	is 200 years old	, is the oldest in the village.

↑ ↑

by the way; as you (may) know: as you are (well) aware;
as you may (or may not) have heard; as everyone knows

↓ ↓

object	Harry Smith, who(m)	you've met before	, lives near you.
	This house, which	we've lived in for years	, is 200 years old

You will remember that non-defining clauses tend
to be formal and are more frequent in written
English, although we do use them in speech,
especially with the addition of phrases like *by the
way, as you may know,* etc. Remember also that

a these clauses must have commas in writing,
and are marked by pauses in speech;
b *that* CANNOT replace *who(m)* or *which* in
non-defining clauses;
c the object form *whom* is still found in this
construction.

Now join these sentences:

1 Mary's just flown to Australia. She hates flying, as
you know.
2 The people there were very polite to me. As you
may have heard, they can be rude.
3 That grandfather clock was sold for £500. By the
way, it's over 150 years old.
4 Ron James has just become champion again. He's
been champion for the past 3 years.
5 George Orwell is probably best known for *Nineteen
Eighty-Four.* He also wrote *Animal Farm.*

B2 Describing a further action (or actions), or specifying
what was happening or what someone was doing, using
the Present Participle -*ing* form

1 In the sentence 'Winston went slowly, resting several times on
the way', *resting= and (he) rested*. Study these examples, then
rephrase the following sentences in the same way.

He bumped into me, knocking the glass out of my hand. (= . . . and he knocked . . .)
They ran after me, shouting my name every few minutes. (= . . . and they shouted . . .)
Cut the cloth carefully, making sure the lines are straight. (= . . . and make sure . . .)

   1 The official studied my passport and checked all the details.
   2 She walked slowly up the stairs and held on to the handrail.
   3 The police searched the building and looked into every room.
   4 He spoke carefully and gave plenty of examples.
   5 I stood and watched the match for a while, and then walked
      on. (*Be careful!*)

2 In the sentence 'It was the police patrol, snooping into people's
windows', *snooping= who were snooping*. For progressive
actions like this (after *It is/was*), the relative pronoun and
auxiliary verb(s) are often omitted.
Practise these exchanges and adapt them to the prompts below:

A: What's/What was that noise? | A: Who's/Who was that at the door?
B: Oh, it's/it was only John chopping wood in the garden. | B: Oh, it's/it was only the postman bringing the post.

   1 flag – flap against flag-pole outside   **1** salesman – sell silk scarves
   2 lift – stop on the floor above   **2** neighbour – want to borrow some sugar
   3 children – come in back door   **3** someone – ask the way to the town hall
   4 builders – work on the site opposite   **4** woman – want to know if a Mr Green lived here
   5 helicopter – go over   **5** John – ask if he can use the telephone

Note that this construction is also used with *there is/there are*, as in e.g.

There was a large poster hanging on the wall. (= . . . which was hanging . . .)
There are two men staring at us. (= . . . who are staring . . .)

B3 Sometimes we turn sentences around in English to give greater emphasis to what would normally be the
second half, e.g. 'How often . . . the Thought Police plugged in on any individual wire was guesswork.'
Study these two types and then turn the following sentences around in the same way:

a How long he'll stay is anyone's guess. = It's anyone's guess how long he'll stay.
   Who she was remained a mystery. = It remained a mystery who she was.
   What he thought was not important. = It was not important what he thought.

b What they were doing no one knew. = No one knew what they were doing.
   Where she was going I don't know. = I don't know where she was going.
   Why he needs so much money I've never asked. = I've never asked why he needs so much money.

   1 It's up to you how long you stay.   **6** It doesn't matter how much you pay.
   2 I didn't enquire when they were planning to leave.   **7** He won't say where he was born.
   3 We'll never know what really happened.   **8** It's a mystery why he left his job.
   4 I'll never understand why he bought that car.   **9** It's not important how you get the job done.
   5 No one seems to know what he does.   **10** I never understood what it was all about.

C Listening and register

There are many ways in which formal and informal English differ.
Two of the most noticeable are the ways in which people use
relative pronouns, and words like *moreover, consequently, likewise,*
etc. in place of more everyday words and phrases such as *besides,
so, in the same way,* etc.

C1 You are going to hear a sketch from a satirical revue. But first study
these pairs of sentences and notice the way relative pronouns are employed.

informal written and spoken	formal written and spoken
The room (that) he lived in was small.	The room in which he lived was of moderate size.
The people (that) the money is being raised for will be grateful.	The people for whom the money is being raised will be very appreciative.
The laws (that) they had to live by were very harsh.	The laws by which they were forced to live were repressive.

Now look at these clauses, listen, and write down the version the other speaker uses:

PRESENTER/INTERVIEWER:
1a . . . what house I live in . . .
2a _____
3a . . . the last time I was stopped by the police . . .

MR NOONE:
1b _____
2b . . . the doctor and dentist whom you visit . . .
3b _____

Did you notice any other clauses with relative pronouns? Were they formal or informal?

C2 Now study this table, listen to the interview again, and notice how
these words are used. Afterwards, see if you can remember any of
the sentences in which the speakers used these words.

Words expressing	informal/neutral	formal	very formal
result	so	therefore, accordingly, consequently, in consequence	thus, hence
addition	and, also, too, besides (which), and what's more	furthermore, moreover	
opposition	but, however	(and) yet, on the contrary, nevertheless, nonetheless	
comparison	in the same way	similarly, likewise	

C3 Discussion

How much truth do you think there is behind a sketch like this?
Do you think some people are turning into 'robots'?

D Vocabulary: some verb 'families'

Apart from through the grammar we use (pp 48–49), we can obviously specify more precisely what we mean by using the right word. How many different verbs do you know, for example, meaning *to fly*? In each section opposite there is a sentence or two from the text on pp 46–47, together with a group of words related in meaning. Find out what they all mean (using a dictionary if you wish) and then do the exercise.

D1 'In the far distance a helicopter *skimmed* down between the roofs, *hovered* for an instant like a bluebottle, and *darted* away again with a curving flight.'

> to soar; to glide; to float; to swoop

Read this short description and complete the blanks with appropriate verbs:

As I watched from the beach, the bird launched itself from the cliff and immediately _____(1) up to about 200 metres. It stopped, if that's the right word, and seemed to be _____(2), like a boat on water. With wings outstretched, it _____(3) slowly down the length of the beach until it was so low that it _____(4) the surface of the water with its feet. I thought it was going to land in the water, but no, it _____(5) up again, and this time reached a height of about 30 metres, where it _____(6) in one spot, scrutinising the waves below. Then, all of a sudden, its wings almost folded, and neck outstretched, it _____(7) down and into the water and appeared seconds later, a large fish struggling in its beak.

D2 'The black-moustachio'd face *gazed* down from every commanding corner.'
'. . . every sound you made was overheard, and . . . every movement *scrutinised*.'

> to stare; to glimpse; to glance; to peer; to gape; to glare

Complete each sentence with the most appropriate verb (and give reasons):
1   He _____ at me in amazement. (*glanced? glimpsed? gaped? peered?*)
2   She was furious, but said nothing; just _____ at him. (*stared? gazed? glared? gaped?*)
3   The boss _____ everything I write. (*glances? scrutinises? glares? peers?*)
4   He _____ at me in the dim light. (*scrutinised? stared? glanced? peered?*)
5   They _____ into each other's eyes . . . (*stared? peered? glared? gazed?*)

D3 'Behind Winston's back the voice from the telescreen was still *babbling* away about pig-iron . . .'

> to mumble; to chatter; to natter; to mutter; to chat; to grumble

Complete each sentence with an appropriate verb:
1   Don't _____ so much. I can't understand what you're saying.
2   They were all _____ away in some foreign language.
3   It's no good _____ about it: we all feel the same but we've all got to do it!
4   The two old men sat in the park and _____ about old times.
5   The two girls in front of us _____ all the way through the film.

D4 'Down at street level another poster . . . *flapped* fitfully in the wind . . .'

> to flutter; to wag; to wave; to brandish; to shake

Put the verbs in column 2 in the correct order to make sense:

1	2	3
The bird	brandished	its wings.
The dog	waved	its tail.
The boy	shook	to his girlfriend.
The flag	flapped	in the breeze.
The knight	fluttered	his sword in the air.
The man	wagged	his fist at us.

E Exercises for homework

This newspaper article was written on 30th December, 1983. Read it carefully and then do the exercises opposite.

A look at Orwell's 1984

– from the perspective of a closing 1983

YOU may have read the book Nineteen Eighty-Four – now see the year! But don't be surprised if the year bears little relation to George Orwell's story. He intended it as a satire, not a prophecy.

Even so, the book, written in 1948, has initiated widespread debate over where the country is heading. Many of the themes contained in Orwell's novel reflect fears that are still with us today.

He seized on our fear of being enslaved by showing us a people robbed of freedom.

He envisaged a nightmare land dominated by omnipresent authorities who keep checks on every action, word, gesture or thought.

Played down

All this may lead us to survey the political scene in Britain in 1984 with some concern.

R. K. Moseley, whose books on British politics have established him as a leading authority on the subject, played down such fears when I spoke to him at his home in Poole.

By Tim Walker

'True, dictatorships flourish as never before. Torture and imprisonment without trial is the lot of thousands in many parts of the world,' he admitted.

'True, it could be argued that Governments, even in Western Europe, sometimes appear to regard their electorate as Orwell's witless proles, easily manipulated by the mass media.

'But in Britain at least, while we are beset with immense social problems, politically conditions are still very different from those in Oceania, the land of the future that Orwell described.

'Pressure groups opposing aspects of the Government's policies have never been stronger or more articulate.

'On trust'

'Above all, we still have the right to vote the Government out of office. Our rulers know they have the power – but only on trust.

'We are, thank goodness, still a long way from the nightmare of Orwell's Nineteen Eighty-Four.'

You need only pick up a newspaper to find proof of this. In Britain the State has no control over the Press and papers can and do speak out against the Government when they see fit.

In the bleak country Orwell described, the media were controlled by the State, and their sole purpose was to churn out the State's propaganda.

The State even introduced an official language named Newspeak, which precluded people from communicating subversive thoughts.

'Fluffier'

According to Dr Arnold Mason, deputy head of general academic studies at Bournemouth and Poole College of Further Education, our language is actually going in the opposite direction.

'Newspeak was about cutting the language down to the bone and narrowing our range of thoughts. In fact the language is getting fluffier, with many new words being introduced, and others diversifying in meaning,' he said.

But he conceded that politicians were increasingly exploiting the language to suit their own ends, and often used words that hid their real intentions and made what they described appear more acceptable.

They can use evasive gobbledygook like 'anticipatory retaliation' for 'knocking the hell out of the enemy without provocation'.

There was no truth in Orwell's land beyond that which the State told you. Religion, as we know it today, had no place in his bleak new world.

In Orwell's book, mankind had not only turned its back on religion, it had also grown morally diseased.

Mr Michael Bell, secretary of East Dorset Family Concern, saw parallels in Orwell's book with today's society. In Oceania, the public were thirsty for violent executions, and revelled in pornography.

Today these appetites are satisfied by video nasties and merchandise sold in sex shops.

In Orwell's world, family values had been cast aside, with children literally turning on their parents, and marriages, as we know them, obsolete.

'To some extent family values are being eroded,' said Mr Bell. 'But, good grief, it hasn't got to the stage Orwell described. And, with determination, I believe these trends can be reversed.'

Technology

Another trend Orwell examined in his book was the increasing use of new technology.

Mr Peter Jackson, chairman of Dorset Confederation of British Industry, said the book portrayed new technology as an evil, manipulated by the State to keep the population in order.

He said the book encouraged an unhelpful, Luddite-like approach to new technology. 'In fact it is a life-saver. If we turn our backs on new technology we will cease to be competitive, and it will be our downfall.'

'I admit that in the short term new technology does occasionally threaten jobs, but by making industry more competitive it safeguards them in the long term. So there is no reason to fear new technology.

'It improves our quality of life, by releasing us from many of the boring, repetitive jobs, and increasing our leisure time.'

Sometimes people see shades of Nineteen Eighty-Four in the widespread use of information-gathering machines. But Mr Jackson said the machines could hardly be said to threaten our privacy and were there for our own good.

Not the same

'They can help companies spot people who run into debt. That helps them cut overheads, which keeps prices down.

'And it's silly to think of Big Brother when you see cameras monitoring you in shops. It isn't the State that put them there – only store chiefs who want to stop shoplifters forcing up their prices.'

In Nineteen Eighty-Four no one could embark on enterprises that were independent of the State.

'That is certainly not the case today, though of course industry can be affected for better or worse by Government policy. 'As I see it, the trend in industry today is moving away from State control,' he said.

So if you believe all that, free enterprise lives on in England as we prepare to enter 1984. Man and machine are getting along famously, and religion and morality are still important to us.

Saddened?

Big Brother, if he is alive today, must be a sad and embittered man.

E1   Write a summary of the article writer's view of 1984, beginning each paragraph with the starter sentence given, and using the other starters and questions as a guide.
While the writer feels that many themes in Orwell's novel reflect fears in modern society, nevertheless . . .
(What is his general view of what 1984 will be like?)

On the question of politics . . .
(What is the situation in some parts of the world? But what about Britain? And what have people still got the right to do?)

As regards the media and language . . .
(How different is the situation in Orwell's world from the one in Britain in 1984? And what is happening to language, according to one of the people the writer interviewed?)

In terms of society and its values . . .
(Are there any similarities between Orwell's world and ours? And what is happening to family values – again according to one person he interviewed?)

When it comes to technology, . . .
(How did Orwell's book portray technology? And how is it regarded by many now?)

And finally, as far as State control is concerned, . . .

E2   Write a letter to the editor of the newspaper in which this article appeared, putting the opposite point of view. In other words, argue that the world today (perhaps only under the surface?) is beginning to look very much like the world of Orwell's *Nineteen Eighty-Four*. Refer, as the article does, to politics, the media, society and its values, technology and state control. Begin your letter with 'Dear Sir, . . .' and close with 'Yours faithfully,' and sign it.

Unit 6

A1 In pairs or small groups, ask and tell each other about your early childhood. Ask and say
- when and where you were born.
- whether you had any brothers or sisters.
- what you were like as a baby or small child.
- what your earliest memories are.
- what your father's occupation was when you were very young.
- what was happening in the world when you were born, etc.

A2 In groups of four, read and help each other to understand just *one* of these four extracts. Each is from a biography or autobiography. Then do the exercises opposite. Extract **1** is from *Maria Callas* by Arianna Stassinopoulos; **2** is from an article about Eartha Kitt by Andrew Duncan (*Sunday Telegraph*); **3** is from *Unreliable Memoirs* by Clive James; and **4** is from *The Door Marked Summer* by Michael Bentine.

1

Maria Callas

At the same time, both parents were getting ready for the arrival of their new son. Neither of them seemed prepared to consider even for one moment the possibility that their new-born child might be a girl. Their yearnings and primitive logic had convinced them that the new baby would be a son who would take the place of Vasily and make their life, so far away from where he had lived and died, complete. All the little clothes Evangelia knitted were blue, and everything they bought for the baby's bedroom was for a baby boy. 'Ever since Vasily's death,' Evangelia said, 'I had prayed for another son to fill the empty place in my heart.'

On 2nd December 1923, the expected son failed to arrive. Instead Dr Lantzounis brought to the mother a baby girl weighing twelve-and-a-half pounds. The baby clothes would not have been right even if they had been pink: 'You made clothes for a baby like a doll,' Dr Lantzounis told Evangelia, sitting by her bed, laughing and patting her hand, 'but they are too small for this baby. The nurses can't get them on her. She is like a young lamb, she is so large!'

The first words Maria heard from her mother were 'Take her away.' And her mother's first gesture was to turn her eyes from her daughter and fix them on the snowstorm raging outside the hospital window.

2

'I would really like to write a book about my two half-sisters, Pearl and Almeida. We had the same mother, but have all led completely different lives and don't know each other at all. Pearl is a housewife, and Almeida is a nurse'.

Eartha, the eldest, was born when her mother – part Cherokee, part black – was 14 years old. She took her surname from the plantation. 'My father was supposedly the owner's son. I wasn't wanted by anyone, because I wasn't the right colour for any particular group. That's why my mother gave me away when I was about four years old. She was marrying this older black man; I remember cowering behind a door listening to her pleading with him to take both me and Pearl.

Eartha Kitt

'He said, "I'll take Pearl, but I don't want that yellow girl, Eartha Mae, in my house". It wasn't a matter of my mother not wanting me. She had to do what she did, and I have no feelings of bitterness towards her.

'She gave me to a woman I called Aunt Rosa, but I was just left to drag myself up with the animals in the forest. I played with them, ate whatever they ate. Very often it was a toss-up between the dogs, the cats, the birds and myself as to which was going to get the leftover scraps from the table. I didn't talk until I was God knows how old, but I remember everything that happened.'

3

Clive James

I was born in 1939. The other big event of that year was the outbreak of the Second World War, but for the moment that did not affect me. Sydney in those days had all of its present attractions and few of the drawbacks. You can see it glittering in the background of the few photographs in which my father and I are together. Stocky was the word for me. Handsome was the word for him. Without firing a shot, the Japanese succeeded in extricating him from my clutches. Although a man of humble birth and restricted education, he was smart enough to see that there would be war in the Pacific. Believing that Australia should be ready, he joined up.

This isn't the place to tell the story of my mother and father – a story which was by no means over, even though they never saw one another again. I could get a lot of mileage out of describing how the good-looking young mechanic wooed and won the pretty girl who left school at fourteen and worked as an upholsterer at General Motors Holden. How the Depression kept them so poor that they had to wait years to get married and have me. How fate was cruel to both of them beyond measure. But it would be untrue to them. It was thirty years or more before I even began to consider what my parents must have meant to each other. I can't remember my father at all. I can remember my mother only through a child's eyes. I don't know which fact is the sadder.

4

Michael Bentine

When the Armistice came, Pop decided to accept an offer from the Peruvian Government to build their Air Force, which then consisted of a few worn-out early wartime machines, and in 1920 my father, mother and four-year-old brother set out on the SS *Ortega* for a much-delayed second honeymoon, in South America.

It was there, in Peru, that I was conceived and later born in Watford, Hertfordshire, on their return to England, which Ma had insisted on, in order to ensure that I, like my brother, was a British-born citizen.

The date was 26th January 1922 and on that day I became entitled to two passports and dual nationality, British because I had been born in Britain and Peruvian because, under the laws of the Republic of Peru, if a father is a Peruvian his children are too, and his sons are liable for military service in the Peruvian Army. So you can see that for that innocent, new-born baby, life would never be uncomplicated.

When I was a year old my family moved to Folkestone. All the concentrated academic study, the long hours in the factories, the field trials and flying had resulted in my father being constantly assailed by vicious attacks of asthma and bronchitis, and he was forced to retire at the age of thirty-two.

A3 Re-form into different groups of four (one from each of the previous groups) and ask and tell each other about the early life of Maria Callas, Eartha Kitt, Clive James and Michael Bentine. Ask and say

1 when and where the person was born.

2 whether he or she was wanted.

3 how many brothers and sisters he or she had.

4 what he or she was like as a baby or young child.

5 what his or her father was doing (for a living) when he or she was born.

6 what else we learn about the family into which he or she was born, etc.

A4 Stay in the same groups. From what you have learned, and through more question and answer, try to find out

1 which two extracts have most in common.

2 which seems to be the most humorous.

3 which is the most shocking.

4 which is the most sentimental.

5 which gives most information about the person's father.

6 how much all four extracts have in common.

A5 Class discussion

1 Which extract most made you want to read more? Why?

2 Were there any similarities between your own early days and those described in the extracts?

B Communicative grammar

B1 Present Perfect (*have done*) and Simple Past (*did*) to
express ideas in the past.

There are layers of complexity surrounding the concepts of *have done*
and *did*. Study these sentences: *I never met my grandfather.*
                                       I have never met my grandfather.

The first sentence tells us that my grandfather has passed away:
'when he was alive' is understood. The second tells us he is still
alive: 'never met him *yet*' is understood. What is suggested by each
of the sentences in these pairs?

1 I had a lot of good times in England.
  I've had a lot of good times in England.

2 I didn't invite John to the party.
  I haven't invited John to the party.

3 They haven't told their son about the war.
  They didn't tell their son about the war.

4 I went to town.
  I've been to town.

5 I haven't been to the bank today.
  I didn't go to the bank today.

6 I didn't see the boss this week.
  I haven't seen the boss this week.

7 The introduction of the breathalyser had a great effect on people's lives.
  The introduction of the breathalyser has had a great effect on people's lives.

Now complete the questions in the following story with a
suitable form of the verb, Present Perfect or Simple Past.

You're driving along the road when the traffic
in front of you comes to a halt. You ask your
passenger, who has a better view: ....
He mumbles encouraging noises for half an
hour, then the traffic starts moving freely
again. Suddenly the car in front stops and you run
into it. You shout angrily at the driver: ....
He is apologetic and enquires politely: ....
You, still furious, demand: ....
He replies innocently: ....
You give up the argument and drive on. A sign
saying 'Free Drinks' comes up on the left, but
you drive past. Your thirsty passenger,
absolutely incredulous, gasps: ....
You don't answer. After an hour or so, your
engine cuts out and the car glides gracefully
to a standstill. Your passenger asks: ....
You both look sadly at the petrol gauge. He sobs: ....
You mutter something about it looking like
an empty tank. He remonstrates: ....
You mumble something about having a bad
memory and ask lamely: ....
He mentions an AA box, and you hunt frantically
for your membership card, but in vain.
He exclaims: ....

'No,' you reply, somewhat more than relieved: ....
and start walking back to phone the AA for assistance!

1 *'Why / we / stop?'*

2 *'Why / you / stop / so quickly?'*
3 *'I / do / much damage?'*
4 *'you not ever / hear of signalling?'*
5 *'Oh / you not see / my signal?'*

6 *'Why / you not stop?'*

7 *'What / happen?'*
8 *'We / not run out of petrol, / we?'*

9 *'But / you not fill it up today?'*

10 *'you / see / a phone box / back there?'*

11 *'you not come out without your
AA card, / you?'*
12 *'I / just find it / in my wallet,'*

B2 Simple Past (*did*) and Past Perfect (*had done*) to express ideas in the past

You know that the Simple Past *did* is used to express actions at a definite time in the past, and that the Past Perfect is used to describe earlier actions in relation to a 'simple past' action, for example:

They had already closed the gates when I got to the football stadium.

Remember, however, that a *did . . . did* combination is often used to describe two actions occurring at almost the same time, for example:

They closed the gates just as (= the moment when) *I got to the stadium.*

In the following sentences choose between a *did . . . did* combination and one with *had done . . . did* or *did . . . had done*. Give your irregular verbs a polish as you go!

1 She (*ring*) the hospital late last night in case he (*have*) an accident.
2 They all (*leave*) the room in protest when he (*light*) his filthy old pipe.
3 Bond (*foolishly leave*) the country before they (*give*) him his gun.
4 He (*leave*) the company by the time I (*go*) to work there last year.
5 I (*feel*) very tired that morning: I (*not sleep*) well the night before.
6 By the time we (*get*) to the theatre, the curtain (*already go up*).
7 Until I (*meet*) her last week, I (*never speak*) to a real aristocrat.
8 The woman (*strike*) the child when he (*spit*) his chewing-gum on the ground.
9 She (*put on*) weight as soon as she (*go back*) to Italy and started eating pasta.
10 His arm (*keep*) him awake at night because the nurse (*wind*) the bandage round it too tightly. (Consider two possibilities.)

B3 Past and Past Perfect, Simple and Continuous

Study this:

When I got home, they had dinner.	(= I got home, then they had dinner.)
When I got home, they were having dinner.	(= . . . they were in the middle of dinner.)
When I got home, they had had dinner.	(= . . . they had finished dinner.)
When I got home, they had been having dinner for half an hour.	(= . . . they had started half an hour before and were still in the middle of it.)

Now complete the following, using the prompts and the most natural tense form:

1 When the referee finally blew his whistle,
  a seven players / lie / on the ground.
  b one player / already throw / four or five punches.
  c nobody / hear.
  d they / play / 95 minutes.

2 When the brothers went bankrupt,
  a they / open up / new company under a new name.
  b they / already run up / debts of £50,000.
  c the company / run down / several years.
  d they / lose / £2,000 a day.

3 I could tell from her face that
  a she / cry.
  b she / try hard / not to cry.
  c she / find out / the truth.
  d she / already know / the truth.

C Functions: giving explanations for present or past states

English often uses continuous verb forms (*have been doing* and *had been doing*) when drawing conclusions. The Present Perfect *have been doing* suggests that the results of the activity can be seen in the present, and the Past Perfect *had been doing* that the results of the activity can be seen in the past. For example:

Someone's been reading my book! = *I'm sure of it because it's been left open at the wrong page, or someone's moved it.*

They'd been smoking in the room. = *I knew when I went in because the room smelled so awful.*

C1 You notice something wrong or unusual about a third person.

He or she . . .
- is sweating.
- has blisters on his/her hands.
- seems to be feeling dizzy or giddy.
- is hoarse, or has a sore throat.
- seems to have a stiff neck.
- looks as if he's/she's got pins and needles.
- is out of breath and panting.
- has bloodshot eyes.
- is blinking rather a lot.

And/or his or her
- lips are sore.
- teeth are chattering.
- eyes are watering.
- cheeks are swollen.
- fingernails are filthy.
- face looks very pale.
- hands are blue with cold.
- face is very flushed.
- hair is wet.

In pairs, improvise dialogues like this:

A: Why are his teeth chattering?
 or Why is he shivering?
 or His hands are blue with cold!
B: (Yes,) well, he's been standing out in that cold wind!

C2 Do the same, this time putting your questions/remarks in the past, for example:

A: Why was he sweating before lunch?
 or Did he have a temperature at lunchtime?
 or His face was really flushed at dinner.
B: Well, (yes/no,) he'd been running and he was exhausted.

D Register: formal and informal letter styles

D1 Read carefully these extracts from two letters written by the same young woman. Is it just her mood that makes them feel different in tone?

> As you will see from my enclosed curriculum vitae, I am a 24-year-old graduate from the University of Manchester, where I read Social Sciences.
> Since graduating, I have had considerable practical training in dealing with handicapped children of all ages. During the two years in which I was employed as a language teacher in Bordeaux, I spent my vacations in a holiday centre which had been specially established to cater for the needs of mentally and physically retarded teenagers. I feel that the experience I gained there has furnished me with an insight into the problems such people face.
> Since returning to England I have been engaged in voluntary social work in local schools, and am now extremely keen to broaden my horizons at an establishment such as yours.
> Should you wish to pursue my application, I would be available for interview at your convenience. Perhaps you could contact me at ...

What different effect would the letter have had on the reader if the alternative verbs had been used?

read – studied	*feel* – think	*broaden* – widen
graduating – leaving university	*gained* – got	*wish* – want
dealing with – coping with	*furnished* – provided/given	*pursue* – carry on with
was employed – worked	*face* – come up against	*be available for* – come for
established – set up	*returning* – coming back	*contact* – get in touch with
cater for – do something for	*been engaged in* – done	

D2

> ...<u>No doubt</u> the <u>agency people</u> gave you some <u>information</u> about me, so I won't bore you with what I did at school and <u>uni. etc</u>.. <u>I couldn't wait to leave</u>, <u>as a matter of fact</u>, and then, when I had left, <u>I couldn't for the life of me think</u> what to do. <u>In the end</u>, I went over to France for <u>18 months or so</u>, teaching and doing <u>odd bits</u> of social work. Got engaged to a French car mechanic who was running holiday camps for <u>kids</u> out there, but that <u>fell through</u> when it turned out he'd been married twice before! You're not married, are you?!
>
> Since I <u>got back</u>, I haven't really been out with anyone – I've been spending most of my time <u>writing off for jobs</u> actually.
>
> Anyway, if you think there's any point in our getting together, <u>even if nothing comes of it</u>, I'm free most weekends and could come and see you. <u>Let me know</u>.

Find other ways of expressing the words and phrases underlined in the letter. Then decide whether your innovations are similar in tone to the original, or more, or less, formal.

E   Listening and socialising

E1 You are all at a party. None of you knows each other very well. Listen to some of the conversations that are being started around the room. Notice how such conversations begin, and notice too how the first speaker helps to keep things going.

E2 Now you take your place at the party – on your feet! Circulate, and begin conversations with 'lonely-looking' strangers. (When spoken to, you must confirm the questioner's impression and improvise a little background information for him or her.) Here are some opening gambits:

They tell me (that) . . .	*I gather (that)* . . .	*How is it that you* . . .?
I hear (that) . . .	*Is it true (that)* . . .?	*Am I right in thinking* . . .?
How come (you . . .) . . .?	*I've been told (that)* . . .	*Aren't you the man/woman/*
Is it right (that) . . .?	*I understand (that)* . . .	*person who* . . .?

And these are some of the ways you might continue:

. . . you once met / Robert Redford/.   *. . . you've been to / Russia/.*
. . . you've been on the radio/ on TV.   *. . . you once worked as a/ an . . .*
. . . you play / the tuba/.   *. . . you once won a prize for . . .*
. . . you've got nowhere to sleep tonight.   *. . . you were born in / America/.*

No doubt you will think of many more with which to 'challenge' your fellow-guests. If any conversation seems to be going on too long, excuse yourself politely and join someone else: also, don't be afraid to interrupt someone else's conversation (with, for example: *Excuse me for butting in, but . . . I couldn't help overhearing what you were saying . . ./but aren't you the person who . . .?* etc.).

F Vocabulary: some more verb 'families'

Have a good look at this collection of everyday action words, verbs
which may not always be on the tip of your tongue when you need
them.

wash clean rinse boil dip	push shove	squeeze pinch grip	cut slice chop saw	tear rip
	fix stick glue press	wrench jerk	cook boil grill fry	lift raise pick up prop up
hit pat tap knock hammer strike	throw toss spin flick roll	drop lower	fold bend crumple screw up	turn screw twist stir tighten loosen
rub scrub polish wipe scrape scratch stroke	wind wrap tie thread	pull drag haul drill pierce prick	put down lay rest	pour sprinkle spread cover

F1 Demonstrate the meaning and use of the verbs,
either verbally or by gesture!

F2 Look at and listen to how someone comforted a
baby:
'No, it was no trouble at all. I just went upstairs,
picked him up, put him over my shoulder and
patted him a few times. Then I laid him down on
the bed and covered him up – and he was asleep.
That's all there was to it!'

Now in pairs or small groups tell each other how
easy it was for you to do the following. (You
probably won't want to stray outside the Simple
Past very often, but can you find the right verb at
the right time?) Then describe other such tasks.
1 Put up a shelf in the kitchen.
2 Make a salad.
3 Change a wheel on a car, or mend a puncture
on a bicycle.
4 Dress a wound, or revive someone who had
fainted, or stop someone's nosebleed.
5 Rescue a piece of toast from burning badly,
and then eat it.

F3 Look at and listen to how someone has tried to
combat insomnia:
'I've tried everything. I've tried putting a drop of
whisky in my late-night coffee. I've tried going
without coffee completely and sucking mints
instead. I stuck a wooden board under the
mattress for a few months, and then I ripped out
the springs. I even sawed a few inches off the
bedlegs, but it was no good. I've tried propping
myself up on three pillows, and I've even tried
counting sheep. But nothing seems to work!'

Now in pairs or small groups, tell each other
about your (vain?) attempts to
1 get a bloodstain out of a shirt/blouse.
2 get flowers or vegetables to grow in your
garden.
3 stop a tap dripping.
4 get a particular dish to taste 'like mother
makes'.

Tell each other about other similar problems that
you've tried to solve.

G Exercises for homework

G1 This is a very sloppy letter of application from a Mr B Smith. Read it carefully and then rewrite it for him so that he stands a better chance of getting the job.

Dear Sir,

   I saw your ad. in the paper about a good, well-paid job taking foreigners around Britain, and I'm quite interested.

   I went to the normal sort of schools and got most of the 'O' Levels I took plus a few CSEs; that was in 1978 or '79. Since school, I've been around quite a bit. I had about two years in a school near Bristol looking after their social and sports programme and have spent a few summers showing tourists round England, which I quite liked. I presume that that experience could be useful in some way at your place.

   I'm fairly good at a number of sports and I'm quite keen on music – most kinds – and drama.

   I'm pretty sure that I could do the job you're advertising. (You didn't actually mention the exact salary in your advert. Perhaps you could let me know, if you're interested in me.)

Yours,

B. Smith

P.S. I'm 24, by the way, and single.

P.P.S. I could come for an interview any time.

G2 Study this last autobiographical extract by the American actress/singer Doris Day. Then write 250 words on your own family background. Considering the points that Doris Day did might help you order your ideas:

– where and when you were born (and any reason why you were given your name);
– your first house/your first town (compared with your present situation);
– your father's profession;
– something to typify your mother;
– where your parents originated from (and perhaps their parents).

See if you can incorporate some of the expressions and sentence patterns you met in the texts at the beginning of this Unit as well. And watch your tenses!

   I was born Doris Kappelhoff, named by my mother in honour of her favourite movie actress, Doris Kenyon, a silent-screen star of that year, 1924. (I now live on Crescent Drive in Beverly Hills, and, as bizarre fate would have it, a few houses away from me, on the very same street, lives Doris Kenyon, my namesake, a beautiful, vibrant, chic lady whom I occasionally see.) My parents lived at Greenlawn and Jonathan streets in a red-brick, two-family house in Evanston, a moderate-income Cincinnati suburb. I was born in that house, attended by a good German midwife as my two brothers had been before me.

   My father, William, was a music teacher – primarily piano – and choral master, while my mother, Alma Sophia, was a true hausfrau. She moved the furniture around a lot and my father would constantly fall over it.

   Both my parents were born in downtown Cincinnati but their parents were German immigrants. My mother's father came from Berlin. His family was quite wealthy but he ran into trouble when he refused to join the German army on the grounds that he didn't believe in military activity. There was no war then, but he refused to become a part of any military buildup that might lead to war, so he left Germany, forsaking the lucrative family business. He came to Cincinnati, where there was a large German community, and he opened a pretzel factory.

Unit 7

IT'S WRITTEN ALL OVER YOUR FACE... OR IS IT?

A1 It has been said that we learn a lot about people's moods and emotions from their faces, and particularly from their eyes. If that is so, what might this man be expressing in each picture? – fear? terror? delight? pleasure? anger? sorrow? worry? ecstasy? sadness? boredom? Briefly write down what you think, and why. (And by the way, *are* they a man's eyes? How do you know?)

A2 Discuss what you think with the rest of the class. Use sentences like this:

In the top/middle/bottom picture, I'm sure he must be /amused about something/.
or *he must be /smiling about something/.*

He can't be /bored/ – just look at his eyes.
or *He can't be /thinking/ – just look at his eyes.*

He could/might be /screaming in terror/. Anyway, he looks as if he's /screaming/.

(I think) there's (just) a hint/a trace of /amusement/ in his eyes.

The creases in the corner of his eyes/The furrows between his eyebrows suggest he might be /smiling/.

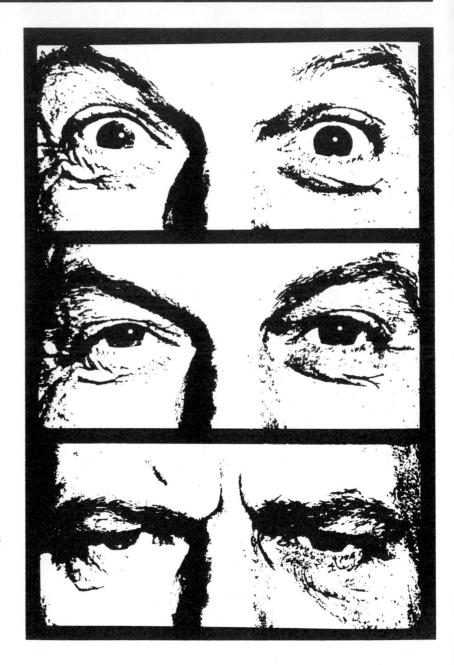

62

A3 Listen and discuss

1 Study these photos carefully and write down what emotion or feeling you think each girl is (or might be) expressing. Don't show your 'answers' to anyone else yet.

1

2

3

4
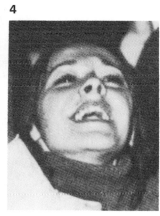

5

2 You are now going to hear part of a radio programme. Listen carefully and then discuss the questions below.
  a What was said about about our ability to judge people's emotions and feelings from their facial expressions? Do you agree or disagree? Why?
  b What did one of the speakers say affects our interpretation of facial expressions? What examples were given of what we need to know? Can you think of others?

c What emotions or feelings did the panellists suggest the girls might be expressing in the photos? How close were they to what you wrote down in exercise 1 above?

3 Having listened to the last part of the programme, were you surprised to find out what emotions the girls were really expressing? Why?/Why not?

B Communicative grammar

You will know that we use *can, could, may* and *might* to ask for or express permission, that we use *can, is/are able to, could* and *was/were able to* to express ability, and that we use *mustn't* and *couldn't* or *wasn't/weren't allowed to* to express prohibition. But let's look at the ways we use modal verbs to express:

1 possibility or supposition
2 assumption or deduction
3 obligation (and absence of obligation)

B1 Expressing possibility or supposition with *could, might* and *may*

1 Can you honestly answer these questions with certainty?

Look at picture 1:   What nationality are the two men?
                      What are they doing?

Now cover the picture: What nationality were the two men?
                      What were they doing?

2 In situations like this you have to assume or suppose, like this:

| I think they | could / might / may | (well) | be Portuguese. / be having an argument. / have been Hungarian. / have been having an argument. |

Now write down what you think the people in the three photos might be doing, what might have happened, etc.
Then check with the rest of the class.

B2 Expressing assumption or deduction with *must* and *can't*

If you have reasons for being more certain about who people are (or were), what they are (or were) doing, etc., then use sentences like this:

| I'm sure they | must / can't | be Portuguese / be having an argument / have been Hungarian / have been having an argument | because . . . |

1

2

In pairs, tell each other what you can *deduce* from the photos using *must* or *can't*, and give reasons.

3

B3 Expressing obligation with *must, have (got) to* and *need to*, and absence of obligation with *don't have to, haven't got to, don't need to* and *needn't*, (and prohibition with *mustn't*)

1 Read this, look at the drawings and do the exercise:

Gestures

'A gesture', wrote Desmond Morris in his book *Manwatching*, 'is any action that sends a visual signal to an onlooker. To become a gesture, an act has to be seen by someone else and has to communicate some piece of information to them.'

The problem with gestures, however, is that, unlike many facial expressions which are readily understood across the world, gestures tend to vary from country to country or from culture to culture, so that a similar hand gesture may mean something completely different in, say, Germany and Indonesia.

Between speakers in the United Kingdom, the gestures here would be quite clear. Say what they mean, or what they might mean, using sentences like this:

It means { you must(n't) / you have (got) to / you don't have to / you need to / (you don't need to) / (you needn't) } do that.

2 What other gestures do you use or do you know which express obligation, lack of obligation, prohibition or warning? Describe and/or show them and say what they mean.

3 An English-speaking friend is coming to your country and is worried about about what to wear, what do, what not to do, etc. Write down pieces of advice about clothing, social behaviour, etc. that he/she ought to know, and then discuss them. For example:

You mustn't smoke in the street. / You won't need to bring any warm clothes with you. / You needn't worry about the language – everyone speaks English.

You may need to use these future forms: *You will/won't have to . . . You will/won't need to . . .*

4 There is a problem with *need* in the past. Study this:

I *didn't need to go* to town. (= *There was no need for me to go*, but the listener still doesn't know if I went or not. It's ambiguous.)
I *needn't have gone* to town. (= I definitely went to town, but discovered later that *there was no need for me to have gone.*)

Rephrase these sentences using *didn't need to* or *needn't have* as appropriate:
a There was no need for her to have cooked so much. (We couldn't eat it all.)
b There was no need for them to ask the way. (They had been there before.)
c There was no need for me to have run. (The meeting started late after all.)
d There was no need for us to buy lunch. (We had taken sandwiches with us.)
e There was no need for you to have made your bed. (I would have done it for you.)

C Functions: expressing regrets, and speculating

C1 There are many ways of expressing regret in English. Look, and listen to this young businessman telling a colleague about something he regrets:

> 'I meant to have told you. (*What?*) You know I went to evening classes last year to get that exam in accountancy. (*Yes, I know. You said.*) Well, it turns out it was a complete waste of time. (*How come?*) I passed the exam, but I needn't have done the course at all. I could have done something a lot more interesting. (*Why?*) Well, I only did it because they said I needed it for promotion – and then they said they'd promote me without the qualification anyway. (*I don't believe it.*)'

In pairs, improvise versions of the young man's experience around these situations:

1 bought an expensive book instead of borrowing from the library
2 took out too much holiday insurance – didn't have enough spending money
3 had expensive repairs done on motorbike – would have been cheaper to buy new one
4 rushed home to see film on TV – had seen it – missed important local club meeting
5 booked tickets for a concert weeks ahead – plenty of tickets at the door – concert hall half empty

C2 1 Look at picture a) and practise this conversation. Then adapt it to improvise similar conversations about the people in pictures b) and c). Note that speaker A is suspicious and speaker B is defensive.
  A: What's that man doing down by the river?
  B: I don't know. I can't see very well. He might be feeding the ducks. I suppose. Or he could be throwing stones in the river. Or he may just be having his lunch.
  A: Oh, come on! I'm sure he can't just be having his lunch. Look at him. He must be throwing away evidence of a crime or something.

a)

c)

b)

2 Now cover the pictures and improvise the same conversations in the past, for example.
  A: What was that man doing down by the river yesterday lunchtime? etc.

D Vocabulary and register

There is quite a difference between the way we describe emotions and feelings in everyday speech and the way in which emotions and feelings are described in literature.

D1 Look at the examples and say what you notice about the language used in the sentences from novels and short stories and then in the spoken sentences (in speech bubbles).

Her face registered utter boredom . . .

He smiled briefly, but there was too a hint of apprehension deep in his eyes . . .

As the realisation of the true horror of the situation dawned on him, his face became a mask of terror . . .

'She looked bored stiff...'

'He smiled, but you could see he was worried...'

'When he realised what was happening he looked terrified...'

D2 Cast your eye over these nouns and adjectives to do with emotions and feelings:

fear	– afraid	pleasure	– pleased	fury	– furious
fright	– frightened	amusement	– amused	anger	– angry
terror	– terrified	ecstasy	– ecstatic	apprehension	– apprehensive
horror	– horrified	happiness	– happy	worry	– worried
sadness	} – sad	excitement	– excited	surprise	– surprised
sorrow	}	boredom	– bored	astonishment	– astonished
disgust	– disgusted	aggression	– aggressive	reflection	} – thoughtful
contempt	– contemptuous	suspicion	– suspicious	meditation	}

Now read these brief extracts from novels and short stories and describe the characters' emotions or feelings to a partner verbally:

1 The faces of all the men in the line expressed their communal sorrow . . .
2 Disgust was written all over her face . . .
3 Her eyes displayed her pleasure, tinged with a trace of suspicion about the man's intentions . . .
4 The boy sat at his desk resigned, a picture of boredom, waiting for the next lesson.
5 Together, poring over their game of chess, the two old men formed a single study in reflection . . .
6 Fear gripped them . . .
7 She allowed a flicker of surprise to cross her face . . .
8 Somewhat surprisingly, in the face of such an attack, his face expressed mild amusement, not the indignant anger expected by the others . . .
9 Her face glowed with happiness . . .
10 No words could adequately have expressed the utter contempt in his eyes as he surveyed the boy's rough handiwork . . .

D3 If you've ever seen yourself as a 'novelist' or a 'short story writer', now's your chance! Read these few lines of 'spoken English' and then rewrite them as if for a paragraph in a novel or a short story. Try to use the kinds of phrases employed in the sentences above.

'Carol looked happy and excited when she went into the cinema. She was looking forward to the film because friends of hers had been very enthusiastic about it. She wasn't even thinking about Donald. It was pretty gloomy and there were a lot of people in the cinema, so she didn't see him at first. When she did spot him, she was surprised: he said he was staying home to work. Then she saw he was with another girl and she became very angry and suspicious. When he happened to look across and see her, he looked decidedly embarrassed.'

E Read and discuss

This poem was written by Ian Serraillier. Read it
and discuss the questions below.

PRISONER AND JUDGE

1

The prisoner was walking round and round the prison yard.
He had a low forehead and cruel eyes;
You couldn't trust him anywhere.

He dressed up as a judge; he put on a wig and robes
And sat in court in the judge's place.
And everyone said:
 'What a deep forehead he has, what learned eyes!
 How wise he looks!
 You could trust him anywhere.'

2

The judge was sitting in court in the judge's place.
He had a deep forehead and learned eyes;
You could trust him anywhere.

He dressed up as a prisoner; he put on prisoner's clothes
And walked round and round the prison yard.
And everyone said:
 'What a low forehead he has, what cruel eyes!
 How stupid he looks!
 You couldn't trust him anywhere.'

E1 About the poem:
 1 Why did the poet say 'You couldn't trust him
  (= the prisoner) anywhere'?
 2 When and why *could* you trust the prisoner?
 3 Why did the poet say 'You could trust him
  (= the judge) anywhere'?
 4 When and why *couldn't* you trust the judge?
 5 What is implied by 'a low forehead' as
  opposed to 'a deep forehead'?

E2 In small groups discuss this question: Do you
agree or disagree with the following? Give
reasons and examples.
You can learn everything you need to know about
a person from
 1 his or her hair
 2 his or her eyes
 3 his or her facial expressions and gestures
 4 his or her clothes – especially footwear.
When you have discussed all aspects of the
question, appoint a spokesperson to report back
to the rest of the class.

F Exercises for homework

F1 Put in the correct form of the modals and verbs in these sentences.
Example: You've got it wrong again. You (*can't*) (*pay attention*)
when I explained it.
You write: You can't have been paying attention when I explained it.

1 I think they (*might*) (*finish*) the meeting by now. I'll go and see.
2 There's a lot of noise coming from that room. They (*must*)
(*have*) a good time.
3 People were coming out crying with laughter. The film (*can't*)
(*be*) that funny, surely.
4 I (*not need*) (*phone*) John because he promised to phone me.
5 I phoned him, but then found that I (*not need*). He had written
me a long letter.
6 We (*may*) (*get*) a specialist in to talk on this subject. We
haven't got anyone suitably qualified on our own staff.
7 You (*can't*) (*do*) the job yet! I only gave it to you ten minutes
ago!
8 The Smiths aren't here yet. They (*could*) (*look for*) somewhere
to park the car.
9 We (*not need*) (*be*) so suspicous about that man. I checked his
references later and found he was a perfectly bona fide
representative for James and Son.
10 I got no answer when I rang his house earlier. Of course, he
(*might*) (*work*) in the garden or something.

F2 Imagine you attended an interview for a job which you had applied
for in writing. You were disgusted at the way you were treated,
however, and at the way the interview was conducted. Below are
the notes you wrote in preparation for a letter of complaint to your
local Employment Council. Read them carefully and then write the
letter, beginning like this:

'*Dear Sir,*
Yesterday I attended an interview for a job with a local company and was disgusted . . .

- Interview late — must have waited nearly 1 hour — no apology!
- Interviewer made me feel definitely inferior — kept smirking!
- May have made a few mistakes — may not have answered all questions fully — but I tried — was polite.
- Can only assume — interviewer must have had bad day — still no excuse.
- Must have mislaid my application form too — had no notes — surely didn't need to ask <u>everything</u> again !?
- Wasn't begging for job.
- Hope this was isolated case — if not, I might as well apply for job as interviewer. Couldn't do worse!
- Any action I could take against company?

So that's how it's done!

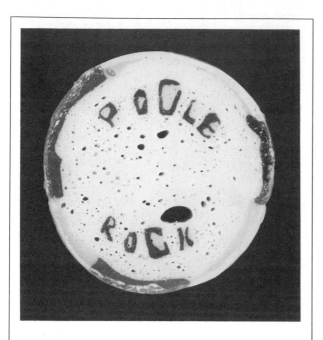

A1 Have you ever wondered how they get the lettering in rock or the colours in striped toothpaste? Read these explanations and then do the exercises.

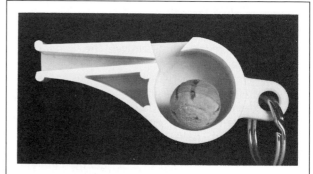

THUNDER IN THE WHISTLE

ROCK WRITING

Any message, in any language, can be reproduced in lettered rock – if it's short enough. Britain exports lettered rock to more than 50 countries. Much of the lettering is skilled work done by hand. The coloured sugar letters – about one metre deep from front to back – which form the actual message are stood along the length of a bed made of sugar and glucose. Another layer of sugar and glucose is placed on top with the rest of the lettering on top of that. A final layer of sugar and glucose makes the 'sandwich' complete. It is then folded into a one-metre cylinder, and the thin red outer casing wrapped around it. The roll weighs about 50 kilos. It is stretched by machine, pulled out onto tables about ten metres long, tapered by this time in the shape of a snake, and then rolled by hand to the required diameter, before being cut with shears.

Football referees, Boy Scouts and retired railway guards will be grateful for the pea in the whistle. How did it get there? The whistle wasn't, in the first place, built round the pea. And if it's a good whistle it almost certainly has, not a dried pea, but a bit of cork inside. The cork is ground and shaped on a lathe, then steam heated in a sort of glorified steam cooker to about 90°C, which makes it pliable. It is then inserted into the whistle with a special blade – like a small boy using his knife to rob his piggy bank. As it cools it recovers its spherical shape. Natural cork is expensive, but is nearly always used in the best whistles (it stands up better to moisture, keeps its shape, rolls satisfactorily and is light enough to be blown about). That tiny, bouncing ball of cork is enough to transform a common-or-garden whistle into what the trade calls a 'thunderer'.

HOLDING THE LIQUEUR

Liqueur chocolates can be made by hand, but mass production is more usual. Chocolate is poured into moulds at a carefully regulated temperature. The moulds are then closed and spun so that the chocolate clings to the inside surface, leaving a hollow in the centre. When the chocolate has set, the liqueur is injected through a small hole, which is then sealed.

Hand-making requires care and patience. The liqueur is prepared in syrup form and cast into moulds, which have been imprinted in trays filled with starch. The liqueur is left in the moulds for a day, during which some of the sugar separates and crystallises to form a crust around the shaped liqueurs. Each is taken out by hand and the film brushed off ready for it to be dipped in chocolate. Conditions have to be just right from start to finish or the whole process is ruined.

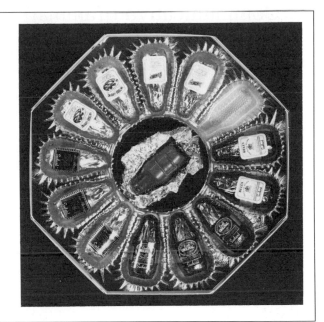

TIGER IN THE TUBE

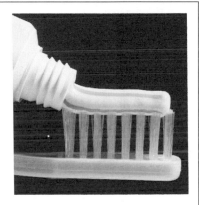

For those who have time to reflect first thing in the morning, two-tone toothpaste is something to reflect on. How do the stripes come out so precisely red and white? Why not a murky pink? The explanation is that the red and white toothpaste lie separately in bulk in the tube. When you press the tube to put the toothpaste on your brush, both colours are forced out. The red paste, which is the first to be loaded into the tube in manufacture, comes out through five holes in a plastic insert in the neck. The white can escape only through the main nozzle. It all sounds a little more simple from the manufacturer's point of view than in fact it is. His problem is to keep the colours from mixing prematurely as they lie side by side in the tube. He solves it by adjusting the relative viscosities – that is, flowing properties – of the two. And for our next trick . . .

A2 Explain, as well as you can (and by gestures and drawing if you need to), to another student
1 how lettered rock is made.
2 how they get the 'pea' into a whistle.
3 how liqueur chocolates are made.
4 how they keep the colours separated in striped (or two-tone) toothpaste.

A3 What can you learn from the text?
1 'Coloured sugar letters' are 'sugar letters which are (or have been) coloured', 'a dried pea' is 'a pea which is (or has been) dried', and so on. How many more phrases like this can you find in the explanations, and what do they mean?
2 'It is stretched by machine, pulled out onto tables about ten metres long, tapered by this time into the shape of a snake, . . .' means 'It is stretched by machine, *it is* pulled out onto tables . . ., *it has been* tapered by this time . . .'. How many more examples of the passive can you find like this where *it is, they are*, etc. or just *is, are*, etc. have been deleted?
3 'Much of the lettering is skilled work done by hand' means 'Much of the lettering is skilled work *which is* done by hand'. How many more examples can you find where *which is, which are, which has been* or *which have been* have been deleted?

A4 Project: 'Explain it to me' (see Teacher's Guide Unit 8)

B Communicative grammar: the passive for impersonal explanations, reports, etc.

B1 The passive is often used in the formal, impersonal language which is needed for (scientific and technical) explanations, rules, regulations, reports and so on. Just to remind yourselves of the passive in different tenses, study the sections below and then do the exercises.

1

Present Simple	The chocolates are always packed on the same day they are made.
Present Continuous	The new factory is being built now. (They started 6 weeks ago.)
Present Perfect	This process has been used for hundreds of years.
Past Simple	Your order was received exactly a week ago.
Past Continuous	The factory was being built when I was here last year.
Past Perfect	The result had already been announced before we arrived.
Future	The goods will be sent/are going to be sent tomorrow.
Future Perfect	It will have been finished by the time you return.

Remember we usually avoid forms like *has/had/will have been being done* (and *will/can/may/should/might be being done*), perhaps not surprisingly! They're almost impossible to say!

2 A *by*-phrase containing the agent (i.e. who does or did the action) is sometimes added e.g. *The boy was found by the police near the church*, but it is only required when it supplies essential information, as in these examples:

'Macbeth' was written by Shakespeare. / I've been stung by a wasp! This village is being ruined by heavy traffic trundling through it.

3 You may not have realised it, but there is a certain element of an agent in many prepositional phrases with *by*, as in these examples:

(made/done/produced) by hand/by machine; (done) by mistake/by accident; (sent/carried/taken) by air/by plane/by sea/by ship/by road/by lorry/by car/by land; (informed/warned) by letter/by cable/by telegram/by post/by (tele)phone.

B2 Rephrase the following sentences beginning with the words given in brackets:

1 Someone usually collects the post late in the afternoon. (*The post . . .*)
2 Someone is considering your application now. (*Your application . . .*)
3 No one has typed those letters yet. (*Those letters . . .*)
4 Goya painted that picture about 200 years ago. (*That picture . . .*)
5 They were closing the doors when we got to the theatre. (*The doors . . .*)
6 Someone had already sent the parcel by lorry before I could collect it. (*The parcel . . .*)
7 We will inform you of the exam results by letter. (*You . . .*)
8 Someone will have checked the order again by the time you come back. (*The order . . .*)
9 Someone always makes these special chocolate liqueurs by hand. (*These . . .*)
10 People are always criticising me! (*I . . .*)

B3 In pairs, practise the dialogue on page 73 and then adapt it as necessary with the prompts given.
The situation is this: you go back to a shop, office, garage, or whatever, where you left a job to be done. It is the second time you have been back and the job still hasn't been done.

A: Good morning, sir/madam. Can I help you?

B: I hope so. I left two films to be developed a fortnight ago.

A: May I have your name, sir/madam?

B: Yes, it's Smith. I came in a week ago because I was told they'd be done by then, but apparently they were still being developed.

A: Oh, yes, I remember, sir/madam. My colleague told me. I'll see if they're done now. (*pause*) I'm very sorry, sir/madam. They're still not ready yet.

B: This really is too bad! Can you tell me when they *will* be ready?

A: They'll be done by this time tomorrow. I promise.

B: Good. Well, while I'm here, a friend asked me to get these photos enlarged.

A: Of course, sir/madam. What's the name, please?

B: His/Her name? Jones. Can you tell me when they'll be done?

A: Yes, they'll be ready by Saturday. And I really must apologise for your job taking so long.

1 *At a dry cleaner's*: a suit, trousers, a dress – cleaned, dyed
2 *At a shoe shop*: shoes, sandals, boots – mended, soled, heeled, soled and heeled
3 *At a tailor's*: a dress, trousers, a coat – altered, lengthened, shortened, taken up, let down, taken in, let out
4 *At an accountant's*: annual accounts – prepared, balanced, audited
5 *At a secretarial agency*: letters, a report – (clean-)typed, photocopied

C Vocabulary: past participles as adjectives

C1 As you have seen from combinations like *a dried pea* (= a pea which is/has been dried) and *lettered rock* (= rock which is/has been 'lettered'), past participles occur quite frequently as adjectives before nouns. Study these combinations.

an acquired skill	a wasted journey	
a finished product	a hand-written report	
a guaranteed result	a (pre-)recorded talk/interview/programme	
the required diameter/length etc.	hand-made }	{ chocolates/sweets
the estimated cost	hand-finished	parts/goods
a carefully regulated temperature	factory-made }	{ components
a controlled environment	shop-soiled	articles
a damaged article	custom-made }	{ shoes

lettered rock	frozen food	striped toothpaste	added luxury
whipped cream	powdered milk	tinned fruit	wasted effort
coloured glass	processed cheese	trained personnel/staff	skilled labour

C2 Rephrase these sentences, changing the information in brackets to an adjective:

1 For supper we had some meat (*which had been tinned*) and salad.

2 The woman took the article (*which had been damaged*) back to the shop.

3 Putting a 'pea' into a whistle is a skill (*which has to be acquired*).

4 Goods (*which are made by hand*) are more expensive than goods (*which are made in a factory*).

5 The window was made of hundreds of pieces of glass (*which had been coloured*).

6 The product looked beautiful (*when it was finished*).

7 The manager wouldn't accept reports (*which were written by hand*).

8 They showed an interview with the Prime Minister (*which had been recorded before*).

9 I hate cheese (*which has been processed*).

10 The real cost of the job was nothing like the cost (*which had been estimated*).

D Listening

You are going to hear part of a slide-sound presentation about how pottery is made at the Poole Pottery.

D1 Study these photos and then listen to the commentary. Write the numbers 1–6 on a piece of paper and, as you listen, write the letters of the photos in the correct order as the processes are described on the tape.

A

D

B

E

C

F

D2 Check your answers with the rest of the class. Then listen again and make notes ready to give the same commentary yourself.

D3 In pairs, and using the photos and your notes, describe the different processes to a partner.

E Register: formal (written) and informal (spoken) explanation

E1 This is part of an entry in an encyclopaedia called *How It Works*. In pairs, study it and, by discussion, help each other to understand or work out what some of the unknown vocabulary means (or might mean).

AEROSOL spray can

Aerosol spray cans have been used as convenient packages for an ever-increasing range of products since they first came on the market in the early 1950s. The enormous variety of products available in spray cans includes whipped cream, hair lacquer, fly killer (and other insecticides), paint and perfume.

A spray can is normally made of tinplate with soldered seams, though for products that are stored under high pressure, an aluminium can is used. At the top, there is a simple plastic valve to control the spray. From the bottom of this, a flexible 'dip tube' runs down to the bottom of the can.

The can is filled with the product to be sprayed and the propellant, a compressed gas such as butane or Freon. The gas is partly liquefied by the pressure in the can, but there is a layer of free gas above the liquid. As the can is emptied, more of the liquefied gas vaporises to fill the space.

The valve is normally held shut by the pressure in the can, and by the coil spring directly below the valve stem. When the push button is pressed, it forces the valve stem down in its housing, uncovering a small hole which leads up through the stem to the nozzle in the button. This allows the product to be forced up the dip tube by the gas pressure in the can. The nozzle is shaped to give a spray or a continuous stream.

Aerosol cans are filled on the production line by inserting the product, putting the lid and valve on the can and forcing the propellant in backwards through the valve.

Below: cross section of a typical modern aerosol spray. Gas pressure produced by the volatile propellant forces liquid down the can and up the dip tube to the nozzle when the valve is opened.

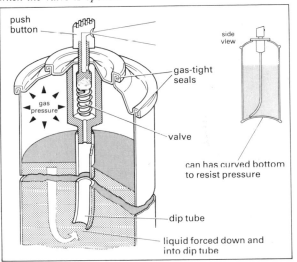

push button
gas pressure
side view
gas-tight seals
valve
can has curved bottom to resist pressure
dip tube
liquid forced down and into dip tube

E2 Now read the passage more carefully individually and make notes on how an aerosol spray can works.

E3 In pairs again, explain how it works as simply and as informally as you can. Use your notes and point to the diagram as and when necessary. Begin like this:

A: Do you know/Can you explain to me how an aerosol spray can works?
B: Yes, actually it's quite simple really. You see this push button at the top?
A: Yes.
B: Well, it's really a plastic valve that controls the spray.

Student B continues the explanation using these expressions and constructions as necessary:
This here is the . . . which . . . and which . . .
The can is filled with . . . . Look, here.
The more (hairspray) you use, the more . . . until . . .
What happens is this. When you . . , . . .
This in turn allows . . . and then . . .
As soon as / Every time you . . . , then . . .

Student A asks for further explanation or clarification with:
And then what?
So what happens then?
But how does . . . ?
But I don't quite see what happens when . . .
And expresses understanding with:
(Oh,) I see / I understand.
Yes. / (Yes,) I've got that.

F Exercises for homework

F1 The following tips on cutting your motoring costs have been written in a very impersonal style using a number of passive constructions. Read the tips carefully and then rewrite them as a handout for the man in the street. In order to make your version less impersonal (or more informal), remember to

1 use active verb forms where you can in place of passive constructions;
2 use imperative forms (*Do . . .* and *Don't . . .*);
3 use *you, your car*, etc.;
4 use simple sentences wherever you can.

You might begin: *Ten things you can do to make a little petrol go a long way.*

The heavy cost of motoring

Ten courses of action to be taken in order to 'make a little go a long way'

1 Ensure that your car is always properly tuned and serviced.
2 Ensure that the tyres on your car have been inflated to the correct pressure.
3 The grade of petrol recommended by the manufacturer should always be used.
4 The choke should be employed sparingly and always pushed in as soon as the vehicle will run smoothly without it being used.
5 Other drivers' actions must be anticipated at all times.
6 Excessive braking must be avoided. Fuel is wasted most when braking hard.
7 Any acceleration should be made smoothly.
8 A sensible cruising speed is advised. Up to one third more petrol can be consumed at 70 mph as compared with a speed of 50 mph.
9 No unnecessary weight should be carried in the car, since more fuel is consumed, especially when accelerating or climbing hills.
10 Wind resistance is increased by a roof rack. If one is fitted to your vehicle, it should be removed when not in use.

(More information about petrol saving can be obtained from the Department of Transport.)

F2 This is an extract from an account of one night's shift for an AA (Automobile Association) patrolman in Central London. The shift lasts from 8.00 in the evening until 8.00 the following morning. Read it carefully and then write the letter he might have written to a friend describing the night. Begin like this:

I like the job, but the night shift seems to be getting busier and busier. Last night, for instance, I'd hardly clocked in when we were called out to a Morris Minor in the Mall. We quickly . . .

The nightlife of an AA patrol

A night on the roads is hard work whatever the weather. Here is a shortened account of one of our patrols in Central London on one Friday night. As over 90 per cent of our members join for the 24-hour Free Breakdown Service, this article will confirm that their judgement is sound.

2020 hours
A non-starting Morris Minor in the Mall is the first call. The driver is amazed at our promptness – a mere five minutes. The failed petrol pump was put right and the driver headed towards Buckingham Palace.

 2255 hours
Three jobs later. Two calls come through. A Cortina with a flat battery and a Jaguar which will not start. No one is in attendance at the Cortina so a note is left on the windscreen by the AA.

 2340 hours
The Jag is again on the move after a faulty ignition switch is mended, so the patrol returns to the Cortina. There, a shivering driver looks on while his car is started for him.

 0040 hours
A Cavalier in Piccadilly has no driver so we move on to a Fiesta with the keys locked in the car. An entry is effected.

 0114 hours
Back to the Cavalier – the lady claims she ran down the road after us – soon she is laughing and the engine is roaring too.

 0245 hours
Two jobs later a couple are sitting frozen in their Fiat, not too happy. But the car is running again almost immediately and the wife blames the husband for leaving the lights on.

 0340 hours
Two phantom cars elude us – a Triumph Herald and a Renault just cannot be found. We hope they got going on their own, pity they didn't let us know.
We take a break.

 0530 hours
Two more jobs behind us. We attend another Cortina with a flat battery – we also act as newspaper boys when we find a bundle of papers addressed to the Europa Hotel.

 0735 hours
Daylight; and the last job is a blocked carburettor – this is fixed in fifteen minutes. We head back home.

Another successful night – with 18 jobs completed in all!

Activity 2 (see Teacher's Guide Unit 8)

Unit 9

What was that you said?

'Defenceless' Japanese was karate expert

Black belting for the hotel mugger

A1 In groups of three or four, read and study together *one* of the newspaper articles on these pages.

AN INTRUDER who attacked a tiny Japanese lecturer in his hotel room ended up in the corridor begging a passerby: 'Help, this man is trying to kill me.'

Karate expert Satushi Takahashi, 36, was wearing only underpants and slippers. His assailant was armed with a metal bed leg, a court heard yesterday.

But despite the odds, the karate black belt disarmed him.

Satushi told an Old Bailey jury he was getting ready for bed when somebody knocked on his door saying he was the manager.

'I opened it halfway and saw a very tall man, over six feet, holding a metal object.

'I blocked his attack with my right hand and both of my legs. He was knocked to the floor and I kicked him on the head with my soft slippers. I could have killed him with my skills but I tried not to over-injure him.'

I said: 'If you don't want to be killed please be a good boy' and we walked up the corridor.

A middle-aged man came up and the defendant begged for help, saying: 'This man is trying to kill me.'

Satushi added: 'My family and friends in Japan have enjoyed this story very much. I have told it many times.'

Security men took away the attacker, William Chalmers, with a suspected broken nose, the court heard.

Chalmers, 27, of South London, Camberwell, denies aggravated burglary. The trial continues.

DAILY MIRROR, *Friday, March 11, 1983*

Short sharp lecture in karate

By a Correspondent

A SLIGHTLY-built university lecturer from Tokyo yesterday demonstrated to an Old Bailey jury karate skills which had an intruder begging for mercy.

'I could have killed him, but I didn't want to over-injure him,' said Mr Satosai Takahashi, aged 36.

Mr Takahashi, a karate black belt, demonstrated the moves he made in tackling the intruder. He used Mr Charles Fisher, defence counsel, as a stand-in.

The barrister kept his wig and gown on and Mr Takahashi took his arm and twisted it, gently up his back, while putting him off balance with some nifty footwork.

Mr Jeffrey Rucker, prosecuting, told the court that Mr Takahashi, in England on research into languages and philosophy, was stranded in London on July 12 last year because of the train strike. He could not get back to Cambridge and booked into the Regent Palace Hotel, Piccadilly.

As he settled down with a book there was a knock on the door and a male voice announced that he was the manager.

Mr Takahashi who was confronted by a man brandishing a heavy metal bed leg, 'reacted with lively speed'. He trapped the man's arm in the door, disarmed him, and demanded to know: 'What is the meaning of this?'

When the man, alleged to have been William Chalmers, 27, unemployed, of Camberwell, London, managed to wriggle free, Mr Takahashi chased him down the corridor in his underpants and disabled him with karate kicks and punches, breaking his nose.

He grabbed Mr Chalmers and marched him to the security office, while Mr Chalmers pleaded with other startled guests: 'Get this madman off me, he's trying to kill me.'

Mr Chalmers, who claimed he had been looking for a friend, pleaded not guilty to aggravated burglary at the hotel.

The trial continues.
The Guardian, March 11, 1983

Daily Mail, Friday, March 11, 1983

Karate black belt gives court demonstration

Mr Takahashi tries a little legal arm twist

Daily Mail Reporter

SMILING Japanese lecturer Satushi Takahashi, small but powerfully able to look after himself, gave an Old Bailey jury a demonstration of the martial arts yesterday.

Using a somewhat wary barrister as a model, Mr Takahashi showed how, while wearing only his underpants, he disarmed an intruder at a London hotel.

A smiling Judge Peter Slot, cautious for the welfare of defence counsel, cautioned: 'Don't be too rough on him.'

Mr Takahashi, a karate black belt, grasped the lawyer's wrist. Mr Charles Fisher, who was holding a metal bed leg alleged to be the weapon in the case, looked apprehensive as his arm was twisted behind his back.

'Would you like a short adjournment after that?' asked the beaming judge. Mr Fisher shrugged and returned to the legal kind of defence.

Mr Takahashi told the court he was getting ready for bed when a 6ft. man armed with a metal object appeared at the door of his room at the Regent Palace Hotel in Piccadilly.

Mr Jeffrey Rucker, prosecuting, said Mr Takahashi squashed the door on the man then pulled him into the room and set about disarming him.

Cornered

The intruder, the court heard, tried to escape the Oriental attention by running up the corridor. But worse was to come.

He was cornered by 36-year-old Mr Takahashi and tried to fight him off. Mr Takahashi told the jury: 'I blocked his attack with my right hand and both of my legs.

'He was knocked to the floor. I kicked him on the head with my soft slippers. I was wearing only underpants.

'When he stood up and he did not try to attack me any longer, I said: "If you don't want to be killed please be a good boy", and we walked up the corridor.

'A middle-aged man came up and the defendant begged for help, clinging to him and saying: "This man is trying to kill me".'

Then, the court heard, three security men came running up and took the intruder away with a suspected broken nose.

Smiling, Mr Takahashi added: 'My family and friends in Japan have enjoyed this story very much. I have told it many times.' Mr Fisher retorted: 'I expect you have dined out on it.'

The man alleged to be the hotel intruder, 27-year-old William Chalmers, unemployed, of Addington Square, Camberwell, South-East London, denies aggravated burglary.

The trial continues today.

A2 Still working in the same groups, note down the relevant information, if any, which your article gives you about:

1 *the intruder:*
   a his name, age and present occupation
   b his physical build and height
   c his home address
   d what injury he suffered
   e what he was charged with
   f what his plea was
   g what his defence was
   h what the verdict was

2 *the karate expert:*
   a his full name, age and occupation
   b his physical build
   c his reason for being in England
   d his reason for being in that hotel

3 *the action:*
   a where exactly the fight took place
   b who witnessed the aftermath
   c when the security men became involved
   d what was unusual about the court proceedings

A3 Without referring back to any of the articles, exchange the information in your notes with students from the other groups. Like this:
'It said in *The Mirror* the man was tiny.'
'In *The Guardian* it described him as slightly-built.'
'I think the *Daily Mail* report called him "small".'
or 'It didn't say anything about that in our article.'

A4 Using information from all three articles, write the statements you imagine the two central characters in the story gave to the police that fateful night.

B Communicative grammar: reporting

B1 Basic sequence of tense changes

You will no doubt remember the principles for tense changes in reported speech; in effect, the verbs move one step backwards when the reporting verb is in the past.
'This man is trying to kill me!' → *He said the man was trying to kill him.*
'I was looking for a friend' → *He told the court he had been looking for a friend.*
'Will you do what you did?' → *He was asked if he would do what he had done.*
Run through the statements and questions below and report them in this way, beginning your sentences: *I told him (that)* . . . or *I said (that)* . . . (You will notice there are certain elements that cannot be faithfully reported. Omit them.)

1	I'll never leave you, darling.
2	You did well to get such a high mark.
3	It's your fault that everything went wrong.
4	All right then, I'll climb the ladder if you hold it steady.
5	I don't think it's fair to give me all the extra work to do.
6	You haven't got the right uniform on, you fool!
7	I'm sorry I wasn't able to come.
8	You always look so elegant, you know.
9	I'm not going to listen to another word of what you're saying.
10	I was nowhere near the scene of the crime.
11	We can increase your salaries as long as you're prepared to work longer hours.
12	If you don't do it of your own accord, I'll make you do it.
13	You're a heartless person who may ruin everything.
14	You've helped a lot, and I'm very grateful.
15	Look, I know I'm not the most organised person in the world.

B2 Gerund and infinitive constructions

To create slightly richer English, we often report people's comments with one of these verbs:

- *congratulate sby on doing, compliment sby on doing, criticise sby for doing, accuse sby of doing, thank sby for doing, blame sby for something happening*
- *apologise for doing, object to doing, admit (to) doing, deny doing*
- *refuse to do, threaten to do, agree to do, offer to do, promise (sby) to do*

Go through the sentences in **B1** once more and report them, using each of these verbs once. For example: *He criticised me for not having the right uniform on.*
Remember: the simple gerund – *doing* – can normally express past events as well as present and future ones: sometimes, however, the perfect form – *having done* – still sounds and reads better, particularly if it avoids ambiguity.

B3 Imperatives

These forms normally rely for report on such verbs as these:
ask, warn, order, invite, remind, advise, encourage, beg, urge
The transformation is usually: '(Don't) go away!' → *He told me (not) to go away.*
Use one of the listed verbs above to report each of these things, recently said to you.

1	Don't forget to lock the door, will you?
2	Come and have dinner with me.
3	Go on! Jump! You can do it!
4	Go on! Change your mind! Go on! Go on!
5	Don't leave your money lying around.
6	Lend me a hand, will you?
7	Empty your pockets!
8	Please, please, stay with me!
9	Wait a few days, that's best.

B4 Exclamations

These are normally left 'untouched' in conversation (He said 'ouch'.) but in more formal English they may be reported with:
She/He expressed (her/his) sympathy / relief / contempt / amazement / approval / disapproval / annoyance / disbelief.

Listen and report the following utterances in the same way, using one of the nouns each time.

1	Thank Goodness!	**5**	What? No! Never! Impossible!
2	What a nuisance!	**6**	Tut! Tut! Disgraceful!
3	Aah! You poor thing!	**7**	Huh!
4	Good Heavens!	**8**	Mmm. Lovely!

B5 Modal verbs

Conventionally, *will* changes to *would*, *can* to *could*, *shall* to *should/would*, *may* to *might* and *must* to *had to*.
Could, would, should and *might* do not normally change, and we have to suffer the occasional ambiguity in the report. (For example, *He said he could do it* is a report of both 'I can do it' and 'I could do it'.)
Must creates most problems and possibilities.

a *had to* is fine if the original has a *have to* flavour, a general present.

b *would have to* is preferable if there is a future connotation.

c *was/were to* reports an order accurately, albeit a little formally, while *mustn't* can safely go to *wasn't/weren't to* or *wasn't/weren't allowed to*.

d *must* itself is often acceptable in reports; *should* is a common alternative.

e In deductions, ('You must be mad!') no change occurs in British English, but American English allows *had to*.

Report these statements, beginning: *I said . . .*, but first work out what *must* means in each case. Is it *have to? Will Have to? Should?* An order? An assumption?

1	We must leave early.
2	We must remember he's only twelve.
3	You must be here at nine.
4	You must be delighted!
5	You must practise as often as possible.
6	We must invite them round one evening.
7	You mustn't open the door to strangers.
8	You must change trains at Birmingham.

B6 Adverbs of time and place and other non-verbal changes

The most important modifications from direct to indirect speech are:
today→*that day* (often omitted)
tomorrow→*the next day/the following day*
yesterday→*the day before/the previous day*
now→*then/at that moment/at that time*
ago→*before/previously*
here→*there*
this→*that/the/it*
that→*that/the/it*

This and *that* require special care. 'Listen to this' for instance would become:
He asked me to listen/listen to him/listen to what he was going to say (not: *He asked me to listen to that!*)
Report these questions, beginning: *She asked me . . .*

1	Do you know where he is now
2	How do you think you'll feel tomorrow?
3	Did you find this bag here yesterday?
4	Were you here an hour ago?
5	What's that cat doing here?
6	Why are you here today?

B7 Game: 'What did you say?' (see Teacher's Guide Unit 9)

C Listening, reading and comparing

C1 Split the class. Half of you read the article below while the other half listen to a radio news item related to it. Make notes, ignoring each other's different activity.

LEO the tramp had the removal men in yesterday.

British Telecom workmen uprooted the public phone box in which he has lived for the last five months and carted it away.

Leo was out on business at the time – appearing in court on a vagrancy charge. After spending a night in the cells.

But later he revealed that he's on the lookout for a new address. He said: 'I want to find another phone box – they are warm and cosy.

'I like to look after the community and keep the boxes tidy.'

The workmen moved in on Leo's detached residence at No. 01–622–6710, Wandsworth Road, South London, while he was still sipping his morning cuppa at Clapham police station.

Three hours later all that was left were three plastic bags.

But neighbour Emily Lancaster, 62, was horrified to learn that the tramp had lost his home.

She said: 'He was a lovely man who didn't hurt anybody.

'He wouldn't even take twigs off trees to burn to keep himself warm. He said they were all God's creatures.'

Leo meanwhile was appearing at Lavender Hill Court where he was charged with wandering in the street and living in a phone box. He pleaded guilty and was conditionally discharged.

Afterwards he set off carrying three plastic bags holding £100 in cash, two transistor radios – 'to get a stereo effect' – a copy of the Daily Mirror, plus batteries, glasses and mysteriously, make-up.

The money was given him by well-wishers and he was on his way to open his first bank account.

Leo, 51, said: 'I think I'm the richest man in the world. They've taken away my home but I'm still free to choose what I do.'

C2 Now in groups of four (two listeners and two readers), exchange information and fill in details that the other two have not received. See if there are any contradictions in the two versions of the story.

C3 Now reverse roles – listeners and readers – and follow the same procedure for this article and the corresponding news broadcast, i.e. listen and read, and then exchange information.

HOME for Mick Mease is a little wooden hut with no mod cons. But he has refused £30,000 for it.

The hut, measuring 10ft by 12ft, is surrounded by land a local development corporation wants to build on. Mick has turned their offer down flat.

Mick, a 59-year-old retired demolition contractor, said yesterday: 'I have told them what to do with the money.

'I've been here for 17 years and here I stay.'

Mick bought the site in Newark Road, Peterborough, in 1966 for £1,000.

His only water is from an outside tap, but he does have a phone, a TV set and other electrical goods.

The land is wanted for industrial development but Mick is stubbornly staying put.

He said: 'Nobody wants to move home at my age. In any case, I like the fresh air.

'I've got a cooker, washing machine, a freezer and my happiness. No one is going to take that away from me.'

A development corporation official said last night: 'Mr Mease occupies a small island in a sea of land which we need.

'Time is getting short, and we are already building close to his property.

'Unless he is prepared to move into the alternative accommodation we are offering, we shall have to acquire the land by compulsory purchase.'

The spokesman added: 'The property and land have been professionally valued and we have made an offer based upon that.'

D Socialising

D1 Listen to a woman telling a friend about an experience she had. Why did the friend find it incredible?

D2 In pairs, improvise similar accounts in which one of you was confronted with contradictory comments, opinions or advice:

1 Three doctors' diagnoses of your bad leg
2 Three garage estimates for repairs to your car
3 Three teachers' criticisms of your English
4 Three newspaper reviews of a recent film

E Register: newspaper headlines

E1 Study these headlines and discuss in groups a) what they mean and b) the special language features they contain.

Your discussion probably referred at some stage to the following points: a) the frequent deletion of articles – *a/an/the* b) the use of Present Simple for Past or Past Perfect c) the use of passive forms with the auxiliary deleted d) the use of noun as adjective. See how many concrete examples of these features you can find in the nine headlines, then express them in more normal sentences. For example, about the helicopter: *A helicopter was shot down while attempting to rescue people or property in danger.*

Posters issued of most wanted man

Stolen gold find for angler

WELSH SPEAKING DECLINE HALTED

Millions being wasted, say Union Leaders

Lawyer's Son Found Guilty of Bribery

BANKER ACCUSED OF FRAUD

Mystery Gang Jailed for £20m Forgeries

Youths Beaten Off By Pensioner

HELICOPTER SHOT DOWN IN RESCUE BID

E2 Another common feature of headlines is the use they make of puns and plays on words. (In 'Black Belting for the Hotel Mugger', *black belt* recalls a mark of rank in karate, but *belting* is also another word for a *beating*.) Can you spot the play on words in these examples? Note also how the future is often indicated with a *to*-infinitive.

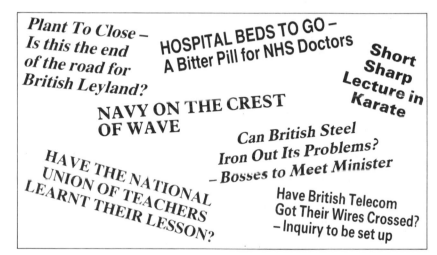

Plant To Close – Is this the end of the road for British Leyland?

HOSPITAL BEDS TO GO – A Bitter Pill for NHS Doctors

Short Sharp Lecture in Karate

NAVY ON THE CREST OF WAVE

Can British Steel Iron Out Its Problems? – Bosses to Meet Minister

HAVE THE NATIONAL UNION OF TEACHERS LEARNT THEIR LESSON?

Have British Telecom Got Their Wires Crossed? – Inquiry to be set up

E3 Group work

These ten headlines are chronologically mixed up. (The story started in 1949 and lasted, in fact, until 1966.)

1 First, express the headlines in more standard English.
2 Now rearrange them into a logical sequence, as you think they appeared.
3 Finally, write a short account of the Timothy Evans affair, based on them.

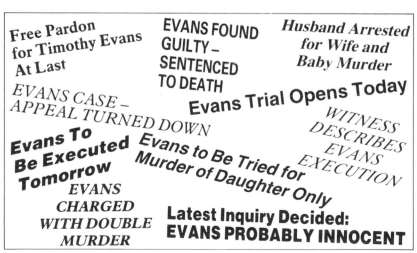

Free Pardon for Timothy Evans At Last

EVANS FOUND GUILTY – SENTENCED TO DEATH

Husband Arrested for Wife and Baby Murder

EVANS CASE – APPEAL TURNED DOWN

Evans Trial Opens Today

WITNESS DESCRIBES EVANS EXECUTION

Evans To Be Executed Tomorrow

Evans to Be Tried for Murder of Daughter Only

EVANS CHARGED WITH DOUBLE MURDER

Latest Inquiry Decided: EVANS PROBABLY INNOCENT

F Vocabulary: the media

Read this sour letter, written to the editor of a newspaper, then do the exercises below in groups of three.

Sir,

At the outbreak of yet another industrial dispute, with newspaper proprietors, editors, journalists and printers all making their own news, may I express the fervent hope that the edition in which you print this will be your last.

For the past few decades, our national press has been the single most divisive element in this country – far more so than education, religion or politics. You serious, 'quality' papers now only address yourselves to a few million people (those running the country) who can follow or are interested in your right-wing editorials, your pseudo-intellectual leaders, those 'in-depth' analyses of current affairs and the high-level business coverage – for the managerial classes only.

Meanwhile the popular press, sliding fast into a civil war for higher circulation (do they really sell 12 million copies a day?) and greater advertising revenue, fill their pages with sensational scoops on the private lives of TV soap-opera stars, exclusive interviews with mediocre celebrities, human interest dramas (interest?), gossip columns, ghost-written articles, infantile cartoons, comic-strips and soft pornography.

Someone who has breakfasted on a diet of on-the-spot reports from correspondents in every corner of the globe, interspersed with glossy adverts for villas in Barbados and a crossword for those of IQ 140+ will have nothing to say to a person whose knowledge of international affairs and foreign news is limited to a few lines on a 'killer earthquake', the US dollar and the Queen's visit to Australia, whose classified ads have been for mail-order second-hand anoraks, and whose mental agility has been tested in guessing where the deleted football was in the original photograph.

Your industry has helped to make a social, political and intellectual chasm within the nation. Let it die, I say.

Television, much maligned as it has been, might prove our saviour. True, inane chat-shows, situation comedy series, never-ending serials and fatuous quizzes with lunatic comperes will not save the country. True, many sets rarely transmit more than the signature tune of the Evening News and might well explode if tuned to a serious studio discussion or documentary. However, if the ever-increasing number of channels and the ever-hotter ratings battle for every unsuspecting viewer do not get out of hand, then the 'box' represents a better bet than you do to unite our deeply divided people.

I am,

Yours faithfully,

1 Summarise together, in more simple terms, the argument of the letter and the man's attitude to the popular press, 'quality' newspapers and television.

2 Explain (or find out) the meaning and give examples of the words and phrases underlined above.

3 Could this letter be a comment on the national daily press in your country? Could the same accusations be made?

4 Which parts of a newspaper do you always/usually/rarely/never read? Why?

5 Think of a piece of news you read about in two different newspapers recently. How was it differently reported?

6 How do you think newspapers will change in form over the next decade or two? In the face of competition from cable TV, teletext, etc., will they survive into the next century, do you think?

7 Still in groups, compose a letter to a TV company, complaining about the low standard of programmes broadcast and the damaging effect this is having on the whole population, especially the young.

G Exercises for homework

G1 Here are some of the scribbled notes you took as Minutes Secretary at a recent meeting of the College Students' Union. Now your job is to write them up properly, reporting what members had to say, in readiness for the next meeting. You should begin:

As chairperson, Juan Carlos opened the meeting by welcoming
everyone and commenting how nice it was to see so . . .

Juan Carlos: (chairperson) – welcome all – nice to see so many – apologies for absence received from Abdul, Kristina. On the 1st item on agenda – college library.

Esther: – organisation of lib. generally v. good – compliment staff. – v. efficient – good service.

Michel: agree – but suggest new system – students take turns to supervise – lunchtimes – etc when free time.

Carmen: too much emphasis on science subjects – think many studs. want more light reading – relaxation important.

Fritz: not agree – remind – library not a newsagent's kiosk

Yoko: need wider range of books – lib. not expanding as it should – very few publications – many books never borrowed – new policy recommended – must set up a committee.

Fatima: very often books wanted not available – fines (for late return) not high enough – suggest double

G2 Read these two articles about the Loch Ness monster, that famous (or infamous?) Scottish tourist attraction. Imagine now that you are Erik Beckjord. You have been asked to supply a commentary for the parts of the video film which actually show the creature. Write about a minute's tapescript for each 'sighting'.

G3 Write a letter to the editor of one of the newspapers, complaining about his wasting valuable space on this latest absurd claim. Refer to things said in this and other similar articles and express your growing impatience with the never-ending coverage given to stories like this.

NESSIE SURFACES AGAIN

THE Nessie-spotting season has started again.

An American team yesterday claimed to have made two sightings of the Loch Ness monster and got them on video film.

Wildlife photographer Erik Beckjord, of the National Crypto Zoological Society of the US, said: 'We got film of an object 15 to 20ft. long and about 250ft. out from the shore. The second sighting was two days later on Saturday at 1 p.m. when something stuck out of the water and went down again,' Mr Beckjord said.

Film-makers claim Nessie sightings

A team from the United States, which has been monitoring the surface of Loch Ness with a video camera for the past week, believes it may have seen the monster on two occasions.

The first claimed sighting was towards the eastern end of the loch. The team says it saw an object about 15ft. to 20ft. long, crossing the waves and raising its 'head' out of the water. The second, from a point over Urquhart Bay, much farther along the loch, was of an object about 30ft. long moving about three feet below the surface.

The team of two, from the National Crypto Zoological Society and led by Erik Beckjord, a wildlife photographer, has been scanning the surface from points along the shore with a camera capable of filming for 240 hours without a break.

Unit 10

A1 Did you know that the average man has 2.21 phobias, the average woman 3.55?! In small groups, discuss how you think *you* would react to – shall we say? – rats, in these circumstances:
- on a cinema screen (life-size or larger-than-life, two or two thousand).
- graphically described in a novel (an army of attackers or on a dinner plate).
- making noises in the room next to yours (ground floor or tenth floor).
- jumping on to your bed (in the dark or with the light on).
- in your hand (dead or alive).

Go on to consider how varying circumstances might alter your attitude towards: a 100-storey building; motorbikes; a fairground ferris wheel; snakes. Report your findings to the rest of the class.

A2 Read through the text on the page opposite, answering these questions as you go. Then compare your answers with your neighbours' and discuss any differences.

1 Which of these statements is implied by the opening lines?
   a Some people might be upset by the picture on the page.
   b Not many people would worry about a real spider on their neck.
   c The sight of spiders might be enough to kill some people.

2 Which of these would a person suffering from one of the phobias mentioned dread?
   a Being locked up in an airing cupboard for a day.
   b A weekend in the desert.
   c Being lost in a maze.

3 Which of these qualities does the text state an RMN must have?
   a An ability to improvise.
   b Patience.
   c An easy-going, sociable nature.

4 Which is the most accurate description of the leaflet's approach?
   a It is educational and informative rather than persuasive.
   b It is quite aggressive, hard-line recruitment.
   c It is both encouraging and warning would-be nurses.

A3 Class discussion

Which member(s) of the class do you feel would be most suited (in terms of character and attitudes rather than specific qualifications) to be the following? And why?
1 a company director   **5** a lift attendant
2 a solo round-the-world yachtsman   **6** an astronaut
3 a nurse in a geriatric ward   **7** an actor/actress
4 a TV news reader   **8** a steeplejack

Let the chosen class members react with their own comments, for example:
I could probably . . . , but I'd be absolutely hopeless at . . .
I wouldn't mind the . . . , but I don't think I could take the . . .
I'm sure if I had to . . . , I'd simply . . .
. . . wouldn't worry me, but I'd be scared stiff if . . .

A spider down the back of the neck is enough to give anyone the squeeby-jeebies.

But finding pictures of them crawling over the page of a magazine is hardly likely to send shivers down your spine or have you running for your life.

This would be ridiculous. Or so you might think.

But for some people, just the thought of spiders can fill them with fears on a scale you'd find hard to believe.

In their mildest form, these feelings amount to little more than a clammy uneasiness. Like the sense of

Which is just as well, for making someone face up to the apparent ruins of his life is no less demanding than helping someone overcome an irrational fear of spiders.

Or simply caring for him on a day-to-day basis.

And because each person's problem is different, you can't always fall back on set methods to help you. Your ingenuity and imagination are working overtime from the minute you come on duty.

Perhaps this is the kind of challenge you're looking

Could you talk someone out of running away from this page?

panic you may have experienced as a child closing the door on yourself in a cupboard.

On a more serious level, they can develop into an acute anxiety attack. In a blind panic you have only one thing on your mind. To escape.

In this state, the fear of finding a spider in the bath, or in the kitchen sink, can turn everyday events like washing or doing the housework into terrifying ordeals.

When people develop fears quite out of proportion to the threat of the thing they are afraid of, this fear is called a *phobia*.

There are many different types of phobia. One of the commonest is *agoraphobia* (the fear of open spaces), when you're literally terrified of venturing outside your own front door.

Other relatively common phobias appear, on the surface at least, to be rather absurd. Like the fear of wearing shoes, getting dirty, stroking cats or having a bird fly near you.

People with serious phobias openly acknowledge that their feelings are irrational. But when faced with them, they cannot control their fear. When things get to a point when their phobia prevents them from carrying on life as normal, they seek help.

Assessing someone with a serious phobia, working out the correct programme and putting it into action, takes immense skill.

And teamwork. As a Registered Mental Nurse (RMN) you don't work alone. You're part of a team of other highly trained professionals, including psychiatrists, clinical psychologists and social workers.

for, but do you think you could be suffering from a mild sort of 'phobia' yourself? A fear of working in a 'mental hospital'.

As an RMN you quickly learn how a normal mind can become ill just as a normal body can.

And that psychiatric hospitals, like general hospitals, are there not to keep people in, but to help to get them back to a normal way of life.

Few people know that over half the patients admitted to psychiatric hospitals are home again within a month.

Or that nine out of ten of them leave within a year. Or that some psychiatric nurses only work in hospitals on very rare occasions.

But having said this, nursing the mentally ill is not for everyone.

To begin with, the training takes three years. With hospital and community experience, practical assessments and tough written exams.

But the way we see it, if you can overcome your own fears, you may well have what it takes to help others overcome theirs.

You could do both by writing to the Chief Nursing Officer, P.O. Box 702, (MI/12), London SW20 8SZ, for more information.

Nursing

B Listening

B1 You are going to hear a woman being interviewed. Divide into two groups; half of you look at the questions on the left, half at those on the right.

Listen, then tell the others whether these statements are true or false.
1 Mrs Kaye is not afraid of trees.
2 They drove past that house by chance.
3 Her husband wanted to buy it.
4 Driving near trees is a nightmare for her.
5 She's got trees in her garden.
6 She is terrified of all trees.
7 It's probably the leaves that frighten her.

Listen, then recall for the others what the man says about
1 earlier conversations.
2 a tree-lined avenue.
3 getting used to that house.
4 trees in her garden.
5 evergreen trees.
6 rubber plants.

B2 In small groups, discuss briefly what might be the cause of Mrs Kaye's phobia and similar ones you know of. What advice would you give her? Might there be a cure?

C Communicative grammar: expressing likely and unlikely conditions with *if*

C1 Conditional sentences (1)

There are two main types of conditional sentence in English. In the first type, the condition relates to an event that is entirely possible, but uncertain. This is most often in the future: *If you can overcome your own fears, . . . ,* but sometimes in the present: *If you really want to know, . . . ,* and sometimes pre-present: *If I've upset you, . . .* Study the clauses below, and notice that any combination of half-sentences, left and right, is possible.

If he finishes work at seven again, . . .	*. . . he won't want to go out after dinner.*
If he's working at Head Office this afternoon, . . .	*. . . he'll be feeling too tired to go out later.*
If he's had another long day at the office, . . .	*. . . he'll have had enough of business for one day.*
If he's been working until now, . . .	*. . . he'll have been working late every day this week.*

These structures are often used for everyday arrangements: *If you push, I'll sit in and steer* and for personal dilemmas: *If I buy her a present, she'll say I've been wasting my money, and if I don't get her anything, she'll be upset.* (Note that *may* and *might* can replace *will.*) In the exercise below, we treat rather larger world issues.

Complete the half-sentences as naturally as possible.

1 If we haven't reduced pollution in our cities by the year 2000, . . .
2 People will soon be living to a much greater age if . . .
3 Unless a division is made between sport and politics, . . .
4 Jams will go on getting longer and longer if . . .
5 A generation of almost entirely non-smokers might appear one day, if . . .
6 If a solution to the problem of juvenile violence is not found soon, . . .
7 If we are doing all our shopping by computer twenty years from now, . . .
8 We will soon have passed the point of no return on nuclear weapons unless . . .

C2 Conditional sentences (2)

In the second type of conditional sentence, the tense of the
condition does not relate directly to the time it represents. Study the
tense sequences in the clauses below, noting that any combination,
left and right, is possible.

If I wasn't/weren't such an idiot, . . .   *. . . I wouldn't be in this mess now.*
  (but you are!)   (but you are!)

If I wasn't/weren't studying English, . . .   *. . . I wouldn't have spoken to her.*
  (but you are!)   (but you did!)

If I hadn't lost my passport, . . .   *. . . I would be going home today.*
  (but you have, or did!)   (but you aren't!)

If I hadn't been feeling so confused that day, . . .   *. . . I wouldn't have been behaving like that.*
  (but you were!)   (but you were!)

Note also that *could* and *might* can often substitute for *would* in
these structures. In this type of sentence, the conditions are:
1) extremely unlikely: *If you had to walk . . .* 2) tentative in polite
requests, suggestions, advice etc.: *Would you mind if I asked you?*;
3) unreal: *If I was 20 years younger, . . .; If you had gone there to
live, ...* Now do these exercises for each category.

1 Consider hypothetical consequences for these unlikely conditions.
  a If people stopped getting married, . . .
  b If twice as much was invested in new industries, . . .
  c If greater contact could be established between East and West, . . .
  d If more people got into the habit of locking their cars, . . .
  e If television started showing more programmes about . . .
  f If we could convince our politicians that . . .

2 Re-express the comments on the left, using the openings on the right.
  a Do you mind if I don't come?   (*Would it be all right if . . .?*)
  b Can you let me have it tomorrow?   (*I would be very grateful if . . .*)
  c Shall I leave you alone?   (*Would you prefer it if . . .?*)
  d Can I take this with me?   (*Would you mind if . . .?*)
  e Why don't you go for a walk?   (*You might feel better if . . .*)
  f Shall we paint it green?   (*Wouldn't it look better if . . .?*)

3 Complete the sentences below by putting in a suitable form of
the verbs in brackets. Three possible consequences are suggested
for each unreal condition.

  a If I (*not take*) an examination tomorrow,
     I (*accept*) their invitation for last weekend.
     I (*come*) out with you tonight.
     I (*dance*) in some discotheque now.

  b If he (*not start*) smoking when he was 15,
     he (*be*) a rich man today.
     he (*not lie*) here in hospital.
     he (*afford*) that car last month.

  c If my present salary (*be*) higher,
     I (*not plan*) to leave next month.
     I (*not spend*) my last holiday at home in the garden.
     I (*go*) out more often.

  d If I (*not stand*) under the ladder to catch you when you fell,
     you (*break*) your leg.
     you (*not smile*) now.
     you (*still be*) there now.

D Functions: hypothesising; inviting, offering and countering opinions

D1 In groups of four, practise this conversation:

A: Would you ever emigrate, do you think?
B: No, never!
C: No? What if you had lost your job and were offered a super one abroad?
B: I don't think that would tempt me, no.
D: But suppose you fell in love with, say, a Canadian, wouldn't you go and live there with him/her?
B: Oh no! No, he/she would have to come here.
A: What, even if he/she had a really good job and you were out of work?
B: Well, I suppose then I might. It would depend on . . .

Now improvise similar hypothetical discussions in which three of you try to persuade the fourth that he/she would, in certain circumstances
 – steal.   – marry someone he/she didn't love.   – refuse to pay a bill.
 – kill someone.   – go on an Amazon expedition.   – go on strike.

D2 Look at this opening of a questionnaire designed to find out people's phobias.

1 If you were stuck in a lift with 24 people for 24 hours, do you think you would **a** panic and start screaming? **b** sit calmly in a corner? **c** keep the others happy with a song and dance?	*testing for claustrophobia*
2 If you had been the first person to climb Everest, would you have **a** danced for joy? **b** coolly calculated how much you could make out of it? **c** felt sick?	*testing for a fear of heights*
3 If one day you have to watch a surgical operation, do you think you will **a** faint? **b** enthusiastically ask to be allowed to lend a hand? **c** look away only when you have to?	*testing for a dread of operations*

In pairs, make up six further multiple-choice questions, using similar structures, that would test for the following:
 – a fear of travelling   – a dread of insects   – a horror of noise
 – a phobia about fire   – an aversion to foreigners (= xenophobia)   – a 'thing' about the telephone

Try out your questions on another pair, and comment to the class on your findings.

D3 Complete and practise these exchanges, noting the 'argumentative' conditional forms.

 1 A: I wouldn't have thought military service did any harm, myself.
     B: You wouldn't think like that if you had to . . .
 2 A: Personally, I would have said the defence budget was money well spent.
     B: You wouldn't feel that way if you had seen . . .
 3 A: I'd say the army helps/helped make men out of boys.
     B: You'd think differently if you spent a year . . .
 4 A: Wouldn't you agree that the training serves a purpose?
     B: You wouldn't say that if your studies . . .

Improvise exchanges in which A feels it's not so
 – difficult to give up smoking.   – hard to bring up a baby.
 – tiring to run a marathon.   – difficult to overcome a fear of water.
 – unpleasant to live in New York.   – bad to work as a coal-miner.

E Vocabulary: some prefixes and suffixes

E1 'Dylanphobia' is not in your dictionary, but sixties' parents suffered
from it, probably even more than from Beatlemania. First, read this
(pseudo-?) intellectual magazine article, seeing if prefixes and
suffixes can help you understand new words.

He was 'the spokesman for a generation', 'the arch-rebel in a decade of
rebellion', the dissident musician who 'sat behind a million pairs of eyes
and told them how they saw'. He was a hero for extroverts and
introverts alike, an intermediary between over-excited undergraduates
and under-privileged down-and-outs. Pre-Beatles and post-'flower
power', he was the loudest and most eloquent voice of anti-
establishment protest, pounding out his three-chord message of non-
conformity. Champion of the down-trodden underdog, he peopled his
world with outsiders and misfits, beggars, immigrants, ex-convicts,
petty criminals, hypochondriacs, deserters and refugees. The victims of
his verbal assaults included any opponents of personal freedom:
parents, lawyers, ultra-conservatives, profiteers, congressmen, neo-
fascist senators, aristocrats, megalomaniacs, presidents of the super-
powers. Though a hypersensitive critic of his country's values, he was
nonetheless a patriot, passionately pro-American, with a deep respect
for his fellow human beings. He touched the sub-conscious of young
America uniquely in the sixties, the symbol of a whole counter-culture
and a forerunner of today's vast movement towards peaceful co-
existence.

E2 Consider the meaning of these prefixes above: (of degree) *arch-*,
super-, *hyper-*, *ultra-*, *over-*; (of attitude) *pro-*, *anti-*, *pseudo-*,
counter-, *fellow-*, *non-*, *co-*; (of time and order) *pre-*, *post-*, *ex-*,
neo-, *fore-*; (of position) *sub-*, *under-*, *trans-*, *inter-*.
See how many common compounds you can make, using these and
the words below. Through examples, show how they might be used
in full sentences.

> *war attack Romantic star author standard Communist*
> *hero modern Continental rival student man paid*

E3 Consider the endings of the types of people above: *-er*, *-ac*, *-at*, etc.
Find more people from the lines of definitions below. We are looking
for someone who:

-ar	lies – begs – steals from houses is an academic
-ant	assists – applies – emigrates – is accused in court
-or	visits – navigates – prosecutes – gives blood
-eer	auctions things – climbs mountains – volunteers
-ic	criticises – makes people laugh – repairs cars
-ot	flies planes – loves his country – is very stupid
-ee	is employed – is being trained – is nominated – controls footballers
-al	plays for money – has a military rank (3 or 4) – damages/ruins property
-ent	opposes – receives – acts for you – is under medical treatment
-man	works with a camera – is in business – speaks for others – sells
-ist	is involved in science / chemistry / economics / physics
-ian	is involved in politics / mathematics / music / electricity

Now try the exercise again, covering the suffixes on the left.

10

F Exercises for homework

F1 A fear of the truth

Two young single men are contemplating the
trials and tribulations of parenthood. Write out
their conversation, putting in a suitable form of
the verb in brackets.

A: Tell me, if you had a nine-year-old son now,
would you let him watch the news on TV?

B: Well certainly, if he (*be*) interested. I (*not do*)
my job as parent and educator if I (*not do*),
would I?

A: I'm not so sure. I think I (*may be*) afraid that
he (*be*) influenced in a bad way.

B: By the news?

A: Well yes. I think if as a child I (*see*) the sort
of things they show nowadays, I (*be*)
frightened out of my wits. I (*probably be*) a
deeply disturbed young man now.

B: Don't be silly. If you (*not allow*) children to
see what is happening in the world, they
(*get*) a terrible shock when they (*be*) older.

A: Maybe so, but I do feel it (*be*) better if they
(*not be*) exposed to as much horror and
violence as they are today.

B: I suppose you (*be*) happier if television (*not
be*) invented and then we (*can*) all go back
to the Middle Ages and we (*not have to*)
know what (*go on*) around us.

A: No, I'm not saying that. But if children (*see*)
bombs and shooting every night on the news
and talk the next day about what they (*see*),
they (*grow*) up thinking that sort of thing is
normal.

B: Well, isn't it? Look, you (*not argue*) the way
you are if you (*ever visit*) a country where the
people (*never see*) a television set. I assure
you, you (*not want*) a society that (*have*) no
idea of how their government (*behave*) or
what changes (*take*) place. I suppose when
you (*get*) married and (*have*) children, you
(*think*) it's all right if they (*watch*) 'Tom and
Jerry' and (*read*) *Little Red Riding Hood* and
really horrific stuff like that.

A: Oh, that's not fair! Look, if I (*know*) you
(*feel*) so strongly about it, I (*not bring*) the
subject up.

92

10

F2 A fear of failure

Write a new version of the story below, re-expressing each sentence beginning with the word or words given in brackets.

Example:

A visit to Budapest nowadays normally entails a trip to see the Chain Bridge. *(If . . .)*

You write:

If you visit Budapest nowadays, you will probably go on a trip to see the Chain Bridge.

1 It was constructed over the Danube some hundred years ago. (*It has . . .*)

2 It was only built because a Scotsman named Adam Clark wanted to produce a perfect piece of architecture. (*It would never . . .*)

3 It is one of the finest examples of its kind in Europe today. (*There are . . .*)

4 Clark was very proud of his craftsmanship. (*Clark took . . .*)

5 He decided to stake his reputation on his work. (*He made . . .*)

6 'I'll throw myself off my bridge if anyone can find anything wrong with it,' he said. (*He told people that . . .*)

7 From that time a fear of failure drove him on. (*He was . . .*)

8 Several times only his obsession with perfection stopped him giving up. (*If . . .*)

9 In the end, Clark decided that two ornamental lions on either side would improve his masterpiece. (*In the end, Clark decided that if . . .*)

10 When he had finished the bridge, he invited criticism of it. (*On . . .*)

11 Someone pointed out that the lions didn't have tongues. (*It was . . .*)

12 Adam Clark did as he had promised and threw himself to his death. (*True . . .*)

F3

Using your dictionary where necessary, write definitions of the difference between the following pairs.

For example: a masochist / a sadist

Although both take pleasure in pain, a masochist delights in his own suffering whereas a sadist enjoys cruelty done to others.

1 an atheist / an agnostic   **5** a dictator / a tyrant
2 a pessimist / a fatalist   **6** a patriot / a nationalist
3 a sceptic / a cynic   **7** a communist / a socialist
4 an optimist / a romantic   **8** a fanatic / an extremist

Later, compare your definitions with those of classmates.

F4

Go back and re-read the advertisement on page 87, then write a letter to an out-of-work friend of yours; summarise the content of the piece and suggest that she/he might do well to consider such an opportunity.

Did I ever tell you about....?

A1 You are going to hear Alan telling friends two jokes involving American visitors to Europe. You have two tasks to follow your listening:

1 Write a suitable sentence for the 'bubble' in each of the cartoons.
2 What do the two jokes tell us about the attitude of some English people towards Americans?

You will have noticed that most of the narrative in the jokes is in the present. (Alan says *he says* twenty-seven times altogether!) This is typical of many such stories. Can you think of one and try to tell it in the present?

A2 You will hear another example of a present narrative in the next listening text. Gordon is describing to Nicolette a play he went to see last night. Nicolette has heard of it, but hasn't seen it. Listen, then complete the sentences below. Try to convert the informal spoken language you hear to something more formal – a style you might read in an encyclopaedia or drama compendium.

1 The play is to some extent autobiographical because ....
2 The play spans a period from .... to ....
3 The central character is ....
4 His life and work change when ....
5 Economic necessity, therefore, forces...
6 Tragedy strikes the family ....
7 The hero's life however turns full circle..
8 An added attraction of the production is the fact that ....

Now choose a film or play or book you are pretty sure your partner has not seen or read. Give a brief description of the characters, plot and message (if any) in the same style and with the same assortment of tenses as in the one you heard.

A3 It is not only in specialised narrative such as jokes and film plots that present tenses are used for story-telling purposes. Listen to Ron describing a frightening experience he had some years ago, and notice how, to heighten the dramatic effect, he sometimes brings the story into the present. While you are listening, look at this picture. See how many differences or inconsistencies you can find between his account of the event and the way it is represented in the picture.

A4 When you are listening to someone commentating on an event he is watching, you might expect to hear a predominance of present tenses. Notice in the next passage, however, how regularly the Simple Present form is used to describe what is happening at this very moment.

A bored young man is twiddling the dial of his radio in search of some music. He moves through a number of stations, but can only find a series of commentaries on sporting events. Listen, and tick which six of these ten sports or events you hear described. *Check you know the sports first.*

– football	– diving	– sprinting
– the long jump	– tennis	– motor racing
– the shot put	– the high jump	
– chess	– gymnastics	

Compare your answers with those of the rest of the class, and give reasons.

B Communicative grammar

B1 Present tenses in narratives

In the listening texts you have witnessed some perhaps unexpected uses of present tenses:
1 *he says* when *he said* might seem more reasonable;
2 *he's visiting England* for *he was visiting England*; and
3 *he can't afford to live* for *he couldn't afford to live*.
It is not *essential* that you should use these yourselves when relating anecdotes and telling funny stories, but they will help to make you sound more natural and colloquial. Their usage cannot be classified as either good or bad English; it is, quite simply, very common.

B2 Stative verbs

You have probably learnt that stative verbs – ones like *love, forget* and *notice* – are not commonly found in the continuous form. This is true, but ignoring the possibility of the continuous completely is to deny yourself a lot of good, colloquial English. Most of these verbs can be used in the continuous form when:

a *we are stressing the temporary or 'now' aspect*
  'You're forgetting that . . .' and 'I'm hating every minute of this.'

b *we are describing a trend (often the start of it) or a process of change*
  'People now are realising . . .' and 'I'm forgetting a lot of my French.'

c *there is a future aspect*
  'I'm seeing my lawyer tomorrow; they're hearing my case on Thursday.'

1 In the sentences below, decide if only one form is acceptable (*do* or *is doing*) or whether either may be used, with or without a difference in meaning or emphasis.

  a That soup (*smell*) good already.
  b I (*not trust*) him any more.
  c (*you not forget*) that she's only 15?
  d I (*already regret*) what I said.
  e (*you not wish*) you'd gone with them?
  f She (*look*) younger every day.
  g Was that the bell or (*I hear*) things?
  h I (*think*) of going to Bath on Sunday.
  i I (*think*) people (*notice*) the difference in the economic climate.
  j Men (*at last recognise*) the right of women to act more as they (*want*) to.
  k I (*know*) he (*feel*) the strain of his new position of responsibility.
  l Look at that child! I (*suspect*) he (*love*) the attention he's getting.

2 With some such verbs there may be a clear difference in meaning if the continuous is used. Compare the *thought process* and *opinion* in:
I'm thinking about/*considering* his offer.
I think it is/*consider* it a generous one.

Comment on the differences here:

  a He appears to be very busy.
    He's appearing at The Ritz next week.

  b She has corns on her feet.
    She's having treatment for them.

  c I suspect he's rather stupid.
    I feel he's being rather stupid.

  d I'm measuring/weighing this box.
    It measures 50cm/weighs 50g.

B3 Future forms

Study each response to statements **1** and **2**, noting the form of the verb and the bracketed rationale for its use. In the jungle that is the future in English, these forms are of course sometimes interchangeable; however, these are guidelines which, if followed, should eliminate most error and misunderstanding.

1 | I think it's going to rain. | (imminently – I see clouds)

  a What a pity! The final starts in ten minutes.   (timetabled programme)
  b Oh no! I'm working outside this afternoon.   (arranged personal programme)
  c It's OK. I'll do the shopping.   (offer)
  d It'll be all right; we won't get wet.   (assurance/reassurance)
  e Shall we postpone our game?   (suggestion)
  f Oh dear, the roads will be wet tonight.   (result of what's going to happen)
  g I think perhaps I'll take my umbrella, then.   (coming to a decision)
  h It'll be raining from now until bedtime.   (continuous action over a period)
  i I'll be standing at the bus-stop when it starts.   (picture of a future point in time)
  j Perhaps it will have stopped by tea-time.   (the normal 'perfect' concept)

2 | I'm going to buy a car. | (thought-out plan/intention)

  a Don't forget the road tax is going up next month. — (announced, fixed decision)
  b You? No! I think I'm going to faint! — (nothing I can control)
  c Right, I'll buy one, too. — (sudden decision)
  d You'll regret it. — (warning)
  e I suppose you'll get/be getting it on HP? — (educated guess/forecast)
  f Will you bring me into work each morning? — (request)
  g Shall I help you to choose it? — (offer/suggestion)
  h Will I have the chance to drive it? — (predict for me)
  i Oh, so you'll be driving to work again soon. — (deduced future habit/consequence)
  j Mm, I'll be getting a new company car soon. — (in the normal course of events)

B4 Now comment on the two different responses to each of the questions/statements below. How do they reflect different attitudes or facts being communicated?

1 There's a train strike tomorrow, you know.
  a That's no problem, I'm going by bus.   **b** That's OK. I'll go by bus.
2 He still doesn't know about the plan.
  a That's OK. I'll be seeing him tomorrow.   **b** All right, I'll see him tomorrow.
3 My wife's arriving back while I'm working.
  a Don't worry; I'm going to pick her up.   **b** No problem. I'll pick her up.
4 What are you going to have for dinner?
  a I think I'm having curry.   **b** I think I'll have curry.
5 Do you want to play? We need an eleventh player.
  a Well, OK. Shall I be goalkeeper?   **b** Well, all right, but will I be goalkeeper?
6 Do you think you'll see the news on TV tonight?
  a I doubt it. I'll be playing squash at nine.   **b** I'm not sure. I'm playing squash at nine.

B5 Charles and Daphne are arguing about a party they're supposed to be going to this evening. Change the bracketed verbs into the most natural-sounding future forms.

DAPHNE: You haven't forgotten we (*go*) to Jane's party this evening, have you?
CHARLES: Unfortunately, no. What time (*it start*)?
DAPHNE: Half past seven. They (*start*) early because Phil and Sue (*catch*) an early plane tomorrow morning, so they (*not want*) to be late home.
CHARLES: Who else (*go*), do you know?
DAPHNE: Well, I expect Jack and Ann (*be*) there, and I know Joan (*go*).
CHARLES: Oh, no! I suppose she (*tell*) everybody all evening about the colour of the new kitchen she (*buy*) soon or the way she (*have*) her patio extended.
DAPHNE: Come on, the taxi (*be*) here soon. What (*you wear*)?
CHARLES: I don't know. (*I look*) all right in this?
DAPHNE: Well, not really, no. I imagine all the men there (*wear*) suits and ties.
CHARLES: Well, which of my suits (*I wear*), then?
DAPHNE: Look, I (*not tell*) you what to wear. You (*have to*) make up your own mind.
CHARLES: Oh, I (*wear*) that old grey one with the hole in the sleeve, then.
DAPHNE: (*you be*) in this foul mood all evening? If you (*be*), I (*not go*), and that's that!
CHARLES: OK, I'm sorry. I (*try*).
DAPHNE: Get dressed, then, or everyone (*go*) home by the time we get there!

C Functions: being a good listener

C1 Practise this conversation in pairs, one of you narrating from the left column, the other choosing from the selection of comments on the right to keep things going. Try this several times, changing roles after each.

I have this recurring dream, you see, in which I'm a wooden statue. Well, when I say 'statue', I look like one, but . . .	*prompting, making assumptions* Really it's you? / You can still see and feel? / Underneath you're human, you mean?
Exactly. And I'm standing alone in the middle of a kind of desert, . . .	*checking, recapping* What, in the middle of nowhere? / You say you're all on your own? / What, miles from anywhere? / Did you say you were made of wood?
Yes. Then slowly a crowd of people come and group themselves around me, . . .	*encouraging continuation* Then what? / What do they do? / So what happens then? / And . . .?
Well, they're all holding burning torches, you see. And my wife's always with them, and it's always her who steps forward first and lights the base of the statue.	*expressing sympathy/concern* How frightening! / That sounds terrible! / What a thing to happen! / Poor you! / That's dreadful! / That must be awful!
Anyway, when she looks up – and this is the strange bit – her face has got half her features and half yours!	*expressing shock/disbelief* No! / Really? / Mine! / Honestly? / Good Heavens! / Never! / You're joking! / That's incredible!
Yes. And then she starts – or the two of you start – neighing like a horse or sort of braying like a donkey!	*thinking aloud* It makes you think. / It makes you wonder. / It's a funny old world.
Mm. And the next thing is, the flames are moving up and up round my waist and chest, and then just as they're about to lick my neck, . . .	*anticipating* That's how it finishes, I suppose? / That's where it ends, is it? / Don't tell me! You wake up?
Yes. That's it. I must have had that dream a dozen times, you know.	*launching one's own story* Funny; it reminds me of when I . . . / Odd you should say that; I once . . . / That's interesting what you said; did I ever tell you about the time I . . .?

C2 One of you invent your own dream to relate, the other improvise responses, questions, encouraging noises as above.

C3 Finally, tell your partner a short story *in the past* and note what changes become necessary in some of the listener's comments.

D Register: formal letters and saying what's in them

Read this letter of appointment through, then fill in the spaces with appropriate details. *Do not show anyone what you are writing.*

> Further to your interview of last Thursday, we have pleasure in offering you the post of .... at our .... branch, to commence on .... and terminate on ....
>
> You will be required to work between the hours of ...... and ......, Monday to Friday (with .... free for lunch), and you are asked to be on the premises not less than ..... minutes before the start of each working day. Any work done in excess of ...... hours per week is voluntary and qualifies for payment at special overtime rates. Participation in fortnightly training sessions outside normal working hours is compulsory, and will not be remunerated separately.
>
> Your basic salary during the first ...... months of your employment will be £...... (.................... pounds) per week. For the period between .... and .... £...... (.............. pounds) per annum.
>
> Your salary will be paid into your bank account on the last working day of each calendar week. You will receive written notification of the gross amount due and of statutory deductions made.
>
> During the first ...... months of employment, you will not be entitled to any period of holiday. Thereafter holiday may be granted at the discretion of your immediate superior.
>
> We should like to take this opportunity of congratulating you on your appointment and would ask you to send us written confirmation of your acceptance of our offer as soon as possible.

Pass your completed letter to another student. Now tell your partner – a friend – the terms of your appointment and compare them with his/hers. Use informal English beginning: *I've got to . . ., They pay . . ., I'll have to . . ., I get paid . . ., I won't get . . ., They don't give me . . ., I start . . .,* etc.

E Listening and socialising

Each comment below is a conversational response to a sentence you will hear on cassette. Within each group of four, indicate which response is suited to which stimulus, first, second, third or fourth.

Group **1**
  a I'm not surprised.
  b I wouldn't be surprised.
  c It's up to you.
  d How was I to know?

Group **2**
  a That doesn't surprise me.
  b I doubt it.
  c I'd rather not, if you don't mind.
  d You might as well.

Group **3**
  a That makes a change.
  b I bet you will.
  c So there is.
  d How do you expect me to know?

Group **4**
  a I don't blame you.
  b It all depends.
  c If you insist.
  d Fancy that!

Group **5**
  a What do you expect?
  b It looks like it.
  c You dare!
  d Don't look at me!

Group **6**
  a It serves you right.
  b It makes no difference to me.
  c Never mind: it doesn't matter.
  d Not that I know of.

Such responses are difficult to produce quickly and naturally in conversation. Having checked your ordering above, practise them further in groups, trying to elicit them from each other.

F Reading and role play

F1 Read through this extract from a sports magazine interview in pairs.
Study the use of present tenses and notice especially how the
Continuous form allows us to 'get inside' the action in a dramatic,
emotive way.

ROB: What thoughts go through your head
when you're lining up at the start?

STEVE: Well, I personally try to empty my head at
that point. I tend to look down and avoid
other people's eyes. You find some are
looking around trying to establish some
sort of psychological superiority over the
rest, but I prefer privacy – mental privacy.

ROB: And then when the gun goes off?

STEVE: Well, at first there's a great feeling of
relief that your body's actually moving
freely.

ROB: And while you're running, your mind is
active, is it?

STEVE: Oh yes. You're concentrating most of the
time on your stride pattern and rhythm
and your position on the track.

ROB: Do you think about the others while
you're running?

STEVE: To a certain extent you have to. With
there being a more aggressive element in
the sport nowadays, you have to be
aware of where your legs are and what
other legs are doing. And shoulders.

ROB: How are you normally feeling by the time
the bell goes?

STEVE: Well, by that stage your legs are
beginning to protest a bit and your lungs
are aching – a sort of burning sensation –
and you're running from memory, or
instinct. It's funny, your mind feels
independent of your legs; or vice versa.

ROB: And if you're leading at this point?

STEVE: You're worried that someone's going to
catch you.

ROB: And if you're behind?

STEVE: You're worried that you're not going to
have the pace to get by. Then off the last
bend, when the tape comes in sight,
you're trying to maintain your style but at
the same time increase speed and stride
length. It's like trying to pour a couple of
litres into a one-litre pot. Sometimes it
works – incredibly – quite often it doesn't.

F2 Still in pairs, take it in turns to interview each other with one of you
taking the role of a (fairly famous):

1	parachutist	**3**	racing-driver	**5**	trapeze artist
2	surgeon	**4**	(water-) skier	**6**	theatre actor/actress

Try to imitate the combination of Simple and Continuous forms above.

G Exercises for homework

G1 Using the one in **F1** as a model, write an imaginary magazine
interview, this time with an astronaut who has been 'up' several
times. Concentrate on the person's feelings at specific points on his
or her trips.

G2 A fellow-student wrote this letter to a mutual friend a few days after leaving Britain to return home. You wrote an almost identical letter, but had the foresight to send it a few days before leaving. Read this version, then complete your own.
Your letter begins: *Just a short note to say I'm afraid I won't be able . . .*

> Just a short note to say I'm sorry I couldn't come to say goodbye in person before I left. As you know, I took my final exams on Friday and was writing compositions until six o'clock. When they had finally finished, there was a little celebration for all the students who were leaving and by the time I got home – about half-past nine, I suppose it was – I was absolutely shattered. Then of course I had my packing to do, and after that I had to tidy up the place a bit. As I left at seven the next morning, I didn't have time to contact anybody. Before I knew it, I was back in my office working again and my holiday had become just a memory.
> Thanks for everything. Best wishes for the future, and kind regards to Helen.

G3 First, read through this advertisement, then do the exercises that follow.

A new way of looking at kitchen walls

AKS are pleased to announce a revolution in kitchen units, the overthrow of reactionary cupboards and a brand-new regime for your run-down walls. Any questions?

Well yes, how much do I pay?
It costs as much as you want to spend.

What do I do?
You just give us a call, and we pop round for a chat.

Sounds OK. What choice do I have?
You choose the colours, patterns and materials; we advise. When you give us the nod, we measure up and send you an estimate.

Then what?
You sign on the dotted line – no obligation, of course. Then we go away and build the units to your specifications.

How long does that take?
You tell us when you want them. Then one weekend when you're not inviting royalty to dinner, we send a couple of eager beavers around. You sit back, make a pot of tea, they instal your brand-new kitchen. No mess. No fuss.

When do I pay?
Ah, not until all the work has been done and you're completely satisfied.

Can this be true?
We guarantee it!

1 Write a short letter to a friend, enthusing about the outcome of your answering this advert. Begin:
   'I felt I just had to write and tell you about our fantastic new kitchen.'
   Try to incorporate some of these openings:
   'What was so amazing was that . . .' 'One big advantage was that . . .'
   'Another great thing was that . . .'
   'What really impressed us was . . .'
   'And the best thing of all was that . . .'

2 Write an advert in a similar style for a Book Club which is persuading people to enjoy the benefits of being a member. Use these prompts as an outline:
   what advantages? – new way of buying books – cheaper, safer, more convenient
   how? – fill in form or phone – send 5 books on trial – 14 days – return if not satisfied – receive 3 books every month – accept minimum of one
   what sort? – wide variety – literature, best-sellers, romance, thrillers, sci-fi
   how long? – terminate membership whenever – no obligation
   how much? – big savings – substantial discounts – some less than half price – postage and packing – one free novel every year

A1 'Like starting school, going to your first job or getting married, retirement is a time of excitement tinged with nervous anticipation and perhaps a little fear.'

1 Have you ever thought about old age or retirement?
2 Are you looking forward to retiring? Why?/Why not?
3 What kinds of problems do people face when they retire?
4 And how do old retired people feel about other people's attitudes towards them?

A2 Who better to get an opinion from than a retired person? Read this article written by a retired gentleman for a national British newspaper. Work in pairs (labelled 'A' and 'B'). You're looking for different information (see p.103), but you need to read the whole article.

LIFE DOESN'T END AT 65

Not all pensioners are 'old' and poor

ARTHUR GODFREY

Retired

I DON'T mind being called a pensioner because I am one. But I do object, very strongly, to being labelled an 'old age pensioner' because the word 'old' is relative and if, at 65, I appear to have more energy, more new ideas, and more initiative than many of my younger brethren, why should I be labelled 'old' and they 'young'?

The term old age pensioner is one the politicians, local and national, like to conjure up, emotively, when arguing against a measure they are opposing whether or not pensioners as a group are themselves much concerned about the issue.

Of course there are pensioners who are short of funds; who need supplementary benefits, and have to watch their spending.

But there are many more, as the monthly over-50s magazine *Choice* makes clear in every issue, who not only have adequate incomes but suffi-cient capital to study the investment market.

Today, there are many more young people who need the resources of the State and the real sympathy of politicians than old age pensioners most of whom, after all, have their homes, an inflation-proofed regular pension, with supplementary benefits given, almost without question, if they need them.

The pensioners are wooed by the politicians, I suspect, only because they have votes, and usually use them. Many of the young people, cynical about politicians of all parties, either do not vote or prefer to support one of the fringe parties who are no threat to the three main ones.

Apart from their pensions, OAPs get a number of concessions denied to younger people whose circumstances are much more difficult. They get free, or subsidised, bus and train fares;

Churchill and Andropov did not give up at 65

concessionary charges at hairdressers and other service shops, and at many exhibitions and shows. Whatever their capital resources many get rate rebates, the cost of which often falls on young couples with children. They also get rent rebates.

The result of all this is that the pensioner is practically brain-washed into considering himself (or herself) as a lesser citizen than his younger contemporaries. Just as, for the first time in their lives, probably, they have the time, and the freedom, to do their own thing, society is impelling them to regard themselves as back numbers, and the under-privileged.

Oddly, the politicians themselves rarely think of giving up when they reach pensionable age. In the USSR, Mr Andropov became leader at the age of 69; Sir Winston Churchill became a war-time Prime Minister at 66, and carried on for years afterwards, as have many others, in many different fields, before and since the war.

So let's drop the term old age pensioner and such euphemisms as senior citizens and the like. Just call us retired people if a term has to be used and, with other people being forced, or induced, to give up work before the statutory pensionable age, this can mean anyone from the age of 50 to 80 plus.

A retired person may, or may not, need extras from society, as is the case with younger people. But there is surely no case for lumping them all together, and putting a label on them, for the benefit of the politicians.

'A' pairs read to find out

1 what Mr Godfrey doesn't mind, and why.
2 how politicians use the term 'old age pensioner'.
3 how Mr Godfrey feels about help for young people.
4 what kinds of financial concessions or benefits pensioners get (in the UK).
5 what Mr Godfrey says about politicians retiring.

'B' pairs read to find out

1 what Mr Godfrey objects to, and why.
2 how well or badly off most pensioners are, according to Mr Godfrey.
3 why politicians apparently 'woo' pensioners.
4 what many pensioners are made to feel by the rest of society.
5 what Mr Godfrey feels about terms like 'old age pensioners' and 'senior citizens'.

A3 Now form groups of four – one 'A' pair and one 'B' pair – and ask and tell each other what you found out from Mr Godfrey's article.

A4 Tell each other about retirement in your own country. Say

1 at what age men and women have to retire, and whether you agree with those ages.
2 how much old age pension retired people receive, if any, and how most old people manage on it.
3 what else is provided for elderly people (e.g. clubs), if anything, and how a lot of old people spend their time.

B Communicative grammar

B1 The prospect of retiring from full-time employment is daunting for many older people. Read what some people said when interviewed about their imminent retirement:

> Rather than just sit and do nothing, I'd prefer to find another 'part-time' job . . .

> I just can't wait to have the time to sit and watch the world go by . . .

> I can't see how I'll ever get used to being retired. I've always been so wrapped up in my work.

> I admit to being a bit apprehensive at the thought of retiring . . .

> Yes, I'm looking forward to taking things easy a bit. But you won't catch me sitting around doing nothing all day . . .

> At last I'll be able to get round to doing all those things I've always wanted to do, but never had the time.

Which of the people above do you think have the right attitude to retirement? Use sentences like: *The person who said that . . .*
Which of them have the wrong attitude, do you think? Why? What did they say?

B2 Verb + *to* + gerund constructions to express preferences, anticipation, etc.

In the sentence *I'm looking forward to the party*, the verb is *look forward to* (not simply *look forward*). This is why the gerund is used after *to* in, for example, *I'm not looking forward to going to the dentist.*
Study the ways we can express certain emotions using verbs with *to* + gerund (and other constructions) and then do the exercise.

anticipation	I'm looking forward to having a good rest at the weekend.
	I (just) can't wait to leave school.
preferences	(Generally,) I prefer reading a good book to watching TV.
	(Given a choice,) I would rather go out than stay at home.
	I (would) prefer to go on working rather than retire.
objection	I object (strongly) to being made to retire.
	I don't like the thought of having to do that (at all).
habits	I'm getting/I'll never get used to going to work every morning.
	Over the years she's grown/become/got accustomed to driving everywhere.
admission	I admit to being a bit short-tempered at times.
	(I admit I'm a bit short-tempered at times.)
determination/ intention	I'm determined } to get round/down to tidying my room this week. I mean/I intend }
agreement/ consent	I { agreed to { consented to } his buying a motorbike as long as he took lessons.

Join these sentences beginning with the words in italics:

1 You'll work for Mr Knight. *You'll have to get used to* it.
2 I have to get up at six now. *I suppose I'll become accustomed to* it.
3 He ran into the back of my car. *He admitted to* it.
4 You haven't booked seats for the concert yet. *Will you ever get round to* it?
5 I like working with other people. But *I prefer working on my own.*
6 I wanted to have an extra week's holiday. *The boss agreed to* it.
7 I read those reports at the weekend. *I finally got down to* it.
8 I have to do more work than the others. *I object to* that.
9 I'm going to the States for a year. *My father's finally consented to* it.
10 We were going to the beach for the day. *We were all looking forward to* it.

B3 Verb + noun/pronoun + participle *-ing* constructions

One of the speakers in **B1** said *You won't catch me sitting around doing nothing all day.* He could have said: *You won't find me sitting around doing nothing . . .* This means: 'If you think I'll be sitting around . . ., you won't find/catch me at it'.

1 Study these examples:

catch	The police caught him stealing.
find	They found the girl hiding in the cellar.
get	He means to get them all dancing by the end of the evening.
start	If this music doesn't start your feet tapping, nothing will.
keep	He kept us waiting for hours.
leave	I left her playing the piano.
don't want } *can't have*	We don't want/can't have you doing nothing. (=You won't be doing nothing: we don't want/can't have that.)

Now join these pairs of sentences, beginning with the words in italics:

a They were playing cards. That's how *we left them.*
b I don't want to stand around for hours. *Please don't keep me.*
c You want to waste your time? *I can't have you* doing that.
d My coat's hanging behind the door. *You'll find* it there.
e He was climbing over the wall. *They caught him.*

2 One of the speakers in **B1** said he wanted to 'sit and watch the world go by'. Verbs like *see, watch, notice, hear* and *feel* can be followed by an infinitive without *to* or a participle *-ing* form. But there is sometimes an important difference. Look at this:

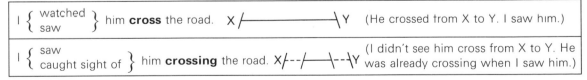

I { watched / saw } him **cross** the road.	X/——————\Y	(He crossed from X to Y. I saw him.)
I { saw / caught sight of } him **crossing** the road.	X/--/——\--\Y	(I didn't see him cross from X to Y. He was already crossing when I saw him.)

a You are going to hear a conversation between a policeman and an elderly woman immediately after an attempted bank robbery. Listen and answer these questions:
Would Mrs Smith make a very good witness in court, do you think? Why?/Why not?
What did she see, hear and feel? And what about her friends?

b Now listen again and make notes. Then write up her statement beginning: *I was standing outside the bank . . .*

C Functions: emphasising emotions and facts with the verb *do*

C1 When Arthur Godfrey wrote in his article (p 102) 'I don't mind being called a pensioner . . . but I do object very strongly to being labelled an "old age pensioner"', he was making special use of the verb *do* to emphasise the strength of his feelings.

This use of the auxiliary *do, does* and *did* corresponds to the stress or emphasis put on other auxiliaries (*will, must, is, have,* etc.) in sentences like 'I won't work on Saturday, but I *will* work for you on Sunday'.

You may already know that *do* is used to give extra persuasive emphasis to orders and invitations (e.g. *Do take a seat./ Do please try to be there.*) and to add extra politeness (e.g. *You do understand, I hope, why we can't come.*) – but now listen to and note the way it is used in the following:

a *Same verb, same tense – emphasis on the positive:*
They say I don't understand: but I *do* understand, honestly.
She thought I didn't hear the phone, but I *did* hear it. (I preferred to ignore it!)
I thought you weren't going to France, but you *did* go in the end, didn't you?
He doesn't think we've worked out the project in enough detail, but he *does* think we're going in the right direction.

b *Same verb, different tense – emphasis on the second (for correction):*
He owns, or (at any rate) *did* own, the shop on the corner.
She works, or (at least) *did* work (at one time), at the hospital.

They lived, or $\left\{ \begin{array}{l} \text{should I say} \\ \text{rather} \end{array} \right\}$ they *do* live, in a small flat in London.

c *Different verb, same tense – often a resigned attitude to one activity followed by an objection to or hatred of another:*
I don't mind washing up, but I *do* object to drying up.
It's all right writing the report, but I *do* hate having to read it out in public.
Cleaning the car's all right, but I *do* dislike having to check the oil and water.

C2 Complete the following as in the examples above:
1 I don't feel particularly sorry for old people with money, but . . .
2 He didn't manage to save *very* much when he was working, but . . .
3 She doesn't mind making the beds in the morning, but . . .
4 He earns, or . . . (*past correction*) . . ., a very good salary.
5 You weren't going to apply for that job, but in fact . . .

C3 Now in pairs practise these short conversations and improvise similar ones with the prompts below:

1 A: You know Frank Grey, don't you?
 B: Yes, he lives in the house on the hill.
 A: Well, that's what I was going to tell you. He *did* live there, but he's moved.

 a Mary James – teaches at the college – left
 b The Greens – own a small hotel in town – sold it
 c Ray Large – works for the local council – made redundant

2 A: Can you wash the car?
 B: All right. I don't mind washing it, but I *do* hate drying it off.
 A: Well, if you wash it, I'll dry it off.

 a paint the living-room – get everything ready
 b take the minutes of the meeting – type them up
 c write the invitations for the party – address the envelopes

D Vocabulary: euphemism and polite language

D1 According to the *Longman Dictionary of Contemporary English*, a euphemism is 'the use of a pleasanter, less direct name for something thought to be unpleasant' in order not to give offence.
Euphemism must not be confused with slang: in fact, the more polite or refined the company, the more euphemism will be used, not slang. Nor must it be confused with an everyday expression for something legal, technical or medical. For example, the expression *to have a heart attack* is not a euphemism: it is an everyday expression for what a doctor would call *to suffer a coronary thrombosis*. Here are examples of quite common English euphemisms:

a senior citizen: an old age pensioner	*to be in the family way:* to be pregnant
to fall asleep / pass away / pass on: to die	*to be short of funds:* to have little or no money
elderly: old	*a disruptive influence:* a nuisance
the powder room / cloakroom: the ladies' lavatory	*a fib/to fib/a fibber:* a lie/to lie/a liar
a refuse collector / sanitary engineer: a dustman	*to be/get tiddly/tipsy:* to be/get drunk
to pay a visit / spend a penny: to use the toilet	

D2 Rephrase these bald sentences using euphemisms to make them more socially acceptable:

1 I'm going to use the toilet.
2 Sue's in the ladies' lavatory.
3 That boy's a nuisance in the class.
4 That girl tells lies all the time.
5 He's just got a job as a dustman.

6 The girl down the road's pregnant again.
7 Mrs James, the old lady who lived in the house on the corner, died yesterday.
8 We'd like to invite some old age pensioners to the party.

D3 Euphemism, however, is also used in a rather sinister way. Read this extract (right) from an essay written by George Orwell in 1946. What does it say about language and politics? How true is it today?

D4 The following sentences are all taken from recent political speeches and reports. Discuss what they really mean:
'There was a frank and open exchange of views.'
'We have never been pro-euthanasia.'
'There are conflicting views among members of the Government about recent proposals regarding adjustments to the present taxation situation.'

In our time, political speech and writings are largely the defence of the indefensible. Political language has to consist largely of euphemism, question-begging and sheer cloudy vagueness. Defenceless villages are bombarded from the air, the inhabitants driven out into the countryside, the cattle machine-gunned, the huts set on fire with incendiary bullets: this is called *pacification*. Millions of peasants are robbed of their farms and sent trudging along the roads with no more than they can carry: this is called *transfer of population* or *rectification of frontiers*. People are imprisoned for years without trial, or shot in the back of the neck or sent to die of scurvy in Arctic lumber camps: this is called *elimination of unreliable elements*. Such phraseology is needed if one wants to name things without calling up mental pictures of them. Consider for instance some comfortable English professor defending totalitarianism. He cannot say outright, 'I believe in killing off your opponents when you can get good results by doing so.' Probably, therefore, he will say something like this:
'While freely conceding that such regimes exhibit certain features which the humanitarian may be inclined to deplore, we must, I think, agree that a certain curtailment of the right to political opposition is an unavoidable concomitant of transitional periods, and that the rigours which certain people have been called upon to undergo have been amply justified in the sphere of concrete achievement.'
The inflated style is itself a kind of euphemism.

E Exercises for homework

E1 Complete these sentences with the correct form of the verb in *italics*
– gerund -*ing* form, participle -*ing* form, infinitive with *to* or infinitive
without *to*.

1 I could never get used to (*eat*) a big breakfast every morning.
2 When he was eighteen, his father agreed to his (*buy*) a motorbike.
3 We watched the plane (*climb*) until it disappeared in the clouds.
4 Isn't it about time you got round to (*mend*) the puncture in your tyre?
5 She says she'd prefer (*go*) out to work rather than (*stay*) home and (*do*) housework all day.
6 I found your purse (*lie*) behind the sofa where you dropped it.
7 They looked up and caught sight of a lorry (*hurtle*) down the hill towards them.
8 Don't ever let me catch you (*do*) anything like that again.
9 Most students object to (*have*) (*do*) too much homework.
10 He's a very professional entertainer: he always leaves his audience (*want*) more.

E2 Below is a table from an official survey carried out about retired
people in Great Britain in the late 70s. Study it carefully and then use
the information in it to write a short newspaper article under the
headline SENIOR CITIZENS' 'LIKES' OUTWEIGH 'DISLIKES'.
NOTE: You need not report all the findings, just those that might be
slightly surprising or might interest your newspaper readers: for
instance, the fact that only a small number (5.9 per cent), relatively
speaking, worry about financial difficulties.

Table 15.6.2   Things particularly disliked and particularly enjoyed about life

Things disliked	Grand total %	Things enjoyed	Grand total %
Financial difficulties	5.9	Just happy, enjoys life, no further details	13.4
Own poor health, disability	15.1		
Poor health, disability of other member of household	2.9	Enjoys company of family, friends	29.3
		Enjoys freedom, being at home, because retired	9.5
Loss of partner, consequent loneliness	5.9	Likes being independent	3.3
Loneliness apart from this	7.0	Enjoys indoor hobbies, pastimes (apart from reading)	23.6
Inability to do certain things (not physical)	5.4		
Boredom	3.6	Enjoys outdoor hobbies, activities	18.5
		Enjoys reading	7.1
Complaints about state of society, vandalism, strikes, bad manners, noise, etc.	4.4	Enjoys social activities	16.8
		Has good health	6.7
		Enjoys holidays, excursions	6.9
Other specific complaints	7.5	Likes eating, smoking, drinking	4.8
Nothing disliked particularly	50.9	Other specific enjoyments	4.1
		No particular enjoyments	9.4

E3 Opposite is an advertisement for the Job Release Scheme run by the
Department of Employment in Britain. You are going to take part in
an international English-speaking conference at which you have
been asked to give a brief report on the British Scheme. Read the
advertisement carefully and write a brief summary (100–150 words)
about the Scheme to read out at the conference.

Stop work up to five years early and make every day a weekend.

Looking forward to retirement?

Some people just see it as not having to go to work every day.

To others, it's the chance to spend more time doing the things they really enjoy.

Like spending more time with the grandchildren. Seeing a bit more of the countryside. Developing new interests.

In fact, doing all the things that used to have to wait until the weekend.

But now you don't have to wait until you retire. Take advantage of the Job Release Scheme and every day can be like a weekend.

HOW DOES IT WORK?

The Job Release Scheme enables you to stop work early – up to five years early in some cases.

Until you get your normal State pension, you'll receive a weekly allowance.

The actual amount may vary, but ranges from £45.70 to £67.20. And if you join for your last year before retirement, it's tax-free.

Provided your employer agrees, and takes on somone who is unemployed, you can apply at least 8 weeks before you want to leave work.

ARE YOU ELIGIBLE?

Men can join the Scheme any time from their 62nd birthday. Disabled men can join earlier – from their 60th birthday.

And women can become eligible at 59.

To find out more about the Job Release Scheme and details of changes to the Scheme. Pick up a leaflet at your local Jobmarket.

Do it now. The Job Release Scheme could make life just like one long, enjoyable weekend.

Job Release Scheme

Activity 3 (see Teacher's Guide Unit 12)

OPINION POLL

Sometimes ☐
Yes ☑
No ☐
Never ☐

A1 Have you ever been interviewed for an opinion poll? If so, where and when? And what was the opinion poll about? If you have never taken part in an opinion poll yet, would you agree or decline to take part? Why?

A2 Read this article silently in order to find the answers to these questions:

1 Why does it seem at first glance that 'neighbourliness is alive and well and living in Britain'?

2 Are the British now more, or less, neighbourly than their parents were?

3 Why is Britain now apparently a 'rubalong' society?

4 Where are people the most, and the least, neighbourly?

5 What are the three types of neighbour and what characterises them?

Neighbours
What we think of the folk next door

● *IS NEIGHBOURLINESS dead? To find out the facts about neighbourliness today, The Sunday Times commissioned an opinion poll company to conduct a major survey. Nearly 2,000 adults cooperated in an in-depth interview on their attitudes to their neighbours. Do we like our neighbours or loathe them? Help them or hold them at bay?*

AT FIRST glance the message seems to be: neighbourliness is alive and well and living in Britain.

Consider the following facts:
● Nearly half those we spoke to reckon to know *by name* eleven or more of their neighbours. A quarter know 20 or more.
● Most of our sample think well of their neighbours. Nine in ten say that their neighbourhood is 'friendly', while only five per cent complain that the neighbours are 'nosey' and three per cent that they are 'snobbish'.
● 86 per cent of adults have done at least something to help a neighbour in the past year. Most have done several favours of one kind or another.
● Only one in five people say they've had any problem at all with their neighbours over the past two years. The rest did not have a single complaint.
● Three in five people speak to a neighbour at least once a day. Only one in ten say that they speak to a neighbour less than once a week.

Neighbourliness lives – OK. Or does it? For we also asked: 'Compared with your parents' generation, do you think you have more contact, or less contact with your neighbours than they did?' A majority replied: 'less contact'. Only one adult in seven said they had more contact with their neighbours than did their parents' generation. And our own, personal interviews reflect a real yearning for an age past where neigh-

bours were at the centre of a comforting and protective world.

People think that caring, sharing Britain is disappearing. In its place we have 'rubalong' Britain, the new low-key neighbourliness of the 80s.

NEIGHBOURS aren't the people we know best any more. After wives, husbands and families come casual friends and (for those with jobs) workmates. Fewer than one person in three rate neighbours among their best friends.

NEIGHBOURS aren't the people with whom we share our troubles. If your marriage breaks up, you are 14 times as likely to go to your family for help than to your neighbours. You are nine times as likely to look to the family if there's a death and 20 times as likely to look to the family if you run out of money.

NEIGHBOURS are more likely to be casual acquaintances than intimate friends. Ninety-seven per cent of adults speak to the neighbours at least once a month – but only six per cent have them round for a meal. Fewer than one in five go out for a drink together. Asked what their neighbours are like, most people are startlingly vague – 'friendly' they say, even 'sociable', but they won't rate neighbours as happy or unhappy, quiet or noisy, or in any other personal terms.

But what decides how neighbourly you are? Three factors in particular, our survey shows: what part of the country you live in, how long you have lived there, and what type of place it is.

Northerners really are friendlier than people down south. They are more likely than people in the south to speak to their neighbours at least once a day, more likely to pop round for a chat and more likely to go to the pub or the club for a drink with a neighbour. So it's not surprising that northerners are more likely than southerners to say that people round them are friendly.

But the survey also shows that the relationship in the north is a more drop-in-for-a-chat, informal sort of a relationship than in the south. Northerners, for example, are much less likely to invite their neighbours round for a meal.

The champion neighbours by far are the Scots. They are twice as likely to know twenty or more neighbours by name as the rest of us.

The longer you live in a place, the more neighbourly you are likely to feel. Over half our sample have lived in the same neighbourhood for 10 years or more and among these, nearly three in five knew at least 11 neighbours by name. They are more likely to reckon the neighbourhood friendly, and to chat to their neighbours. This must partly reflect the fact that, if you don't like the neighbours, you try to move.

But, equally, the longer we stay in a place, the more we get to know people and the more important they are to us. Hence the feelings of anger we picked up from our interviews in communities where neighbourhoods have been destroyed in the interests of wholesale redevelopment.

Important, too, is the kind of area you live in. Thus we can compare neighbourliness in the high-class suburbs with those in multi-occupied, overcrowded inner cities; the old working class terraces with the new, classier estates or rural areas.

On every measure, the country comes out as the bastion of neighbourliness. People there know many more neighbours by name, speak to them more often and rely on them for help in emergencies.

For in the end, it all boils down to

Like neighbours ought to be, two elderly ladies gossip over the garden fence in London's Kentish Town

individuals. Surveying our results, they fall, it seems, into three types:

SUPERNEIGHBOURS, accounting for about perhaps a fifth of the population. They know lots of their neighbours by name; they are in and out of each others' houses for a drink and a chat; they look after a key for their neighbours and help out with the kids; they keep an eye on the old and disabled. They are commoner in rural areas than in urban ones, but every district has some and they are literally the life and soul of the community.

ISOLATES, rather fewer in number, perhaps one person in ten. They don't know many neighbours, nor chat to them; they look elsewhere if they need help or support, neither helping nor being helped. They tend to live in deprived inner-city areas, but, again, every area – even the country – has some.

And then there are the rest of us, the RUBALONGS. Neighbours are a fact of life but not its centre; relationships are amiable but not intense – a bit of give-and-take; real life takes place in the home or the workplace rather than in the neighbourhood.

The fear must be that, as time goes by, there will be fewer and fewer superneighbours – and more and more isolates, straining the complex networks that keeps local society functioning at all. Neighbourliness lives – but whichever way you look at it, it clearly is not quite what it used to be.

A3 Read the article again and make a list of all the ways used to describe statistical information in language, for example: 'Nearly half those we spoke to . . .'

A4 Discussion

What do you think would be the results if a similar opinion poll were conducted to find out the facts about neighbourliness in your own country? Do you think the results would be very much the same as in the UK, or vastly different? Give reasons.

13

B Communicative grammar: summarising numbers and quantities of countables, especially people

B1 **1** You are summarising opinion poll figures. Referring (or remembering back) to the survey on neighbours on pages 110–111, make as many sentences as you can using language from the table below. (Study the table carefully for a few minutes first!)

–	every (single) each and every not one hardly any	person viewer listener motorist

–	not one of the none of the hardly any (of the) not many (of the) very few (of the) just a few (of the) some (of the) quite a few (of the) (a great) many (of the) a large number of (the) large numbers of (the) a lot of (the) lots of (the) masses of (the) the (vast) majority of (the) most (of the) all (the)/all (of the)	people viewers listeners correspondents respondents children young people youngsters teenagers colleagues parents middle-aged people OAPs men women companies firms shopkeepers motorists cyclists pedestrians commuters GPs/doctors MPs/politicians	we { asked . . . interviewed . . . spoke to . . . wrote to . . .
about/roughly approximately something like almost nearly just/well over less than more than (no) fewer than	25 per cent of (the) a quarter of the 33 per cent of (the) a/one third of the 50 per cent of (the) half (of) the 66 per cent of (the) two-thirds of the 75 per cent of (the) three-quarters of the 100 per cent of (the) 2 dozen (of the) 4 hundred (of the)	
	one in five (of the) two out of (every) five	

2 Now imagine you are summarising opinion poll figures about these subjects. (Imagine the polls were conducted in the town and in the country, with young people and with older people.) Radio likes and dislikes; the cost of living; education; life 50 years ago; old age and retirement; tastes in music; hobbies and pastimes.

Refer to the table above and make up sentences like this:
Something like 75 per cent of the older people we spoke to were enjoying retirement.
Hardly any of the women we interviewed listened regularly to the radio.

112

B2 This is a summary of some of the results of a survey about British TV. The report which accompanied these figures included sentences like this:
'. . . almost one in two thinks there is too much sport (on TV) . . .'
'Some 20 per cent overall think there is quite enough comedy around . . .'

A survey of your TV likes and dislikes

	Party political broadcasts	Soap operas	Sport	Quiz shows, panel games, etc.	Films	Comedy
Too much	48%	46%	45%	37%	20%	19%
Too little	3%	7%	8%	15%	37%	30%

	Religious programmes	Current affairs	Light entertainment	Drama	Documentaries	News
Too much	16%	15%	13%	12%	10%	9%
Too little	11%	20%	24%	30%	37%	10%

In pairs or small groups, and using the kind of language from the previous pages, tell each other what the survey found about viewers' feelings towards different kinds of programmes. Don't forget the following introductory phrases which we often use when summarising or generalising:

On the whole, . . .   At first glance, . . .   All in all, . . .
In all, . . .   Whichever way you look at it, . . .   Overall, . . .
Altogether, . . .   There is/seems/would seem to be little doubt that . . .
Apparently, . . .   It seems } that . . .   It appears } that . . .
Generally, . . .   It would seem   It would appear

Example: On the whole, about half the people interviewed thought that there were too many party political broadcasts on television.

C Register

Look at how the same information can be reported formally and informally:

formal (spoken and written)	While/Whereas/Although 13 per cent of all respondents expressed the opinion that there was too much light entertainment on television, 24 per cent of those questioned felt that there was too little.
informal (spoken and written)	Some of the people we asked thought there was too much light entertainment on TV, but roughly a quarter said there wasn't enough.

Formal reports tend to use:
— words like while, whereas, although
— precise figures e.g. 24 per cent
— verbs and expressions like expressed the opinion, felt, questioned
— passive constructions e.g. 24 per cent of those (who were) questioned

Informal reports tend to use:
— words like but, though
— approximations e.g. roughly a quarter
— everyday verbs like said, thought, asked
— contact clauses e.g. the people (that) we asked

Now in pairs, tell each other again (informally) about findings from the TV survey, and then write down a formal version of each piece of information as if for a report.
Compare your formal reports with the rest of the class.

D Listening

D1 You are going to hear someone being interviewed in the street for an opinion poll. As you listen, tick the information given as if you were the interviewer/researcher.

Question 6 I am going to read out things that some people worry about these days, and I would like you to tell me from this card to what extent, if at all, you have worried about each one <u>in the last 2-3 weeks.</u>

(Show card)

	A great deal	A fair amount	A little	Not at all	Does not apply	No opinion
Not having enough money						
The education of children						
Unemployment of yourself or members of your family						
Nuclear war/World war						
Your health/Your family's health						
Relation with your neighbours						
Your children						
Relations with your husband/wife/ boy/girlfriend						
How things are going at work						
Growing old						
Vandalism/Crime in this area						
Your housing conditions						

Question 8 I am going to read out a list of things which can affect how happy people are. From this card I would like you to tell me how happy or unhappy you are with each one. (Read down list.)

(Show card)

	Extremely happy	Very happy	Fairly happy	Neither happy nor unhappy	Fairly unhappy	Very unhappy	Extremely unhappy
District you live in							
Education you received							
Your family life							
Health							
Housing conditions							
Job/Employment of you or your family							
Marriage/Partner							
How you use your spare time							
Standard of living							

D2 Check your answers with a partner. Then in pairs, and using the questionnaire above, interview each other. Finally, as a class, and without mentioning names, collate the information (in statistical form if you can) and write a report of your survey.

E Vocabulary: spoken abbreviations

E1 Look at these newspaper headlines, then in pairs read them out and explain them to each other. Cover the rest of the page as you do this exercise.

SRN Accused of Negligence Towards Patients

Rise in Sufferers from TB

FBI and CIA join forces to fight crime

'ID cards will come soon, says MP

PM TO VISIT INDIA

OAPs To Get Increase in Pensions

E2 Unlike written abbreviations such as *mph* and *St*, which we normally say respectively as *miles per hour* or *miles an hour* and *street* or *saint*, the ones in the headlines above are abbreviations which are actually written and spoken as such. Thus we write *SRN* and say /es aː*r*'en/ (= State Registered Nurse). Abbreviations like this, spoken as separate letters, have been called 'alphabetisms': those which are spoken now as complete words, such as *NATO* /'neitəʊ/, are called 'acronyms'. Study these:

an OAP (old age pensioner)
an MP (Member of Parliament)
a JP (Justice of the Peace)
a GP (general practitioner)
an SRN (State Registered Nurse)
a VIP (very important person)
PVC (polyvinyl chloride: a kind of plastic)
PS (postscript)
TB (tuberculosis)
ESP (extrasensory perception)
a P.C. (police constable)
the UN (United Nations)
the PM (Prime Minister)
R.I.P. ('Rest in Peace')

the EEC (European Economic Community)
the AA (Automobile Association)
the RAC (Royal Automobile Club)
the BBC (British Broadcasting Corporation)
the USA (United States of America)
the USSR (Union of Soviet Socialist Republics)
the FBI (Federal Bureau of Investigation)
the CIA (Central Intelligence Agency)
the UK (United Kingdom)
a PTA (Parent-Teacher Association)
NATO (North Atlantic Treaty Organisation)
UNESCO (United Nations Educational, Scientific, and Cultural Organisation)
a UFO (unidentified flying object)

E3 An abbreviations crossword puzzle

Cover the lists above and do this crossword in pairs. Then compare your answers.

Across
1 Russia
4 A British doctor
6 A British magistrate or judge
7 The European Economic Community
10 A British policeman
12 American Federal Bureau of Investigation
13 An afterthought to a letter
14 A British motoring organisation
17 Tuberculosis
18 Prime Minister
19 North Atlantic Treaty Organisation

Down
1 The United States
2 State Registered Nurse
3 British Member of Parliament
5 A kind of plastic
8 Extrasensory perception

9 British Broadcasting Corporation
11 American Central Intelligence Agency
14 Letters often found on tombstones
15 An association of parents and teachers
16 A 'flying saucer'
17 Television

F Exercises for homework

F1 Read this article carefully and answer the multiple-choice questions.

Nearly half of children aged 7 to 16 'have seen a video nasty'

By Richard Evans

More than 3,500,000 children, nearly half of those aged seven to 16 in England and Wales, have watched a 'video nasty', according to a report published yesterday.

More than one in five have seen at least four of such films, declared obscene by various courts, while a third of children have seen a 'nasty' by the age of eight, it claims.

The latest findings of the parliamentary group video inquiry, based on a national survey of 7,000 schoolchildren and parents, follow the publication last November of initial survey results which were treated sceptically by some academics, church leaders and MPs who questioned the research's validity.

But Dr Clifford Hill, director of the research project, said yesterday the new figures were totally accurate. 'All the data has been extensively analysed by a highly competent academic working party. All of us put our academic reputation behind the report.'

The report claims that 45 per cent of children have seen a 'nasty' compared to the original estimate of 40 per cent.

Many children watched the horror films without their parents' knowledge, often in homes of friends or relatives.

The report also says that 57 per cent of the children had seen at least one '18' rated film.

The Rev Peter Liddelow, deputy headmaster of a west London comprehensive school and a working party member involved on the survey, said that the report's figures, far from exaggerating, probably underestimated the problem of 'video nasties'.

He disclosed that 63 out of 73 fourth formers at his school admitted this week to having seen at least one 'nasty'. One boy had seen 29 of the 51 films declared illegal in one court.

'Some boys and girls have had nightmares and then wake up and cannot get back to sleep.

'I find these figures quite appalling. These films are so dramatic and so realistic that children enter into the spirit of these films. It is poisoning and polluting their minds.

'It is going to have a degrading and devastating effect on the generation,' Mr Liddlelow said.

Lord Coggan, the former Archbishop of Canterbury, who attended yesterday's launch, said: 'I think that severe courses of action are called for in regard to these video nasties. The moral welfare of children is quite clearly at stake. It seems impossible even for parents who are concerned to guarantee their children don't see them.'

The statistics portrayed a very serious picture, he said.

The Rev Gerald Burt, secretary of the social responsibility division of the Methodist church, which with the Roman Catholic church withdrew its sponsorship of the research after last year's controversy, said yesterday that he remained sceptical about the latest evidence.

Mr Graham Bright, the Conservative MP for Luton South who is sponsoring a private member's Bill to outlaw 'nasties', criticised the interim report and said yesterday: 'I do question the validity of the research. It points at the problem, but I do not think one can take that as concrete evidence.'

---

1 According to the article, the survey done on 'video nasties' before this one
 A proved that most children have seen at least one.
 B was greeted with some scepticism.
 C should have included information about younger children.
 D was based on too small a sample.

2 How convinced are the members of the research project that the statistics are valid?
  A Not very.
  B Fairly.
  C Reasonably.
  D Totally.

3 Although the statistics are appalling,
  A the problem may not be as bad as it seems.
  B children's education does not seem to be suffering.
  C schoolchildren's moral standards do not appear to be affected.
  D the situation could be far worse than the figures indicate.

4 In Lord Coggan's opinion,
  A it is up to parents to stop their children watching 'video nasties'.
  B the statistics prove that parents are irresponsible.
  C something must be done about the problem soon.
  D the 'video nasties' statistics prove very little.

5 Mr Bright, the Rev Gerald Burt, and the Roman Catholic church all agree that
  A the research which led to the report is suspect.
  B there is controversy about the evidence.
  C 'video nasties' should be banned.
  D the recent figures are valid.

F2 Write a short magazine article of about 300–350 words on the value (or otherwise) of opinion polls.
Here are some questions to get you thinking:

– What kinds of people, organisations and so on use opinion polls? What for?
– How important are opinion polls in advertising?
– How effective can opinion polls be in bringing about social changes?
– How 'true' are the results from opinion polls?
– Do people tell the truth when they answer questionnaires for opinion polls, or do they perhaps say what they think the questioner or survey form would like them to say?
– Do figures from opinion polls influence people in the way they vote at elections, in the things they buy, the forms of transport they use, and so on?
– Should more use be made of opinion polls, do you think, or should they perhaps be banned? (Should someone undertake a survey to find out what people think in general about opinion polls?!)

These are just some of the questions you might consider.

Whatever you decide to do, and whatever aspects of the topic you decide to write about, try to bear in mind that a piece of writing of this nature should have a clear introduction (1 paragraph), a clear development (2–4 paragraphs) and a clear conclusion (usually 1 paragraph).

Unit 14

ATTITUDES TO THE HANDICAPPED

A1 Look at these four stamps, published by the British Post Office to commemorate The International Year of Disabled People 1981.
- Which aspects of disability do they reflect? What are they asking us to remember?
- How effective do you think they are?
- What effect did The International Year of Disabled People have in your country?
- Would you say there had been a change of attitude towards handicapped people recently?
- Can you think of any spheres of life, social, cultural, economic or political, in which such a change is still necessary?

A2 Read these lines, part of an information leaflet published to accompany the stamps above. Then do the exercises that follow.

No one knows exactly how many disabled people there are in the world, but estimates suggest the figure is over 450 million. The number of disabled people in India alone is probably more than double the total population of Canada.

In the United Kingdom, about one in ten people have some disability. 'Disabled people' in this context are those who are physically handicapped, deaf, hard of hearing, blind, partially sighted, speech impaired, mentally handicapped, mentally ill, or suffer from handicaps such as epilepsy. Disability is not just something that happens to other people: as we get older, many of us will become less mobile, hard of hearing or have failing eyesight.

Disablement can take many forms and occur at any time of life. Some people are born with disabilities. Many others become disabled as they get older. There are many progressive disabling diseases. The longer time goes on, the worse they become. Some people are disabled in accidents.

Many others may have a period of disability in the form of a mental illness. All are affected by people's attitude towards them.

Disabled people face many physical barriers. Next time you go shopping or to work or visit friends, imagine how you would manage if you could not get up steps or kerbs, or on to buses and trains. How would you cope if you could not see where you were going or could not hear the traffic? But there are other barriers: prejudice can be even more formidable and harder to break down and ignorance inevitably represents by far the greatest barrier of all. It is almost impossible for the able-bodied to fully appreciate what the severely handicapped go through, but the International Year of Disabled People was of enormous value in drawing attention to these barriers and showing that it is the individual person and their ability, not their disability, which counts.

Answer these questions:

Paragraph 1

What aspect of disablement does this paragraph deal with?

Which of the two sentences do you find more thought-provoking?

Paragraph 2

In this paragraph, which specific human functions are referred to?

Paragraphs 2 and 3

How would you summarise the difference in content between these two paragraphs?

Paragraph 3

Which are the two key sentences in this paragraph?

One sentence here is an explanation of another. Which one?

Paragraph 4

Which is the key word in this paragraph?

Which three examples of disability are referred to in the first half of it?

In which areas did The International Year of Disabled People do most good?

A3 Role play in fours

Two of you have composed the article opposite and feel it makes an important, worthwhile statement. Two of you find the tone bland, the approach unoriginal, the message trivialised. You would like to have seen a more powerful, harder-hitting piece of writing. Go through the text, attacking and defending accordingly. Make sure that the criticism is constructive and that detailed alternatives are suggested.

A4 Group discussion: the brighter side

1 Look at this photograph. Where do you think it was taken? What would you say are the qualities the sportsman on the left must possess? What might be the special motivation for such an athlete?

2 How much do you know about the Paraplegic Olympics? What sporting events have you heard of disabled people taking part in?

3 Outside sport, what remarkable achievements on the part of handicapped people do you know of?

4 How has modern technology helped the lot of the disabled? Which inventions can you think of that have enabled them to do things from which their handicap previously barred them?

B Communicative grammar

B1 Look carefully at this model, noting the structure with *too* and *enough* and the use of *the disabled*. We are commenting critically on the extent, degree and suitability of certain things.

> Many store entrances are $\begin{cases} \text{too low or too narrow} \\ \text{not high or wide enough} \end{cases}$ for the disabled to get through.

During the course of a survey you have made these notes on the plight of various sections of our society. Report your findings, using each of the two patterns above.

1 signs and notices – small and unclear – partially sighted people can't read them
2 coins – small and light – elderly and very young people unable to handle easily
3 libraries – inaccessible – old and sick people often can't get to them

4 shop announcements – quiet – people who are hard of hearing can't follow
5 interest rates – unstable – unemployed and less well-off people can't invest safely
6 new laws – vague and unspecific – homeless, socially deprived people don't benefit
7 local councils – low budget – mentally ill people can't be given treatment they need
8 workplaces – inflexible system – blind and deaf people can't find work there

B2 Look at the various aids that one company has produced to help the elderly and the disabled and consider what a salesman has to say about one of them.

> 'It's never very easy – in fact, it's often very difficult, sometimes impossible – for disabled people to pick something up off the floor, so we've designed a special "Helping Hand", so that they can do this sort of thing more easily.'

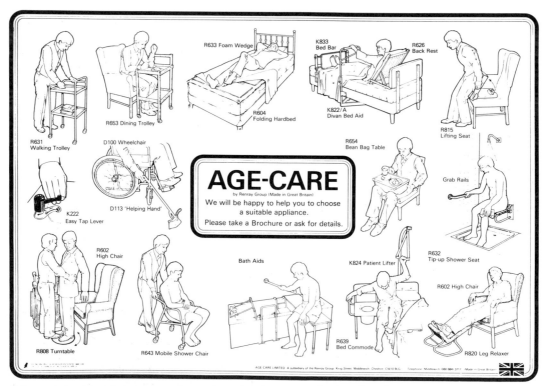

What might the salesman say about the other items on display above?

B3 Study the possible combinations in the box below. Then, using the prompts that follow, discuss our changing world, commenting on past, present and future habits.

It was/used to be	normal/commonplace	for women to wear trousers.
It's always been	quite common	for men to have permed hair.
Nowadays it is	rare/unusual	for babies to be born at home.
One day it will/might be	(almost) unheard of	for films to be shot on location.

1 women/government departments – run
2 teachers/politics in schools – teach
3 parents/children out alone at night – allow
4 people/letters with a ballpoint pen – write
5 referees/footballers – send off
6 people/things on credit – buy
7 men who work in offices/ties – wear
8 police/files on citizens – keep

B4 Practise this exchange with your partner, trying out all given alternatives. Then act out similar ones with the prompts below. Finally invent a few of your own.

A: You know, people keep travelling { to more and more distant places / further and further away from Earth }, but it

seems to me, the further we go, { the more careless / the less concerned } we are with our own planet.

B: Oh, { surely we're no less careful than we used to be / I don't think we're any less concerned than before } ; it's just that it's

{ more difficult nowadays / not so easy these days } to take the right sort of action.

1 aeroplanes – become sophisticated – frequent crashes – a lot of publicity
2 television – get popular – bad programmes – few original ideas
3 teenagers – mature young – great gap/parents – independent
4 sportsmen – be well-paid – unsporting – take it seriously
5 people – get well-qualified – few jobs – difficult to find
6 nuclear war – be discussed openly – seems likely – people/well-informed
7 rich countries – get rich – poor countries/badly-off – develop slowly
8 family unit – get weak – easy divorce – open and honest in relationships

B5 Finally, practise this 'superlative' exchange, with all the given options, and then act out similar ones with the following prompts, changing the names as you wish.

A: { They say / I should think / I'd imagine } Stalingrad was { easily the most horrific / by far the bloodiest / just about the most tragic } battle { of modern times. / in recent history. / in living memory. }

B: Yes, { I believe / I gather / I suppose } it was one of the worst conflicts { in the history of the world. / there has ever been. / the world has ever seen/known. }

1 Picasso (*great painter / influential artist*)
2 the micro-chip (*significant invention / represents dramatic turning point*)
3 The Beatles (*popular group / famous musical quartet*)
4 Mohammad Ali (*exciting boxer / complete athlete*)
5 Armstrong's first steps on the moon (*thrilling moments / fine achievement*)
6 John F Kennedy (*well-loved American president / impressive statesman*)
7 E.T. (*successful family film / profitable movie*)
8 The Vietnam War (*bad war / futile conflict*)

C Read and discuss

C1 In pairs, read this account of a spectacular achievement by a disabled person, trying to help each other fully to understand it. Then do the exercises that follow.

2,500-mile voyage

Disabled yachtsman triumphs

By Craig Seton

Mike Spring, the disabled yachtsman paralysed from the waist down, received a champagne welcome yesterday when he reached Cornwall after an arduous single-handed voyage to the Azores and back – much of it in terrible pain.

Mr Spring, aged 39, a computer programmer from Solihull, completed the 2,500-mile round trip at Penzance, 27 days after leaving Ponta Delgada in the Azores in his 30-foot yacht. He climbed ashore from the 3M Mariner unaided but for his crutches and heavy calipers.

Mr Spring, who broke his back in a road accident in 1969, was cheered as he walked uncomfortably up a ramp but remained modest about his achievement, which began early in June when he set out to prove that his severe disability was no deterrent to such a challenge.

Looking ruddy-faced and happy, he announced himself tired but feeling fine. There was one disappointment. His voyage was intended to raise £20,000 for the Pain Relief Foundation, of which he is a patient. But at the end of the voyage Lord Northesk, the chairman of the Foundation's fund-raising committee, announced that Mr Spring had raised not much more than £4,000, and he appealed to the public to make the trip financially worthwhile.

Mr Spring, who works for the 3M company, which sponsored him on his journey, took only 16 days on the outward voyage to the Azores where he spent several weeks recovering and re-supplying his boat.

Mr Spring said yesterday that one of his constant worries had been pressure sores on his body caused by sitting for too long in one position.

At one stage large waves had washed over the boat, soaking his only dry clothing and putting some of his advanced electronic equipment temporarily out of order.

Though he had often been depressed and wondered why he bothered to do it, there were good moments too. He was frequently accompanied by whales and dolphins, which raised his spirits.

'You are in another world out there', he said. 'It can get you down or it can make you elated.'

His voyage had proved that even severe disability was no bar to the most determined person, but he gave a word of caution to other disabled people: 'It is dangerous out there and I only made it because of the amount I put into it.

'I was worried that people were going to criticise me and say I was utterly mad and foolhardy, so I knew I had to do it properly.'

Tired, but happy, Mr Spring coming ashore on his crutches

C2 Still in pairs, and without referring back to the text, try to relate these facts and figures to context.
For example: Cornwall – where *or* the place
A: I think that was where he arrived back, wasn't it?
B: Yes, I think it probably was.
or No, wasn't that the place he set off from?

1	Penzance	– where *or* the place	**8**	3M Mariner	– what *or* the name
2	39	– how old *or* the age	**9**	1969	– when *or* the year
3	Solihull	– where *or* the town	**10**	June	– when *or* the month
4	27	– how many *or* the number	**11**	£20,000	– how much *or* the amount
5	The Azores	– where *or* the islands	**12**	£4000	– how much *or* the sum
6	2500	– how many *or* the number	**13**	3M	– who *or* the name
7	30 feet	– how long *or* the length	**14**	16 days	– how long *or* the time

C3 In fours, discuss whether Mr Spring's trip was really worthwhile. Two of you think it was, two of you don't. Base your argument only on what you have read and take a minute or two first to make notes, as begun below:

worth it
– tremendous welcome
– proved his point
....
....

not worth it
– financial disappointment
– physical discomfort at sea
....
....

C4 P.S. A happy ending

> ## Disabled sailor raises £20,000
>
> A lone voyage to the Azores and back by Mr Michael Spring, who is disabled, has raised more than £20,000 for the Pain Relief Foundation, despite early fears that his efforts would be a financial failure.
>
> Mr Spring, aged 39, a computer programmer from Solihull, broke his spine in a road accident 14 years ago and is paralysed from the waist down. He sailed alone to the Azores in his 21ft yacht, 3M Mariner, in the summer.

D Listening

You are going to hear Roger, a teacher and writer who suffers from multiple sclerosis, talking to Guy about some aspects of his life as a disabled person. There are four excerpts of their conversation on the cassette. Look at each set of questions before you listen, noting which points you are asked about.

Excerpt One Roger talks about the way people behave towards him. What significance do these phrases have in the conversation?
1 'a blithering idiot'
2 'I'm articulate'
3 'they tend to talk to me'
4 'How's Roger today?'

Excerpt Two We are given an example of people 'trying to help'.
1 Which would you say is true? In this story, Roger occasionally sounds rather like
   a a politician **b** a bitter man **c** a comedian **d** a spoilt child
2 What do's and don't's have you personally learnt from his story?
3 After listening, how would you now approach a disabled person getting on a train?

Excerpt Three We hear about the challenge that faces disabled people.
1 How in his response does Roger slightly distort Guy's opening question?
2 What do people often assume when they see a person in a wheelchair?

Excerpt Four Roger speaks about his personal frustrations and regrets.
1 Does he drive a car? How do you know?
2 Has he been disabled since birth? What indicates that?

E Vocabulary: adjectives and adverbs

E1 'Ignorance inevitably represents by far the greatest barrier.'
In each sentence below, two words are omitted: one an adverb
before the verb it modifies, the other a superlative form. Choose from
the words which precede each section to complete the generally
somewhat formal-sounding sentences.

little	utterly	distinctly	best	latest	strictest
deeply	greatly		least	earliest	

1 I would .... appreciate the chance to meet you at your .... convenience.
2 I .... thought he would be at his .... so soon after the operation.
3 I .... remember telling you that it was all to be in the .... confidence.
4 I .... regret that we shall have to ask you to leave by Friday at the ....
5 I .... reject the suggestion that I was in the .... to blame.

firmly	well	categorically	most	least	worst
freely	confidently		wildest	lowest	

6 She .... admitted that company business was at its .... ebb for years.
7 I can .... imagine that you would want at .... £500 for your old car.
8 We .... expect to get that painting for $100 at the ....
9 He .... denied that he had contemplated murder, even in his .... dreams.
10 I .... believe that ugly professional football today is sport at its ....

flatly	seriously	automatically	best	earliest	worst-off
strongly	sincerely		utmost	slightest	

11 I .... hope they will not demand their money until December at the ....
12 He .... refused to be influenced in the .... by what we had to say.
13 I .... doubt whether this is really in everyone's .... interests.
14 I .... assumed my valuables would be handled with the .... care.
15 I .... disapprove of the .... in our society having to pay tax.

E2 Physical barriers v. physically handicapped

Consider these two sentences: *The surgeons showed technical
brilliance* and *They showed themselves to be technically brilliant*.
The following sentences are taken from an article about a seriously
disabled boy of eleven who was given a new lease of life with
artificial limbs – and a skateboard. Complete the unfinished words.

1 Ten years' medic___ research has made this possible.
2 The boy has overcome many of his physic___ handicaps.
3 He appears psycholog___ well-balanced.
4 The emotion___ strain on his parents has been great.
5 He shows normal ment___ agility.
6 He is intellect___ sound.
7 Some education___ problems remain.
8 Academ___ speaking, he is well up to average.
9 Integration soci___ is not as difficult as one would expect.
10 It is technolog___ a great breakthrough.
11 It is a scientif___ miracle.
12 Such operations raise certain mor___ and ethic___ issues.

F Exercises for homework

F1 Most of the adjectives in the brackets below need some modulation
(e.g. *nice* to *nicely*, *nicer* or *nicest*). Write out the passage in full,
making all suitable changes.

One of the (*mysterious*) disabilities that exist is that of dyslexia,
(*common*) known as word blindness. (*Serious*) affected people have
(*extreme*) difficulty in reading at all (*fluent*). Often the (*short*) a
word is, the (*difficult*) it is for them to decipher (*accurate*). The
problem is (*surprising*) widespread, but (*relative*) few people (*open*)
admit to suffering from it. This is (*hard*) (*surprising*) in that by far
the (*common*) reaction from other people is one of (*mild*) amusement.

Dyslexia is not always (*immediate*) recognised among the (*young*)
and sufferers at school are all too often considered (*educational*)
subnormal. In actual fact, they may be (*intellectual*) at an (*extreme*)
high level and reach (*normal*) (*academic*) standards in other fields.
Doctors have proved (*conclusive*) that the disability in no way
reflects (*low*) than average intelligence, but the fact remains that
dyslexics' embarrassment becomes (*great*) and (*great*) as they get
(*old*), unless they are given (*special*) training.

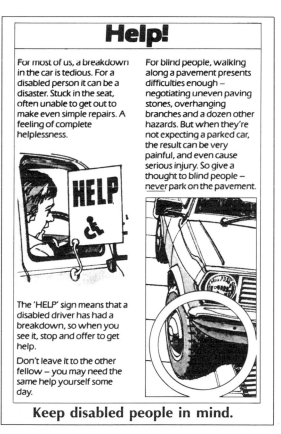

F2 Look at and read the information on the left, then
consider the two pictures below. Write a suitable
text for each of them.

F3 Project: What does it mean?
(see Teacher's Guide Unit 14)

The play's the thing ...

A1 When did you last go to the theatre or the cinema? What did you see?/What was the title of the play or film? Did you enjoy it? Why?/Why not?
Is there any particular scene you remember? Why?

A2 Opposite is the centrefold of a theatre programme. Read it carefully once or twice without taking any notes. Then in pairs, and with books closed, tell each other what you can remember about the plot and these characters: Jack; Algy; Gwendolen; Thomas Cardew; Ernest; Lady Bracknell; Cecily; Canon Chasuble; Miss Prism

Then check your information with the rest of the class. Refer to the programme again if necessary.

A3 Now you will hear part of a rehearsal for an amateur production of *The Importance of Being Earnest*. The part being rehearsed is from the end of Act III.

1 Listen and then answer these questions:
   a What is Jack Worthing's real identity?
   b What happened to him when he was a baby?

2 Listen again and concentrate on the language the characters use in the scene from the play. There are certain words which you might not understand because they are not often used now. They are:
a perambulator: old formal word for *pram*, a four-wheeled vehicle in which you transport a baby
capacious: formal word meaning able to hold a lot, of large capacity
a bassinette: old formal word for a pram
a temperance beverage: a drink of some kind that is not alcoholic

Apart from these 'archaic' words, however, what else strikes you about the language the characters use?

3 Finally, listen again and make notes in order to describe the characters. Some students should make notes on Miss Prism and Gwendolen, the others on Jack and Lady Bracknell. Then describe to each other what impression you have of the characters.

OSCAR WILDE
The Importance of Being Earnest

THE PERSONS OF THE PLAY	THE SCENES OF THE PLAY

THE PERSONS OF THE PLAY

JOHN WORTHING, J.P.

ALGERNON MONCRIEFF

REV. CANON CHASUBLE, D.D.

MERRIMAN, *Butler*

LANE, *Manservant*

LADY BRACKNELL

HON. GWENDOLEN FAIRFAX

CECILY CARDEW

MISS PRISM, *Governess*

THE SCENES OF THE PLAY

ACT I

Algernon Moncrieff's flat in Half-Moon Street, W.

ACT II

The garden at the Manor House, Woolton

ACT III

Drawing-room at the Manor House, Woolton

TIME

The Present

(The play was written in 1895.)

SYNOPSIS OF THE PLAY

Young John ('Jack') Worthing arrives in London from the country, determined to marry the Honorable Gwendolen Fairfax, lovely cousin of his friend Algernon ('Algy') Moncrieff.

Dropping in at Algy's flat, Jack finds that he has to explain that he was adopted by a Mr Thomas Cardew when he was a baby. He also explains that he calls himself Jack in the country, but Ernest in London, so that he can blame his behaviour in London on Ernest, a fictitious brother.

Their talk is interrupted by the appearance of Gwendolen and her mother, Lady Bracknell. The latter is lured into another room by Algy, and Jack proposes to Gwendolen. Gwendolen confesses that she loves him, but partly because of the name Ernest.

When 'interrogated' by Lady Bracknell, Jack is forced to confess that he doesn't know who he is. He was found by Mr Cardew (his guardian) in a handbag in Victoria Station, and was called Worthing because Mr Cardew had a ticket for Worthing!

Act III finds Algy in the country visiting Cecily under the assumed name of Ernest. (Cecily is Jack's 18-year-old ward and the granddaughter of Mr Cardew.) When Jack returns, dressed in mourning clothes, to announce the death of 'cousin Ernest', Cecily tells him that Ernest has come back, and they (Jack and Algy) are forced to meet. The plot becomes even more complicated with the arrival of Gwendolen, and there is, not surprisingly, some hostility between the two girls. All is soon explained, and both men agree to be re-christened Ernest. But their joy is short-lived, because Lady Bracknell arrives in a state of fury, having traced her daughter to the Manor House.

While she agrees to the marriage of Cecily and Algy (her nephew), she will not even consider the marriage of Jack to her daughter Gwendolen. All is deadlocked, it seems, until Canon Chasuble (the vicar) arrives to announce that everything is ready for the christenings and that Miss Prism (Cecily's governess) is on her way. This surprises Lady Bracknell, who demands to see Miss Prism at once.

cont/ . . . .

B Communicative grammar

B1 Look at these two sentences. What do the parts in italics tell us?

> Lady Bracknell, *Gwendolen's mother and an aunt of Algernon's*, is determined to stop her daughter marrying Jack.
> Miss Prism, *the lady who lost Jack when he was a baby*, is horrified when it is suggested she might be his mother.

From your reading and listening, make similar comments about the following:
1 Algy **2** Cecily **3** Jack **4** Gwendolen
5 Canon Chasuble **6** Mr Cardew

Go on to make sentences about the best-known politicians in your country, for example:
Mr L'Etranger, *the Foreign Minister*, has recently . . .

B2 Look at these two sentences, noticing the work that the adjectives are doing:

> Gwendolen, *rich and rather spoilt (as she is)*, is full of silly romantic notions.
> Cecily, *less worldy wise than Gwendolen*, is nevertheless nobody's fool.

From your reading and listening, make similar comments about:
1 Jack **2** Lady Bracknell **3** Miss Prism
You might consider using these adjectives:
pompous prudish debonair handsome upright overpowering

Go on to talk about famous sportsmen and their images, using the same structure, for example:
Bjorn Borg, *cool, calm and collected,* could always . . .

B3 Look at this sentence:
A man calling himself Ernest has greater attraction than one named Jack.
This is an increasingly common way of expressing:
A man who calls himself Ernest has greater attraction than one who is named Jack.
In each of the sentences below, the first space can be filled with an
-*ing* form verb (perhaps with added preposition) and the second
with an -*ed*, past participle form of a verb. The lists of verbs below
might help if you are stuck.

1 A play . . . 'big names' is not always more satisfying than the same play . . . by enthusiastic amateurs.
2 Comedies . . . life as it really is can often say more than dramas . . . with a serious message in mind.
3 Books . . . in our book shops and libraries nowadays seem much more attractively produced than those . . . a couple of decades ago.
4 Teams . . . modestly-talented players who work for each other often do better than ones . . . with individualistic superstars.
5 Cars . . . the assembly line these days are fitted with many more gadgets and gimmicks than those . . . ten or fifteen years ago.
6 People . . . for themselves generally have much greater job satisfaction than those . . . by a large impersonal company.
7 Young children . . . in the country have a very different view of life from those . . . in a big city.
8 Shops . . . genuine discounts on quality products usually make more profit than those . . . with cheap and nasty goods.

coming off leaving offering starring appearing showing portraying dealing with growing up living containing consisting of working

produced made brought up employed performed written published printed filled packed stocked done

B4 Cause and effect, purpose and result

1 Look at this budget sheet for the company's production of *The Importance of Being Earnest*.

BUDGET SHEET

Required expenditure		Expected income
Hire of Hall	70.00	Expected attendance of 800, based on
Rights	42.00	average of last five shows.
Administrative expenses	10.00	
Set construction	45.00	Average seat price of 65p gives box
Paint	15.00	office sales of £520 and profit of £86.
Special lighting	30.00	
Special effects	15.00	Average seat price of 55p gives box
Wardrobe	65.00	office sales of £440 and profit of £6.
Printed publicity	65.00	
Press advertising	35.00	Average seat price of 50p gives box
Direct mail	7.00	office sales of £400 and loss of £34.
Special props	5.00	
Sundries	10.00	Expected programme sales £35.
Contingency allowance	20.00	
Total expenditure	434.00	

Break-even position is achieved by average seat price of 50p.

N.B. The above figures assume that the cost of production of the programme is exactly covered by the advertisement revenue.

2 Below are comments made at a pre-performance committee meeting. Notice the ways in which the purpose of things, the reasons for them and their results can be expressed.

reason/purpose

'The aim/purpose of this production is to wipe out our bank overdraft.'
'We would need to sell 800 tickets at 50p to/in order to break even.'
'We must cover programme costs, { so that money is not wasted there.' / so as not to have to cut into profits.' / in case attendances are down.' }

reason/cause

'As/Since/Because we charged 50p last year, 55p would only be a 10 per cent increase.'
'The high expenditure { is due to / is caused by / springs from / stems from } such big items as costumes, hire of the hall and performing rights.'
'Owing to/On account of / Because of } the rather elaborate sets, production costs will be higher this year.'
'Another { reason why they're so high / reason for them being high } is the need for special lighting and effects.'
'Having made a loss last year, / Being a self-supporting company, / Not having any form of subsidy, } we need to think in terms of real profit this time.'

result/effect

'We have chosen a 'period piece', { with the result that / as a result of which / so } the wardrobe budget is bound to be large.'
'Reduced expenditure would result in/lead to/mean a loss of quality.'

B5 Role play

In groups, re-enact the committee meeting. (Present were: treasurer, secretary, producer, publicity officer, stage manager, wardrobe mistress and set designer.) Discuss together production costs and the fixing of ticket prices, championing and resisting any cuts in your particular area of responsibility. All of you should explain your reasons, motives and deductions, and comment on consequences.

C Functions: extemporising

 Remember how the producer at rehearsal 'got lost' occasionally? But remember how he kept on talking. Listen to this conversation, noting the many tricks of hesitation, digression and avoidance. Note too the variations in the column on the right which the speakers might have used and which you can use in your own improvised conversations below.

A: Wasn't there something you wanted to ask me?

B: Oh yes, now that you mention it, there was something. *Now*   *let me think*
 what was it? Oh dear, *it's completely slipped my mind.*   *my mind's a blank*

A: Wasn't it something about . . .?

B: Yes, that's right. Oh, *by the way*, you owe me 10p for that phone   *while I think of it*
 call yesterday.

A: That's true. I'm sorry. You were saying . . .?

B: Oh yes, *where was I?* Er . . .   *what was I saying?*

A: You were going to ask me something.

B: So I was. Yes. *Hang on a minute.* Yes.   *I'll think of it in a minute*
 It's coming back to me. Well, the thing is . . .   *It's on the tip of my tongue*
 Oh, *before I forget*, your mother phoned; she wanted you to   *I nearly forgot*
 ring her.

A: Oh thanks. But what was on your mind before?

B: On my mind? Ah yes! *I know what I was going to say.* You see,   *I know what I meant to tell you*
 I've been thinking: you and I – *how can I put it?* – we've been   *let me put it this way*
 friends for nearly a year; *in fact*, it's more than a year now, and   *as a matter of fact*
 . . . Look, *on second thoughts*, don't worry about the 10p. You   *come to think of it*
 keep it.

A: Stop changing the subject!

B: *I tell you what:* let's talk about it later.   *I've got an idea*

A: No! I want to hear what you've got to say.

B: Well, the point is: we – *or rather* I – I feel – *or should I say*, I   *at least/or let's say*
 think I feel? – . . .

A: Get to the point!

B: Well, isn't it time . . .? No, *I don't mean that.*   *that's not quite what I mean*

A: What are you trying to say?

B: Well, *to cut a long story short*, . . .   *in a nutshell*

A: Yes?

B: I mean, *to come to the point*, . . .   *to put it bluntly*

A: Yes?

B: Will you marry me?

Now improvise similar conversations, in which one of you finds it difficult to:

1 ask for a loan of some money.   **3** admit to breaking the other's best watch.

2 confess to crashing the family car.   **4** tell a parent of one's decision to marry.

D Register

Read each short set of notes about the life and work of Shakespeare, then combine two or more of the facts given using the prompts which follow. (See the examples with *whose*.) The resulting sentences will exemplify a flowing, albeit somewhat formal, style often welcomed in good written prose.

1 William Shakespeare was born in Stratford in 1564. (His name is now a household word throughout the world.) He spent about 25 years of his middle age in London. He did all his writing there. He retired to Stratford in 1611.

> *Example:* . . ., whose . . .
> *William Shakespeare, whose name is now a household word throughout the world, was born in Stratford-on-Avon in the year 1564.*
> *or: William Shakespeare, whose home town was Stratford-on-Avon, spent most of his middle age in London.*
> *or: William Shakespeare, whose writing was all done in London, was born and died in Stratford-on-Avon.*

   a . . ., where . . .
   b . . ., during which time . . .
   c . . ., at which point . . .
   d It was . . . that . . .

2 Shakespeare wrote 38 plays. (He also wrote a large collection of sonnets.) 18 of his plays were published in his lifetime. He was as famous for his poems then as for his plays. Most of his plays are still performed regularly today.

   a . . ., not to mention . . .
   b . . . as well as . . .
   c . . ., for which . . .
   d . . ., eighteen of which . . .
   e . . ., most of which . . .

3 He wrote comedies and romances. He wrote tragedies and history plays. His tragedies are the best-known. Some history plays are not often read and even less often performed.

   a . . . both . . . and . . .
   b . . . not only . . . but also . . .
   c . . . the latter being
   d . . ., let alone . . .

4 The plays are not uniform in their atmosphere. The tragedies are not all gloom and doom. The comedies are not all jokes and custard pies.

   a Neither . . . nor . . .
   b Just as . . ., so . . .

5 He wrote some ten tragedies. *Hamlet, Macbeth* and *King Lear* are perhaps the finest. The three plays are similar. They all deal with universal themes. Their central characters all die in the closing scenes.

   a . . ., of which . . .
   b Among . . .
   c . . . similar in that . . .
   d One thing . . . in common is that . . .
   e The fact that . . .
   f . . ., all three of whom . . .

6 Hamlet was poisoned. Macbeth died by the sword in battle. Lear died of old age and a broken heart.

   a Whereas . . ., . . .
   b . . ., as opposed to . . ., who . . .
   c . . ., while . . .
   d . . . different in that . . .
   e Unlike . . ., . . .

7 The plays are difficult. They have difficult language in them. Perhaps a person doesn't understand much English. The plays can still be enjoyed.

   a However little . . ., . . .
   b . . ., even if . . .
   c . . . regardless of . . .
   d . . . in spite of . . .
   e . . ., even though . . .
   f . . . on account of . . .

E Vocabulary: theatre and cinema

E1 Read these brief reviews of plays and films showing in London: they are from the 'What's On' section of a magazine. Then in small groups discuss which play or film you would most like to see.

THEATRE

Animal Farm *(National/Cottesloe)*. Peter Hall's adaptation and production of the *1984* man's other hit. *(928 2252)*

The Business of Murder *(Mayfair)*. Now in its fourth amazing year, an undistinguished thriller with Richard Todd. *(629 3036)*

Cats *(New London)*. Feline musical masterpiece, still stunning, thanks to the constant and vigilant re-rehearsal care of director Trevor Nunn and composer Andrew Lloyd Webber. *(405 0072)*

Evita *(Prince Edward)*. Though it's not holding up nearly as well as *Cats*, this musically magnificent Rice-Webber Argentinian extravaganza still bears traces of Hal Prince's original and brilliant production. *(437 6877)*

Master Harold and the Boys *(National/Cottesloe)*. Johannesburg's acclaimed Market Theatre Company visiting the National with Athol Fugard's new play about a white boy and two black waiters. *(928 2252)*

Pack of Lies *(Lyric)*. Award-winning Judi Dench and Michael Williams in Hugh Whitemore's enthralling new play about the neighbourhood of espionage. *(437 3686)*

The Real Thing *(Strand)*. Tom Stoppard's lyrical, Pirandellian play about love and acting, now with a new cast led by Susan Penhaligon and proving a London and Broadway hit despite disgracefully dismissive original reviews elsewhere. *(836 2660)*

CINEMA

La Balance *(18)*. By a new name in French cinema, Bob Swaim, who came from California as an anthropologist and made his way *via* commercials and documentaries and short fictions to celebrity with French audiences as writer and director of this fast-moving, very violent thriller.

The Big Chill *(15)*. College companions, idealists in youth who are now members of the Establishment, meet after long separation at funeral of brilliant and cherished friend; his suicide leads them to assessment of their own lives. Laurence Kasdan, who made *Body Heat*, deals sympathetically with these products of the hopeful Sixties. A cast of rising talents includes William Hurt, Kevin Kline (from *Sophie's Choice*), Tom Benenden, Glenn Close; admirable ensemble playing.

Never Cry Wolf *(PG)*. Fine Disney film, a study of the Arctic white wolves of Northern Canada. A Government biologist sent to investigate reports that the wolves are destroying the caribou herds comes to a very different conclusion: observing a family, parents and cubs, he finds that they live on mice. From his first terrified reaction in solitude to his surrender to the charm of the beautiful animals he is admirably played by Charles Martin Smith; affectionate photography by Hiro Narita; Carroll Ballard directs.

Champions *(PG)*. A tale of courage based on true story of Bob Champion, jockey who had cancer, under treatment recovered and (with a horse which also had recovered from a grave injury) won the Grand National. John Hurt as rider, John Irvin as spirited director, some splendid horses.

The Dresser *(PG)*. Chosen for this year's Royal Film Performance: version of Ronald Harwood's stage play about ageing autocratic star in touring theatrical company and his relations with the others. Brilliant performances by Albert Finney as the old actor and Tom Courtenay as the devoted dresser.

PUNCH April 4 1984

E2 In pairs, read the reviews more carefully and pick out and list vocabulary under three headings: Theatre, 'Common' and Cinema.

Words which might be used in connection with both the theatre and the cinema (such as *cast*, *plot*, *dialogue*, *characters*, etc.) should be listed in the 'Common' column. Then add as many other words as you can think of to each of the three lists. Finally, compare your lists with the rest of the class.

E3 Still in pairs, try to write similar *brief* (3–4 line) reviews or descriptions of two plays and two films that are on in a town or city in your country now. Then read out and compare what you have written with the rest of the class.

F Exercises for homework

F1 Write a synopsis (about 250 words, if you can) of a play, film, short story or novel that you have enjoyed and might recommend to someone else. Write it as simply as possible, using the Present and related tenses like the synopsis of *The Importance of Being Earnest* on page 127 and the play described on cassette in Unit 11 (page 94).

F2 Match the joining words on the left with the phrases and clauses on the right to complete the sentence. We've done one for you.

I always lock my bedroom door at night,

unlike	nobody can come in.
whereas	all the thieves in my area.
regardless of	someone tries to come in.
which	in 25 years my house has never been broken into.
so as not to	most people I know.
in case	my brother very rarely does.
on account of	be disturbed.
even though	the time I go to bed.
so that	the hall, front and back doors.
not to mention	some people find a bit strange.

F3 Read the following quoted opinions on Sir Peter Hall, who in the past thirty years has been Director of Britain's two leading theatre companies (The Royal Shakespeare Company and the National Theatre) as well as the Covent Garden Opera House. Then summarise their content in an article, editing, paraphrasing and ordering the material as appropriate. Try, wherever possible, to use connecting phrases like: *not only . . . but also, on the one hand . . . on the other hand, while, whereas,* etc.

'One becomes very attached to Peter, and one likes to be "in the sun". If you suspected there was a shadow falling on you, then you got very hurt about it' – director

'. . . he's bloody-minded and utterly ruthless' – actor

'We all have this love-hate relationship with him' – director

'. . . the man of the most vision and daring the English Theatre has produced in my time' – actress

'Mr Hall and his company . . . have not only given us a production to remember all our lives; what they have done above all is to demonstrate that great drama, interpreted by men of imagination and understanding has a power and a reality that can make us forget entirely that we are in a theatre.' – theatre critic

'. . . like a super brother' – actress

'Over a working life of twenty years, through exceptional talent, and a capacity for unrelenting work, Hall has established himself as a totally unique figure in the arts – combining the roles of director-producer of theatre, films and opera, impresario, and business administrator with brilliant success' – author

'I do wish he'd stop pretending to be so nice and simple, when he's really very complicated and ambitious and a dictator' – actress

'A brilliant administrator, a very good director and basically, unfortunately, a very nice bloke. It would be much easier if I hated his guts.' – actor

'Peter uses you. He's quite straightforward about it. You benefit, he benefits. No sentiment.' – actress

133

Unit 16

I've never been so embarrassed in all my life!

A1 In pairs or small groups, tell each other about personal experiences you have had which at the time were embarrassing or humiliating. Briefly, ask and/or tell each other:
- what you were doing when you had the experience.
- where and when it happened.
- who else was there.
- what happened, etc.

A2 Now in groups of three, read and help each other to understand *one* of these two embarrassing experiences described by Patrick Campbell. Then do the exercises. (As you read the texts, notice how the writer has used the past tenses – *did*, *was doing*, *had done* and *had been doing*,)

Tooking for a Lowel

1

Even now, after all I have been through, the thought of being unclothed in the presence of women has the power to make me half mad with anxiety. I drum my feet on the floor, perspire, and whistle loudly to drive the memory away.

So far, I, undressed, have come rushing at women twice. One of these occasions was connected with a shaving brush.

I was lying in the bath one morning, when I remembered that I had left my new shaving brush in my overcoat pocket. The overcoat was hanging in the hall.

Everything else was ready and in position. Shaving mirror and soap; new razor blade; toothbrush and paste; hairbrush, comb and brilliantine tin; packet of ginger biscuits and a copy of *Forever Amber* on a chair beside the bath. When I wash I like to *wash*.

Everything was ready, then, except the new shaving brush. I lay submerged for some time with just the nostrils and the whites of the eyes showing, trying to think of a substitute for a shaving brush. Perhaps if the soap were rubbed on with the hand, and worked in? Or the toothbrush might be adapted to serve the purpose? The only difference between a toothbrush and a shaving brush is that one is shorter and harder than the other, and the handle is fastened on in a different direction. But the toothbrush, properly employed, might be induced to work up a lather. I might even, by accident, invent a new kind of

shaving brush, with a long handle and a scrubbing motion. . . .

All this time I knew I would have to get out of the bath and fetch the shaving brush out of my overcoat pocket.

I got out of the bath, in the end, at a quarter past eleven. At that time I had a hairy kind of dressing gown that set my teeth on edge if I put it on next to my skin. I ran out of the bathroom, roughly knotting a shirt about my waist.

In this flat the bathroom, bedroom and sitting room led off a passage. I ran lightly down the passage to the door, where my overcoat usually hangs. Then I remembered I had left the coat lying on a chair in the sitting room. I ran more rapidly back along the passage, leaving footprints on the carpet. Already, I was becoming chilled and a little pimply. Passing the bathroom door I put on an extra burst of speed, and entered the sitting room nearly all out.

It is difficult under such circumstances to make a precise estimate of the passage of time, but I think that a fifth of a second elapsed before I saw the charwoman standing by the window. She must have been dusting the bureau, but when she saw me she froze dead.

I, too, froze. Then I said 'Waah!' and tried to leap out backwards through the door.

The charwoman very nearly got there first. The thought must have flashed through her mind that she would be better off outside in the passage, convenient to the main staircase, and so with a kind of loping run she came across the room.

We arrived upon the mat inside the door simultaneously. The mat went from under us, and we came down. I fell heavily on the feather duster which she was carrying,

134

and the bamboo handle snapped. I thought my leg had gone.

We lay together on the mat for several moments, not shouting or anything, just trying to piece together in a blurry way exactly what had happened.

I came to my senses first. I was younger than she was, and probably more resilient.

I jumped up and made another break for the door. To my surprise I found it was shut, and not only shut but locked. I wrenched at the handle, conscious in the most alive way of my appearance from the back. The door was unyielding. I caught sight of a Spanish shawl draped across the top of the piano, and in a trice I was enveloped in it, an unexpectedly flamboyant figure.

Afterwards I remembered that the door opened *outwards*. I had gained the impression that it was locked by unthinkingly pulling it towards me.

And now the charwoman was also back on her feet. But to my horror I saw that she was taking off her housecoat – slowly and deliberately. It seemed to be her intention to disrobe. But why?

I watched her, wide-eyed. She folded the housecoat into a neat square. She placed it tidily in the centre of the table. 'That,' she said, 'is me notice – and now me husband will have to be tole.'

I fortunately never saw her again.

2

The other incident involving me and women took place when I was fourteen.

On this occasion I was again lying in the bath, but this time it was night, and I was reading *The Boy's Own Paper*. The rest of my family had gone out to the theatre, and I was alone in the house.

The particular edition of *The Boy's Own Paper* which I was reading must have contained a number of bumper tales, because when I came to the last page I found that the temperature of the bathwater had dropped from near-boiling to lukewarm. Checking back later I discovered that this had, in fact, been my longest sitting – ninety-seven minutes.

Taking care not to disturb the water, and set up cold currents, I reached out with one arm and dropped the *B.O.P.* over the side of the bath on to the floor. With the same hand I groped around in gingerly fashion for the towel.

There was no towel. I had placed it on the chair, but now it had gone. I sat up in the bath, chilled, and peered over the edge, hoping to find it on the floor. There was no towel. I sank back into the water again, trying, as it were, to *draw* it round me.

There was no towel in the bathroom of any kind. And slowly I was freezing to death. I stretched out my right leg and turned on the hot-water tap with my toe. Ice-cold water gushed out.

There was only one measure to be taken in this extreme emergency. I gathered my muscles, leaped out of the bath in a compact ball, wrapped the *B.O.P.* round me, wrenched open the bathroom door, and fled down the short passage leading to the linen cupboard. The linen cupboard door was open. I shot into it, and slammed the door behind me. Absolutely instantaneously I discovered that our parlour maid, a young girl named Alice, was in the linen cupboard too.

What Alice and I did was to start screaming, steadily, into one another's faces. Alice, I think, believed that the Young Master had come for her at last.

In the end I got the door open again. It opened inwards, so that I was compelled to advance upon Alice in order to get round the edge of it. Alice, still screaming, welcomed this move with an attempt to climb the linen shelves and get out of the window.

I tried some word of explanation. What I said was: 'It's all right, Alice; I'm tooking for a lowel.' This had the effect of throwing her into a frenzy. She tried to put her head into a pillow cover.

It was obvious that there was nothing more I could do, so I ran back into the bathroom, locked the door, and listened at the keyhole until I heard her run down the passage to the hall, sobbing.

The only other thing I would like to say is that now, whenever I have a bath, I make a list of the things I am going to need, and check it carefully before entering the water.

A3 As a class (or in different groups) tell each other about Patrick Campbell's two embarrassing experiences. Say
  - what he was doing (on each occasion).
  - what he had (already) done or had been doing up to then.
  - what he did, and why.
  - what happened next, and then. . . .
  - who he met and what happened – what she said, what he said, etc.

A4 Discussion
  1 How do you think *you* would have reacted in the situations the writer described? Or how would you have reacted if you had been one of the women?
  2 Thinking of the writer's experiences, and any such experiences you may have had yourself, do you think people learn from such experiences? If so, what do we learn? If not, why not?

B Communicative grammar: narrating past experiences and events

B1 Simple Past (*did*) and Past Continuous (*was doing*) to describe events in the past

When we describe events or experiences in the past, the use of *did* or *was doing* is very important.
Study these two sentences:

> When she saw me, she was dusting the bureau.
> When she saw me, she froze.

The first tells us that she had started and was in the middle of dusting when she saw me. The second tells us what she did when she saw me, or almost at the same time as she saw me.

Remember Patrick Campbell's experiences? Without looking back, try to answer these questions. Write down brief answers, then check them with a partner. (Only look back at the texts when you have done all you can.)

Text 1

a What was he doing when he remembered where he had left his shaving brush?

b What was the charwoman carrying when she fell down?

c And what happened to it when Patrick fell on it?

d What did he do when he found the door was 'locked'?

e What did he do when he saw the Spanish shawl?

Text 2

a What was he reading when he realised the bath water was lukewarm?

b What happened when he turned on the hot-water tap with his toe?

c What did Alice do when she saw Patrick in the linen cupboard? And what did he do?

d What did she do while he was trying to get out of the cupboard?

e What did she do when he tried to explain what he was looking for?

B2 Simple Past (*did*) followed by a present participle *-ing* form for a simultaneous or consecutive action

Study these sentences from Patrick's anecdotes and note what they mean:

'I ran out of the bathroom, roughly knotting a shirt about my waist.'

(= As I ran out of the bathroom, I roughly knotted/was roughly knotting a shirt round my waist.)

'We lay . . ., not shouting or anything, just trying to piece together what had happened.'

(= As we lay . . ., we didn't shout/weren't shouting or anything; we just tried/were trying to piece together what had happened.)

'I lay submerged for some time, trying to think of a substitute for a shaving brush.'

(= I lay submerged for some time and tried/was trying (all the time) to think of a substitute for a shaving brush.)

NOTES:
- The Simple Past can be used for a period of time e.g. *lay for some time*, as long as the period is complete and finished in the past.

- The participle *-ing* form can imply a 'simple' or a 'continuous' action, and a simultaneous or a consecutive or subsequent action.

Rephrase the following sentences, using a participle -*ing* form:

1 We sat and waited for the film to start.
2 I hid behind the car and wondered what to do next.
3 My sisters jumped up and down and screamed with delight.
4 We ran out of the building and shouted at people to keep back.
5 He fell on the feather duster and broke the handle of it.

6 They both made for the door and watched each other warily.
7 I finally came to my senses and wondered why I had acted like that.
8 The big man wrenched at the door and swore all the time.
9 To my horror, the dog came slowly towards me and bared its teeth.
10 I lay awake all night and worried about the problem.

B3 Past Perfect Simple (*had done*) and Continuous (*had been doing*) to describe actions prior to simple past events

Study how *had done* and *had been doing* are used in these sentences. Then join the sentences below in the same way.

I had only gone a few steps when/before I realised that I was being followed.
I had been walking for about five minutes when I realised I was being followed.
It was only when / It wasn't until } I turned/had turned the corner that I realised I was on the wrong road.
It was only when / It wasn't until } I had been driving for half an hour that I realised I was short of petrol.

1 I waited for half an hour. Then there was a knock on the door.
2 I wrote three letters. Then I decided to have a rest.
3 I drove for two hours. I suddenly felt very tired.
4 I looked out of the window. I realised that the man was still outside. (*It* . . .)
5 I heard about the accident. Then John came to tell me about it.

B4 Past Continuous (*was doing*). *was going to do* and *was to have done* to express unfulfilled intentions

Read these beginnings of accounts of experiences. Note that *was doing* and *was going to do* indicate what was going to happen later, and are therefore often followed by a *so*-clause. However, *was to have done* tells us that a particular 'plan' or course of action had already been 'cancelled', and is therefore often followed by a *but*-clause.

I was to have driven to Cambridge that morning, but the car was in the garage being repaired, so I rang for a taxi . . .

I remember the day well. We were going to spend the day down at the beach, so . . .

I was going to London for the day for a meeting, so I had to get up early and go down to the station . . .

Rephrase these 'starters' in the same kind of way:

1 Our plan was to have a meal out that evening, so . . .
2 My plan was to watch the football international at Wembley, so . . .
3 Our plan was to visit my grandparents that day, but we'd had a phone call . . .
4 According to my schedule, I was to fly to New York that day, so . . .
5 Our intention was to get up late (because it was the weekend), so . . .

B5 Game: 'Follow that!' (see Teacher's Guide Unit 16)

C Vocabulary: some compound nouns with an -*ing* element

Compound nouns are very common in English, as you will know.
They help us to describe exactly what we are talking about. This
section deals just with those that contain an -*ing* form.
Look over the examples and the lists and define them or match them
as indicated.

C1 A *shaving brush* is 'a brush (which/that is) used for shaving (with)'.
A *sitting room* is 'a room (which/that is) used for sitting in'.
NOTE the main stress is on the first element, for example:
   a '*scrubbing brush*, '*walking shoes*, '*chewing gum*

Define some of these in the same way.

a swimming pool	a filing cabinet	shaving cream	running shorts
a bathing costume	a steeringwheel	writing paper	swimming trunks
an adding machine	a carving knife	drinking water	working hours
a sleeping pill	a playing field	cleaning fluid	operating instructions
a frying pan	a racing car	chewing gum	eating apples
a hearing aid	a sewing machine	cooking oil	cooking apples

C2 A *revolving door* is 'a door which/that revolves'.
Boiling water is 'water that/which boils (or is boiling)'.
Rising costs are 'costs which/that are rising'.
NOTE the main stress in compounds like this is on the second element, for example:
   a ˌrevolving 'door, ˌboiling 'water, ˌrising 'costs

Match the adjectives with the nouns to make meaningful compounds:

A	B	A	B	A	B
the following	saucer	a paying	pain	sliding	water
a missing	log fire	a reclining	event	rising	doors
a pressing	storm	a tempting	seat	pouring	costs
a roaring	question	a coming	impression	driving	rain
a searching	person	a gripping	guest	running	ambition
a flying	engagement	a lasting	offer	flying	stars
a raging	example	a stabbing	story	shooting	fish

C3 A *long-lasting effect* is 'an effect which/that lasts a long time'.
A *breath-taking view* is 'a view that/which takes your breath away'.
Self-sealing envelopes are 'envelopes which/that seal themselves'.
NOTE the main stress in this compound is also on the last element, for example:
   a ˌbreath-taking 'view, a ˌlong-lasting ef'fect, ˌself-sealing 'envelopes

Again, match the adjectives with the nouns to make meaningful compounds:

A		B	
a man-eating	an eye-catching	event	record (LP)
a long-playing	a far-reaching	job	shark
a long-standing	a world-shaking	drug	decision
a time-consuming	a habit-forming	display	invitation

A		B	
a self-governing	self-raising	wristwatch	politician
a self-respecting	a self-seeking	safe	flour
a self-defeating	a self-supporting	person	colony
a self-locking	a self-winding	scheme	policy

C4 Game: 'Twenty questions' (see Teacher's Guide Unit 16)

D Listening

You are going to hear two anecdotes, personal experiences of the kind people tell over a meal or on other social occasions. Guy tells the first one; the second is told by Roy.

D1 Listen to both of the anecdotes just once and then answer these two questions:
1 What kind of experience did both Guy and Roy have?
2 *Very briefly*, what happened to each of them?

D2 Now listen to each more carefully and make brief notes in order to ask and answer these questions in pairs:

Guy's anecdote
1 What had he recently done? (2 things)
2 What car did he drive?
3 What happened in the first 'incident'?
4 What was the second 'incident'?

Roy's anecdote
1 What reminded him of the experience?
2 What was he asked to do? With whom?
3 Who was there when they arrived?
4 What preparations did they make?
5 What happened when he started?

E Socialising and functions

In small groups of three or four, and using as much of the language you have practised in the Unit as you can, tell each other about personal experiences you have had which at the time were embarrassing, frightening, surprising, disgusting, exciting, humiliating, etc. Begin like this:

A: I've never been so /terrified/ in my life!
B: Why? What happened?
A: Well, . . .

Student A continues to say:
— what he/she was doing, where and when.
— whether he/she was in an everyday situation (in a shop, in the street, etc.) or at a concert, a rather formal dinner, at a job interview, etc.
— who else was there.
— what happened, what he/she/others said.
— what he, she or someone else had done or had been doing before the event in question.

— how he/she felt.
— what happened afterwards, or what has happened since.

. . . and other students in the group:
— express surprise and/or interest with expressions like: *Oh, yes? | No, you've never told me/us (about) that. | Really?/ Good heavens! | Well, well! | Honestly? Is that true?*
— encourage A to continue with questions like: *What happened then/next? | So what did you/the other person do? | How long did you have to . . .? | Did you . . .? | How did you feel . . .?*
— and express sympathy with expressions like: *That must have been /terrible/ for you! | I'm sure I would have been . . . too! | I can just imagine it! | I bet you were!*

16

F Exercises for homework

F1 One particularly common form of the embarrassing situation is that known in English as 'dropping a brick'. When you 'drop a brick', you make a remark or do something which means something unpleasant to the person or people you are speaking to, although you may be ignorant of it at the time. Here are two accounts of bricks dropped by James Herriot, the famous English vet and author, in his own humorous style. Read the accounts carefully and then complete the following sentences, supplying the correct tenses of the verbs.

My absentmindedness, though constant and long-standing, has usually manifested itself in trivial ways. Brushing my teeth with shaving cream and wondering why the new toothpaste tasted so foul and made me foam at the mouth. Stopping in the middle of a veterinary round and trying to think where the devil I was going. Forgetting to put my dog back into the car after a country walk and having to dash back to the spot where, showing more sense than his master, he would be patiently waiting. Enclosing letters in the wrong envelopes with wildly embarrassing results.

However, there are two incidents which, though not world-shaking, may have caused certain people to doubt my sanity.

The first was when my wife asked me to take the sitting-room clock to be repaired. With my two young children in the car I drove into the market place of our little town and, clock under arm, entered the shop. Only it wasn't the right shop: it was the butcher's. My children, who always delighted in their father's affliction, watched giggling as, with my thoughts far away, I stood staring into the butcher's eyes.

I had been a customer for a long time and the good man smiled in anticipation as he twirled his cleaver in his hand and I clutched my clock. This went on for several very long seconds before I realised where I was. There is no doubt I should have calmly purchased a pound of sausages, but my return to the world was too sudden, the prospect of explanation too unthinkable. I merely nodded briefly and left.

The other man in our town who probably thinks I am unhinged is a Mr Craythorne. Some years ago he was manager of Mead's grocer's shop, his children went to the same school as mine, and he and I knew each other quite intimately.

He was standing in the doorway of his shop one day when I passed, my brain, as usual, wrestling with some distant problem, my eyes staring into space.

I heard his voice: 'Now then, Mr Herriot,' and turned a blank gaze on him.

Only fellow sufferers will understand that at that moment I had not the remotest idea who he was. To whom, I desperately cogitated, belonged this very familiar face? Then, as I floundered, I noticed the word 'MEAD' in foot-high letters above the shop window.

'Good morning, Mead,' I cried heartily, giving him a smile compounded of friendliness and relief.

I had gone only a few steps before I realised that my greeting had been not only impolite but somewhat arrogant. I turned back and addressed him again.

'Good morning, *Mister* Mead,' I said.

It was only when I had turned the corner of the street and come to the surface that it dawned on me, too late, that his name was Craythorne and the time was late afternoon.

First incident

1 James once (*leave*) his dog in the country after he (*take*) him for a walk.

2 He (*already go*) into the butcher's shop before he (*realise*) that he was in the wrong place.

3 James (*take*) the sitting-room clock to be repaired when he (*wander*) into the butcher's shop by mistake.

4 His children (*not say*) anything when he (*go*) into the shop because they enjoyed watching him suffer!

Second incident

1 Mr Craythorne (*be*) manager of Mead's grocer's shop for some time before this incident (*occur*).

2 Mr Craythorne (*obviously stand*) in the doorway of the shop for a while before James (*pass*).

3 When Craythorne (*speak*) to him, James (*not answer*) immediately.

4 James (*try*) to remember who the man was when he (*spot*) the word 'MEAD' over the shop window.

5 The ghastly truth of his mistake only (*occur*) to James after he (*turn*) the corner and (*walk*) down the next road.

F2 Imagine for the moment that you found the anecdotes in this Unit fascinating enough to tell someone else about! You're writing a letter to an English-speaking friend to tell him or her about one of them. Choose any one from the Unit and write a brief summary of it in about 100 words as if for a paragraph in your letter. You might begin something like this:

'I read/heard a /funny/ story in a book/on the radio the other day. It was about . . .'

Activity 4 (see Teacher's Guide Unit 16)

Unit 17

A1 Have you ever had a serious accident – fallen off a ladder, been burned, nearly choked or nearly drowned? If so, did anyone help you or save you? How? Tell us about it.
Have you ever saved or helped anyone who was drowning, who had been hurt in a crash, who had been burnt, etc? If so, tell us what you did.

A2 Below is an extract from *The Emergency Book*, a book which describes in detail how to save people who have suffered a heart attack, choking, burns, and so on. In pairs, read the first paragraph. Then one student read 'Precautions . . .' and the other 'The unconscious victim'.

Anybody can drown. It's a fact. Strong swimmers and divers will go under the surface for no known reason. Perhaps a muscle spasm, a sudden attack of illness, a psychological quirk that terrorises them for some mysterious reason. Overconfidence is a deadly enemy for swimmers. Nobody knows for sure. Anybody can drown, but some groups of people are more at risk.

Precautions which should be taken
Swimmer and boater, beware. You are neither as strong nor as skilled in or on the water as you think you are. You shouldn't swim or go out in a boat alone. You shouldn't allow yourself to become so tired that your body is weakened or your mind is apt to become careless. There are several organisations that will teach you to swim. They can also teach you safety-first in the water and in a boat.

There should be rescue equipment, preferably life jackets of some sort, for each person in a small boat. The jacket should be *worn*, not simply left lying about somewhere half forgotten and out of reach. A small boat can be upset quite easily at any time, even in the placid waters of a lake. Small boats are more dangerous, of course, where the water is rougher.

Despite the obvious fact that simple common sense can prevent most drownings, people *will* do stupid things, and it has been shown that many do not bother to use common sense – especially if they're with a group of friends and having a good time.

So there is every likelihood that one day a person in danger of drowning will desperately need your help. It's up to you to prepare yourself for rescue as best you can. Also, there is a bonus in it for you. Your *own* life will be safer because you'll have learned to be safety-conscious and you'll have learned techniques that you can apply to your own survival in case something should happen.

The unconscious victim
If the person you are trying to rescue is unconscious in the water, get him to shore as fast as you can. Tow him by his shirt collar, his hair or his hand, but keep him on his back and try to keep his mouth and nose up out of the water. If there are other people around, you must, of course, send someone for help and tell others to help you.

An unconscious drowning victim needs help fast. If you can't make him breathe on his own in five minutes or so, his body will begin to die. *You must hurry.* You must get air into him in minutes. If his heart has stopped beating, you must give external cardiac compression, just as you would for a heart-attack victim.

If you have reached the victim and he is unconscious and apparently not breathing, you should begin to give mouth-to-mouth artificial respiration as soon as you can, even before you get him all the way out of the water. If you can support his body, you should begin breathing into his mouth, using this technique:
One, wipe any obvious foreign matter from his mouth.

Two, tilt his head back and lift under the back of his neck. Three, put the heel of your hand on his forehead to keep it back and, with the fingers of the same hand, pinch his nostrils closed.
Four, blow air into his mouth. Give him a series of quick breaths. Then give him a breath every five seconds.
Start this series right where you are, standing in shallow water, or clinging to the side of the pool, or in a boat, or anywhere you can support the victim on his back and give help effectively. *Speed is vital.*

A3 Now tell each other what your half of the text said.

A4 The extract above omitted some of the necessary actions to be taken when trying to save a person from drowning. So now study the complete sequence of actions below and, in pairs, explain to each other what to do.

One student should explain, using some of this language:
The first/next/most important thing you must/should do is (to) . . .
After you've /done/ . . ., then you . . .
Above all/Most important of all, you must/ mustn't . . .

The other student should prompt and/or ask for information with some of this language:
What should you do first/next/then/after that?
What do you do if you find that . . .?
What are you supposed to do if . . .?
I'm not sure I understand that. Could you explain it again, or show me what you mean?

Action sequence for drowning victim

1 Lay victim flat on back.

2 Clear mouth of foreign matter.

3 **Commence mouth-to-mouth respiration:**
   - Tilt victim's head back.
   - Place hand under back of neck.
   - Place heel of other hand on forehead and pinch nostrils shut.
   - Blow air into mouth in series of 4 quick breaths, then 1 breath every 5 seconds.

4 If blockage suspected in throat, turn on side and deliver 4 sharp blows with heel of hand between shoulder blades.

5 Administer 4 chest thrusts. Clear foreign material from mouth. Attempt again to ventilate. Repeat blows and thrusts as needed until airway cleared. After successful ventilation, check neck pulse. If no pulse in neck, start cardiac compression.

6 **Continue mouth-to-mouth respiration and cardiac compression until victim revives or help arrives.**

7 You can empty bulging stomach by placing victim on stomach and placing both hands beneath stomach and lifting to help empty it. You can also clear bulging stomach by leaving victim on back, turning head to one side and pressing on stomach to clear it

8 Protect patient from shock by wrapping in blankets to keep warm. Make victim comfortable and reassure him that everything is all right.

B Communicative grammar

B1 *Should* and *ought to* to give advice, and express regret, criticism and probability

You already know of course that *should* and *ought to* are often used when giving advice. But study the examples of this and other uses and then do the exercise below.

advice	You	{ ought to should }	see a doctor about that rash on your leg. be looking for a new job.
regret	I	{ ought to should }	have tried to give her artificial respiration. have been watching the children more carefully.
criticism	You	{ ought to should }	have finished that job last week. have been watching where you were going.
probability	They ought to/should be in France by now. You shouldn't have any difficulty passing the exam.		

What might you say in these situations?

1 A friend tells you she thinks someone at work is stealing things.
2 A friend of yours offered to pick up a prescription for you from the chemist, but forgot. It was important.
3 John is out of work and worried he won't get another job. You know he's got good qualifications. Console him.
4 You saw a bad car crash in which people were injured. You walked away.
5 A friend wasn't listening when the teacher explained what you all had to do. He asks you. Criticise.

6 You fell off your bike. You know you weren't watching the road at the time.
7 Mary's got an important exam tomorrow and you see her reading a pop magazine. You think she's wasting her time.
8 You left some clothes at a dry cleaner's and were told they would be ready by Friday at the latest. It's now Thursday afternoon.
9 You see a friend writing an essay. You were all supposed to have handed them in yesterday afternoon.
10 Your parents are away and you were supposed to ring them last night. You forgot.

B2 Giving formal orders and commands, and expressing prohibition with *to be to (do)*

Notice how this structure is used rather formally, and often with the passive infinitive for notices and written instructions.

You are to stay here.
You are not to move.
You're to do as you're told.
They are to be here by nine o'clock.

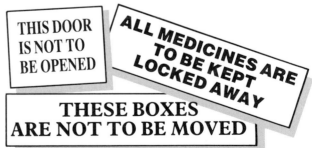

THIS DOOR IS NOT TO BE OPENED

ALL MEDICINES ARE TO BE KEPT LOCKED AWAY

THESE BOXES ARE NOT TO BE MOVED

Write notices for the following. You want to make sure that

1 no one touches a pile of important papers on your desk. (THESE PAPERS . . .)
2 no one removes any magazines from the Library. (NO MAGAZINES . . .)
3 people settle their accounts within 30 days. (ALL ACCOUNTS . . .)

4 no one locks this fire door. (THIS FIRE DOOR . . .)
5 an adult accompanies young children in the swimming pool. (YOUNG CHILDREN . . .)
6 someone cleans and puts away all laboratory equipment at the end of each session. (ALL LABORATORY EQUIPMENT . . .)

B3 Special uses of *will* and *would*

You can already use *will* and *would* to express future ideas, make requests, express conditional ideas and so on, but we also use the words occasionally to express other things in English. Cast your eye over these examples and then do the exercise below.

	will		*would*
criticism	She *will** leave the door open all the time. (=insists on) He *will not/won't* do as he's told. (=refuses to do)	*criticism*	You *would** say the wrong thing, wouldn't you? She *would* wear her best dress! Just like her to be different.
probability/ assumption	That'll be James on the phone (I expect).	*probability/ assumption*	The girl with the blonde hair? That would be John's sister.
habitual prediction	She'll sit for hours reading a book. Given half a chance, he'll talk about the subject for hours on end.	*past habit*	When he was a lot more active, he would go down to the shop and fetch his paper every morning.
timeless prediction (and proverbs)	Accidents will happen. When the cat's away, the mice will play.	*politeness*	I'd be extremely grateful if you would help me.

*NOTE: When used to express criticism in this way, both *will* and *would* are stressed in speech, and cannot be contracted to *'ll* and *'d*.

Rephrase these sentences, using *will/won't* or *would/wouldn't* as appropriate:

1 (It doesn't surprise me that they broke something.) Boys are boys!
2 You can talk to him till you're blue in the face, but he refuses to listen.
3 From the description, the man you were talking about was Jane's boss.
4 You invited them to the party! (You know I didn't want them to come.)

5 I remember, when we were small, we always used to go to the country in July.
6 I'd be glad if you rang me as soon as possible.
7 She insists on wearing her best clothes when she's gardening. (It's so silly.)
8 I expect that's the postman at the door.
9 They're in the habit of playing quite happily on their own.
10 Why is it that children insist on making so much noise?

HE **WILL** LEAVE THE DOOR OPEN ALL THE TIME !

C Register: formal and informal obligation and prohibition

C1 In groups of three, read the three excerpts carefully. Discuss and then write down where you think each was written, by whom, etc. When you have noted down what you think, check with the rest of the class.

1

The Rising Sun Health Farm

You are asked to read and observe the following regulations:

1 Food parcels from the outside world are expressly forbidden.
2 The use of tobacco or tobacco substitutes is strictly forbidden.
3 Alcoholic stimulants are likewise banned.
4 Clients are not to leave the premises without written permission.
5 Any breakages or damage to property are to be reported immediately.

Notes:

a It is essential to build up one's physical capacities steadily. Daily record sheets will therefore be issued each evening; these are to be filled in and returned to the Receptionist before 7 a.m. the following day.
b In the first week, all clients are required to spend at least two hours every day in the gymnasium and a further hour in the activities playground. In the second week, this minimum requirement is doubled.
c It is not advisable to take excessive exercise immediately prior to or after evening salad.
d Conservation of energy is vital. Clients are therefore urged to retire not later than 8.30 p.m.. Attendance a~~t~~ breakfast (6.30–6.45 a.m.) is optional, but recomm~~...~~
e You are reminded that all times of the day, ~~...~~

2

Dear Caroline,

Remember me? That jovial overweight companion of yours at the Social Club? Never again. I am a shadow of my former self.

Life is unspeakably horrible here. We have to be up at dawn! We aren't allowed to eat anything with more than about 4 calories in it, and somehow we're expected to survive on a diet of yoghurt and lettuce! In the morning we're supposed to go on a 20-kilometre run – at least it feels that far – and in the afternoon we're obliged to subject our bodies to a course of so-called massage by a team of heavyweight sadists! They just won't let you rest!

It was a mistake to come. I had to look twice in the mirror to recognise myself this morning. And to think I've got to stay in this wretched place for another ten days! You might have to come and rescue me before

3

Thursday
24th   Day 5

I wrote to Caroline yesterday. I expect the authorities censored it, knowing them. They would! I must find a way out of here. No. That's a sign of weakness. I mustn't think about food. Stop it. Don't be childish. I ought to be strong. It's no good. I can't go on. It's too much for any man. It was all a dreadful mistake, I shouldn't have come here. Nonsense. That's defeatist. They mustn't think they can beat me. I can do it. I'd better stop now, or I shall use too much energy. I must get some rest. This is ridiculous. I've just got to find a way into the village. I simply must.

C2 Still in groups of three, read the excerpts again. Which is the most formal and which the most informal? Why? For example, list the ways in which obligation and prohibition are expressed in each. Discuss your findings with the rest of the class.

C3 Again in groups of three, choose one of the following 'themes' or situations. Then each student in the group write a similar, but shorter, extract like those relating to the Health Farm i.e. either regulations, a letter or a diary. Read your extracts to each other and discuss them when you have finished.

1 Life in a boarding school.
2 Working in a nuclear power station.
3 Working as an agent in the Secret Service.
4 Life in a residential college/university.

D Listening

D1 You are going to hear two people talking about two different kinds of emergency. Before you listen, write this on a sheet of paper:

You should	You shouldn't

Now work in pairs. As you listen, one of you note down the things you *should* do in each emergency, the other note down the things you *shouldn't* do.

D2 Compare and complete your notes. Then compare what you have written with the rest of the class.

E Project: 'Emergency!' (see Teacher's Guide Unit 17)

17

F Vocabulary: noun structures to replace others

F1 One feature of formal spoken and written English is that it uses nouns (with their necessary structures) in place of adjectives, modal verbs and so on. Read these formal sentences and rephrase them in more everyday language. (The nouns to concentrate on are in italics.)

Example: This is a common enough *occurrence*. (=This happens/occurs quite often.)

1 There's every *likelihood/possibility/chance** that he will be late.
2 Please reply at your earliest *opportunity*.
3 You are under an *obligation* to complete the course.
4 Such victims have a *tendency* to resist any *assistance*.
5 We were given the *freedom* to do as we liked.
6 I have every *intention** of complaining.

7 We are making *plans/arrangements/ preparations* for our *departure*.
8 My *advice* to you is not to worry.
9 There is a complete *ban* on all news.
10 *Permission* to use the Staff Car Park is to be obtained from the Principal.
11 There is no *compulsion* (for you) to answer that question.

*Note the use of *every* with these words.

F2 In pairs, read this piece of informal English and rewrite it as formally as you can. Use nouns as above and restructure sentences as much as necessary.

'Nobody's telling you that you *must* learn first aid, but I think you should go on a course as soon as you can. It's quite likely that a friend or a member of your family will have an accident of some kind tomorrow: unfortunately accidents will happen. And if that happens and you haven't been trained in first aid, it's possible you'll just stand by and not only do nothing, but feel helpless, too. I'm already arranging for some of your friends to start a course next week, so if I were you, I think I'd join them. You don't have to go, but please think about it.'

G Exercises for homework

G1 Rephrase the following sentences using the 'starters' given so that they express the same as the original sentences.

1 If I had been him, I wouldn't have touched that old electric fire. (*He shouldn't . . .*)
2 Jane insists on leaving everything till the last minute. (*Jane will . . .*)
3 You must hand in all your work before you leave. (*All work . . .*)
4 They mustn't get any help from anyone. (*They are . . .*)
5 I don't think it'll be difficult for you to persuade him. (*You shouldn't . . .*)
6 It's possible we could arrive before 12. (*There's . . .*)
7 Why weren't you watching the milk? (*You should . . .*)
8 (That boy will have a nasty accident one day.) He insists on touching the sliding doors. (*He won't . . .*)
9 News from the war zone has been banned. (*There . . .*)
10 It's just like her to want to do something completely different! (*She . . .*)

148

G2 The information here about the use of the emergency '999' service in Britain is published by British Telecom. Read it carefully, then use it as a model to write a similar, but more detailed information sheet about the telephone services in your own country for English-speaking visitors. The information sheet you write should advise English-speaking visitors which numbers to dial for Directory Enquiries, the Operator, if they want to make an international call, if they are having difficulty obtaining a number, and what to dial and what to say in an emergency. It should also contain a note about dialling, ringing and engaged tones. (Remember, these may well be very different from those heard on other phones in the world!)

G3 Referring to the 'Action sequence for drowning victim' on page 143, write similar clear instructions on how to deal with some other kind of emergency. You might choose one of the emergencies reported on in the project (page 147). Before you write the instructions, however, study the language used on page 143 very carefully. Among other things, note that the imperative (*Do this . . ., Do that . . .*) is used a great deal and that words like *a/an*, *the*, *his/her*, etc. are often omitted.

999
emergencies

 **Fire**

 **Police**

 **Ambulance**

Cave Rescue

 Coastguard
(sea and cliff rescue)

 **Mountain Rescue**

Dial 999 or the emergency number shown on the number label

Tell the operator which service you want

Wait for the emergency service to answer

Give the telephone number shown on the phone

Give the address where help is needed

Give any other necessary information

Dialling 999 is free

To dial in darkness or in smoke, it will help if you know where the hole or button is on your phone. Remembering where it is and practising finding it with your eyes closed could make an enormous difference in a real emergency.

Other Emergency Services
For other emergencies, eg

Gas ■ Water ■ Electricity
see section 4   NAMES AND NUMBERS

Samaritans
Ashington **814 222** ■ Newcastle **327 272**
Durham **42 727** ■ Sunderland **77 177**

Unit 18

You are kindly requested . . .

1

Guests are kindly requested not to smoke in the dining-room

A1 Here are some fairly typical public notices that you might see in English-speaking countries. You will notice that each uses the passive at least once. This is one thing which makes such notices both impersonal and, at the same time, formal.

In pairs, study them and write down a) where each might be found, and then b) a brief sentence of explanation using the kind of language you would use when explaining it in speech. For example, you might write down for the first:

1 *In a hotel or guesthouse – at Reception, in the dining-room or in written details about meals and mealtimes.*
It means: 'Please don't smoke in the dining-room.'

2

WARNING

ANY PERSON CAUGHT DEFACING
THIS BUILDING IN ANY WAY
WILL BE PROSECUTED

3

N O T I C E

NO MAGAZINES OR
NEWSPAPERS MAY BE
REMOVED FROM THIS
READING ROOM

4 All rooms are to be vacated by 12 noon on the day of departure.

5

NOTICE
Any article not claimed within 3 months after being handed in will be sold.

6 PRIVATE PROPERTY! KEEP OUT!
ANYONE FOUND OR SUSPECTED OF
ENTERING THESE PREMISES WITHOUT
THE OWNERS' PERMISSION WILL BE
PROSECUTED

7 VISITORS ARE ASKED
NOT TO FEED THE ANIMALS
Thank you

8

DANGER
BATHERS ARE ADVISED NOT TO SWIM
BEYOND THE RED MARKERS

9

WARNING
GOVERNMENT PROPERTY.
TRESPASSERS WILL BE PROSECUTED.

10 BREAK IT – AND IT'S YOURS!
Customers are advised that any items broken while being handled will be regarded as bought and must be paid for.

Now check what you've written with another pair of students and then with the class.

A2 Such notices, however, are not always easy to write, and they can be both amusing and ambiguous if not written with some care. The notices below have been collected from various countries around the world where English is a foreign or second language. Again in pairs, read them carefully, work out (if you can) what is wrong with them (using a dictionary if necessary), and then try to rewrite them in correct or unambiguous English.

1

CHILDREN'S HEADS
NEATLY EXECUTED

(A notice in a picture gallery)

2

TEETH EXTRACTED
BY THE LATEST METHODISTS

(A sign in a dentist's)

3

BEWARE!
TO TOUCH THESE WIRES
IS INSTANT DEATH!
Anyone found doing so
will be prosecuted

(A sign on an electricity pylon)

4 If you wish breakfast in your room, please settle on door before night sleeping.

(Instructions found on a label to be put on the outside doorknob of a hotel bedroom)

5

CUSTOMERS GIVING ORDERS
WILL BE PROMPTLY EXECUTED

(A notice in a tailor's)

6 Persons are neatly requested please not to occupy seats in this café without consummation

(A notice in a Mediterranean café)

7

PEOPLES WILL LEFT THE ROOM AT MIDDAY OF TOMORROW IN PLACE OF NOT WHICH WILL BE MORE MONEY FOR HOLE OF DAY

(A notice in a holiday hotel)

Again, check what you've written with another pair of students and then with the class as a whole.

A3 Groupwork: discuss and write

Imagine you are working in a large hotel in your country which caters for (or wants to cater for) English-speaking guests. You have been asked to write a number of notices. In groups of three or four, discuss and write notices telling or advising guests
1 not to leave before paying
2 not to park cars in front of the main entrance
3 not to leave jewellery and valuables in their rooms
4 what to do if/when they want meals or drinks in their rooms
5 what to do if they need clean bed linen
6 what to do if something goes wrong with the central heating/air-conditioning
7 what to do if they want laundry done, etc.
Think of more situations and write as many notices as you can. Then compare with the rest of the class.

B Communicative grammar

The passive structures (which are) practised in this Unit are commonly found in public notices in hotels, self-service restaurants, at the zoo, in shops, in car parks, on the beach, and so on. The structures are also used, however, in other situations, for example in rules and regulations, on registration forms, in formal letters and the like, in other words where a formal style is required. (This is why the passive is often used in explanations like this in textbooks!)

B1 Present Simple passive *is/are done* for orders, official advice, etc.

Examples:
> *Customers are (respectfully) reminded that credit cards are not accepted.*
> *Hotel guests are (strongly) advised to deposit valuables at Reception.*

Note that verbs of ordering, advice, permission, etc. can often be used in the passive with a following *(not) to*-infinitive construction. Such verbs are: *advise, ask, expect, require, request, urge, permit, forbid, allow, warn, invite, recommend*

Work in pairs and write down typical notices you might find in English-speaking countries which

1 advise you to book early for all coach tours. (hotel)
2 ask you not to leave glasses or bottles near the swimming-pool. (hotel)
3 remind you to settle your account before you leave. (hotel)
4 require all passengers to proceed through Customs. (airport)
5 request you to leave dirty walking boots outside. (youth hostel)
6 forbid students to park (their cars) in the staff car park. (college or school)
7 warn walkers not to stray onto private land. (public footpath)
8 remind you that the shop can only accept cheques with a banker's card. (shop or store)

B2 Future passive *will be done* and Present Simple or Present Perfect passive (*is/are done; has/have been done*) and relative pronoun

These constructions again are often found in orders, official advice, etc., but the auxiliary verbs and relative pronoun are often deleted, for example:
> *Anyone (who is/has been) caught damaging property will be prosecuted.*

Note the construction: *to catch/see/discover/find someone doing something.*

Using sentences like *Anyone caught damaging seats will be fined*, say what will happen in your country to
1 a passenger who damages seats in a train.
2 anyone who trespasses on government property.
3 anyone who passes forged bank notes.
4 anyone who provides false information on official forms.
5 anyone found guilty of murder.
6 a customer who steals from a shop.
7 a person who avoids paying income tax.
8 a driver who goes over the speed limit in a built-up area.

Think of other crimes and discuss their respective punishments using the same kind of language.

B3 Passives with modals
Examples:
> *All rooms must be vacated by midday on the day of departure.*
> *All accounts are to be settled by 10 a.m. on the day of departure.*
> *No books may be removed from this reference library without the permission of the Librarian.*

Look at these notices and extracts from rules and in pairs explain to each other what they mean.

Example:

A: What does that mean? 'NO REFUND CAN BE GIVEN'?

B: It means they can't give you a refund (of your money) once you've booked the tickets and paid.

A: Oh, I see.

1 All personal belongings are to be handed to the warden for safekeeping.

2 NO MAGAZINES OR NEWSPAPERS MAY BE REMOVED FROM THIS READING ROOM

3 All room keys must be handed back to the warden at the end of the course.

4 CHILDREN UNDER 14 MUST BE ACCOMPANIED BY AN ADULT

5 All correspondence is to be addressed to the Manager personally

6 NO RESPONSIBILITY CAN BE TAKEN BY THE MANAGEMENT FOR DAMAGE TO OR LOSS OF PROPERTY LEFT IN THE CLOAKROOMS

C Vocabulary: some common adverb-verb collocations

C1 You will have noticed in this Unit that particular adverbs seem to be used with particular verbs. In other words, in a phrase like *You are strongly advised . . .*, the adverb which commonly modifies, or collocates with, *advised* is *strongly*. Study these expressions with common adverb-verb collocations, and then do the exercise.

You are { kindly / respectfully } { asked / requested } / strongly advised / legally entitled / cordially invited / strongly recommended / respectfully reminded / legally required / strongly urged } to do . . .

I was / He was / etc. {
falsely / wrongly } accused (of . . .) / greatly admired (for . . .) / highly delighted (with/by . . .) / unfairly dismissed (for . . .) / completely / thoroughly } exhausted (by . . .) / completely ignored (by . . .) / fully insured (against . . .) / keenly interested (in . . .) / sadly missed (by . . .) / sadly mistaken / highly rated (as a . . . by . . .) / highly recommended (for . . .) / sorely tempted (to do . . .) / promptly / quickly } { told / ordered } ((not) to do)

The job was promptly executed.
The facts were well/widely known.
We were completely lost.
The supplies were badly needed.
Help was kindly/generously offered.
His action was deeply resented.
My offer of help was utterly rejected.

Cover the boxes above and repeat these sentences, adding an appropriate adverb:

1 You are entitled to your money back.

2 His promotion was resented by the others.

3 They were insured against fire.

4 You are invited to the wedding.

5 I was delighted with the present.

6 He will be missed by his friends.

7 The proposal was rejected

8 If you think that, you're mistaken.

9 She was tempted to say nothing.

10 The new hospital was needed.

C2 Role play discussion (see Teacher's Guide Unit 18)

D Listening

The language used in notices, and which you have been practising in this Unit, is also used a great deal in news reports. You are going to hear part of a local radio news broadcast.

D1 Listen once and then say briefly what each news item was about.

D2 Now listen again more carefully and then, in pairs, ask and tell each other

1 what Brian Wide does, and why he is surprised.
2 what his firm is legally required to do.
3 what workers are still badly needed for.
4 why two men appeared in court today.
5 why the man took his employer to court.
6 what he had been accused of.
7 if he had ever been tempted.
8 where the accident happened, and when.
9 if anyone was injured, and how badly.
10 what witnesses have been asked to do by the police.
11 whose death was announced earlier today.
12 what he was greatly admired for.
13 why he will be sadly missed, and by whom.

D3 Now listen again and make notes in order to write out two or three of the items as if for a newspaper. When you write the articles, make up suitable headlines.

E Register

Compare the ways in which requests, orders, statements, etc. are made in speech and in formal written English (e.g. in notices or in printed rules and regulations):

spoken (informal)		written (formal)
'Please don't smoke in the dining-room.'	⟷	GUESTS ARE KINDLY REQUESTED NOT TO SMOKE IN THE DINING-ROOM
'You can't cancel . . .'	⟷	No cancellations can be accepted . . .
'You've got to leave your room . . .'	⟷	All rooms are to/must be vacated . . .
'They won't give you back your money . . .'	⟷	NO REFUNDS CAN/WILL BE MADE . . .

Notice that formal written English tends to use:
1 Passive verb forms.
2 Nouns in place of verbs e.g. *cancellation*, *refund*, *departure*

3 More formal vocabulary e.g. *refund* (= give back), *vacate* (= leave), *deface* (= spoil or damage), *execute* (= carry out or do a job), *premises* (= a building, etc).

E1 Look again at all the written notices on the previous pages (150–153) and, in small groups, quickly tell each other once again (in informal spoken English) what they all mean.

E2 Stay in the same groups. Imagine you are working in a large department store which caters for (or wants to cater for) English-speaking visitors. You have been asked to write a number of notices in English for their benefit. Discuss and write the notices which will tell them about fire precautions, warn them about penalties for shoplifting, guide them to the restaurant or self-service café, tell them whether cheques or credit cards (which?) are accepted or not (and under what conditions), etc. Write as many as you can between you. Then check with the rest of the class.

F Functions: orders, commands, requests and warnings

F1 Compare the variety of spoken forms of orders, commands and warnings with the corresponding notices:

CAUTION!
DANGER
BEWARE!
DO NOT TOUCH!

Look out! Mind out! Watch out!
Watch what you're doing! You must be very careful!
You're to take every possible precaution.
Hands off! Get your hands off! Leave it alone!
(Please) don't touch! You really mustn't touch them.
You're not to touch this under any circumstances.
You will not touch anything whatsoever.

As well as being rather more formal, the longer utterances indicate,
on the one hand, a more measured, less urgent command or warning
and, on the other, a more insistent or more authoritative attitude.
When, and to whom, would you use each of the spoken sentences above?

F2 Compare these two utterances: *Come here this minute!* and *Come
here a minute!* The imperative is common to both. However, the first
sounds like an angry order, possibly from mother to child (*. . . or I'll
give you a smack!*), while the second is a common informal request
(*. . . I want to show you something.*). In fact, the structures we use
for orders, commands, warnings and threats e.g.
Stand up! Keep still! Don't move! Don't you dare! You must tell me!
are often the same as we use for suggestions, offers, requests and
invitations e.g.
*Try a new shampoo. Have a drink! Don't open the window. You
must come too!*

Listen to the statements below and notice how the tone and
intonation varies according to the additional comments or
statements. Then read them aloud yourself.

1 Take off your coat.
  a I want to examine you
  b Make yourself at home.
  c One false move and I'll shoot.

2 Don't be silly!
  a I'll pay.
  b This is serious.

3 You must come more often.
  a We love having you here!
  b Your attendance record is terrible!

4 Now you're not to touch the dishes.
  a I'll do them later.
  b They're valuable!

5 You mustn't say that!
  a It's a very rude word for a little boy to say!
  b Every cloud has a silver lining, you know.

F3 Here are some more statements, some formal-
sounding, some aggressive, some informal and
friendly. Go through them and say who you think
might say them to whom, and when. Then read them
aloud, adding a sentence or two (before or after) in
the same tone.

1 Try it once more with a little less left hand.
2 Do them again and under the nails this time;
and don't come down till they're clean.

3 You must come round to my place one evening.
4 You will not divulge any of this to anyone.
5 You'll sit there until you've said it.
6 You must be more careful when you're changing
down from top to third.
7 You mustn't get confused between commas and
colons.
8 You are to be in the office by five to nine at the
latest.

G Exercises for homework

G1 Finish each of the following sentences in such a way that it means exactly the same as the sentence printed before it.

Example: People had great admiration for him. (*He . . .*)
You write: He was greatly admired.

1 You may not take food off the premises. (*No . . .*)
2 If I catch anyone wasting time, I'll send that person home!
(*Anyone . . .*)
3 You are to send in all your orders by 28 March. (*All orders . . .*)
4 There is a legal requirement for us to employ equal numbers of
men and women. (*We are . . .*)
5 There is deep resentment at the action taken by the
management. (*The action taken . . .*)
6 They will prosecute anyone they catch defacing the building.
(*Anyone . . .*)
7 You may not remove any confidential papers from the office.
(*No . . .*)
8 The law forbids the general public to go beyond this point. (*The
general public . . .*)
9 She showed a keen interest in local history. (*She was . . .*)
10 We would with respect remind all the men that they should
wear a collar and tie. (*All the men . . .*)

G2 You have arranged to meet an English-speaking colleague from
another country at a conference in Britain in April. He/She has just
written to tell you that he/she has lost the information about the
conference and has asked you to remind him/her about registration
dates, cancellation and accommodation. Referring to your own copy
(opposite), write a letter of about 200 words giving all the
information you think he/she needs. You need not bother about your
address or the date: simply begin your letter *Dear* (name), . . .

In order to help you, however, we have circled the important points,
and suggest that you use the following 'starters' for your paragraphs:

Dear..,

I was glad to read in your last letter that you still want to come to
the conference, but was sorry ....

As far as registration is concerned, ...

....

I sincerely hope you won't have to cancel, but if ....

....

You will no doubt want to be resident at the conference, as you
were last year, so ....

I hope that answers all your questions. See you in April!

With all best wishes,
Yours,

Registration

The deadline for registration as a member of the conference at the lower registration fee is 28th February, but as attendance is restricted to 550, those who wish to take part are strongly advised to register as soon as possible. No registration can be accepted for part of the conference only. The full programme of the conference will be posted to all those whose registration form and fees (and accommodation payments) are received in good time; others will receive them at the conference reception table. Would all members of the conference please check in at the reception table as soon as possible after arrival.

N.B. If the conference registration and accommodation are cancelled before 14th March, the fees will be returned minus a £2.00 cancellation charge. NO REFUND WILL BE MADE AFTER THAT DATE.

Cancellation

Every year there are a few members who are unable to attend through illness contracted at the last moment, and they often write and ask for a refund of fees. We appreciate that it is a heavy loss to sustain if you have booked accommodation in a hall of residence and are unable to take it up. However, we are obliged to give our reservation numbers to the College some time before the conference, so that they can order their requirements for catering, and once we have made a firm reservation for a member, we usually have to pay the full cost to the College. We respectfully suggest, therefore, that residential members should view the conference in the same way as, for instance, a holiday reservation and cover their possible cancellation by insurance.

Accommodation

Residential members may check into their rooms from 3 p.m. onwards on Monday 4th April and will be notified of their residence and handed room keys at the reception desk in the covered patio, which will be marked on the map accompanying your registration acceptance. The latest time of arrival is 10.00 p.m. Those likely to arrive after 7 p.m. should notify the Executive Officer before 14th March and she will cancel the evening dinner and make the appropriate refund to those members. All meals are taken in the College dining room.

Members of the conference requiring accommodation should ensure that their registration forms reach the Executive Officer by 28th February. Accommodation will only be reserved if the appropriate payment IS IN OUR HANDS BY THAT DATE (unless special application, giving reasons, is made). No refunds can be made for cancellation after 14th March, nor can any cancellation of nights be accepted during the conference.

Unit 19

YOUR VERDICT!

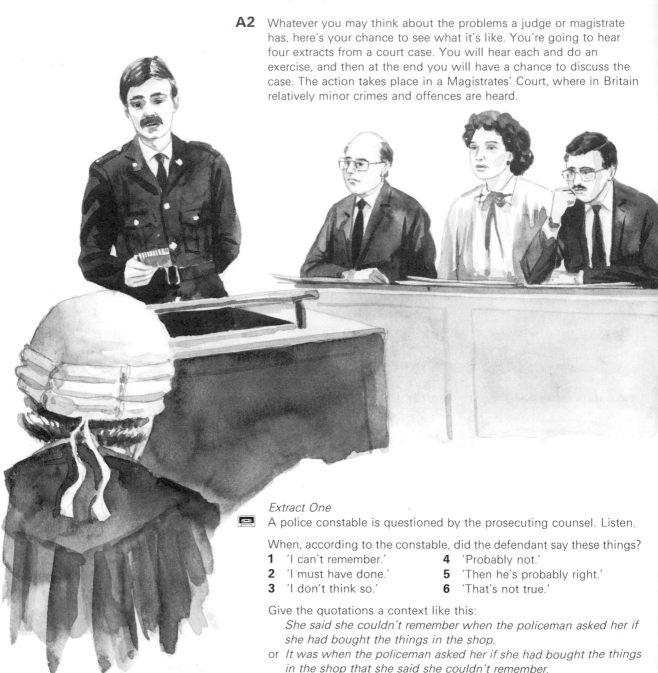

A1 Would you like to be a judge or a magistrate in a court of law? Why?/Why not?

A2 Whatever you may think about the problems a judge or magistrate has, here's your chance to see what it's like. You're going to hear four extracts from a court case. You will hear each and do an exercise, and then at the end you will have a chance to discuss the case. The action takes place in a Magistrates' Court, where in Britain relatively minor crimes and offences are heard.

Extract One

A police constable is questioned by the prosecuting counsel. Listen.

When, according to the constable, did the defendant say these things?
1 'I can't remember.'   4 'Probably not.'
2 'I must have done.'   5 'Then he's probably right.'
3 'I don't think so.'   6 'That's not true.'

Give the quotations a context like this:
   She said she couldn't remember when the policeman asked her if she had bought the things in the shop.
or *It was when the policeman asked her if she had bought the things in the shop that she said she couldn't remember.*

158

Extract Two

The defendant is being cross-examined by the prosecuting counsel. Listen.

Would you say that at any time in this extract Mrs Johns sounds: confident? forceful? irritable? nervous? confused? desperate? clear-headed? aggressive? emotional? flippant?

If so, when? Comment along the lines of: *I thought she sounded rather desperate when she said she couldn't . . .*

Discuss your impressions.

Extract Three

A witness for the defence, Dr Stuart Johnson, a qualified psychiatrist, is questioned by the prosecution. Listen.

Contextualise these figures mentioned by the doctor:
1 100   **2** 20   **3** 1, maybe 2   **4** 2 or 3
5 15th   **6** 18th   **7** 3   **8** 6   **9** 20,000

Comment like this: *A hundred? That was the number of miles he said he had driven that day.*

Extract Four

A character witness speaks on behalf of the defendant, Mrs Johns. Listen.

Which of these qualities does the man attribute to her? Tick as you listen.
courage?   honesty?   kindness?   frankness?   common sense?
devotion?   pride?   intelligence?   generosity?   unselfishness?

Which of his comments illustrate the qualities you ticked?

A3   Role play

In groups of three, take the parts of the three magistrates who have heard this case, and try to reach a verdict (of 'Guilty' or 'Not guilty'). One of you (Student A) feels Mrs Johns is guilty, a second (Student B) disagrees, and a third (Student C) has an open mind – ready to be persuaded by the arguments of the other two. Recall as much as you think desirable of the four taped extracts, quoting and reporting the people concerned in the case. Both Students A and B should attempt to persuade Student C.

When you have come to a decision, compare your verdict with that of other groups.

A4   What was your own *personal* verdict? Give reasons.

B Communicative grammar: reporting what people have written or said

You already know many of the things to remember when reporting what people have said or written in English, such as the sequence of tenses; the use of verbs like *accuse, congratulate, compliment*, etc.; the use of the *to*-infinitive to report orders and commands; and how to report exclamations, modal verbs and adverbs of time and place. (To revise them, look back at Unit 9, pages 80–81.)
When it comes to reporting interviews in the news, minutes of meetings and so on, however, we rarely stick religiously to the exact words spoken. Instead, we tend to paraphrase in order to report the essence of what was said.

B1 Combining reports of questions and answers (formal)

Note the constructions used in these examples (with participles, past and present) to combine reports of questions and answers. Both constructions are fairly formal.

a *'Can you tell us what the Government intends to do now, sir?'*
'Well, it's a little difficult to say right at this moment.'

When he was asked (When) asked On being asked	what the Government intended to do, to comment on the Government's intentions, for a statement about the Government's intentions,	the Minister was non-committal.

b *'Headmaster, would you care to make a statement about the allegations?'*
'Certainly. They are untrue.'
or
'No comment.'
or
'Yes. They are completely unfounded.'

Commenting on the allegations, the Headmaster declared that they were untrue.
Replying to a question about the allegations, the Headmaster declined to comment.
Answering a question about the allegations, the Headmaster stated that they were completely unfounded.

Other verbs used like this are: *agree, apologise, assure, dismiss, argue, admit*

Report these exchanges in the same way:

1 'Do you think the committee was right to do what it did?' 'Yes, I do.'
2 'What do you think of the new budget, sir?' 'I think it's totally unrealistic.'
3 'Mr Long, did you steal the painting?' 'No. But I did buy it from the thieves.'
4 'Jane, is it true you're getting married again?' 'I might – and I might not!'
5 'Do you plan to make any major changes, Mrs Hatchet?' 'No, definitely not. The society will be run as it has been for the past ten years.'

B2 Reporting essential points of a dialogue or discussion

Opposite is the verbatim transcript of part of a meeting accompanied by the relevant section of the minutes prepared by the secretary after the meeting.
1 Cover the minutes and, in groups of four, read (or act out) the meeting twice.

2 Cover the transcript of the meeting and read the minutes carefully. Note the verbs and phrases used to summarise whole phrases and sentences. In the same groups, work through the minutes and try to recall (without cheating and checking back!) *exactly* what was said.

Verbatim transcript of the meeting

CHAIRMAN: If I might move on to the next item on the agenda, the matter of the posters for our next concert. I'm sorry to say that although I offered personally to look into this, I haven't as yet been able to do anything. I must say I hope to do so very soon.

MRS SMITH: With respect, Mr Chairman, that is precisely what you said at our last committee meeting.

CHAIRMAN: No, that's not true at all, Mrs Smith. With respect, I only said I would try to begin to make enquiries.

MR STAINES: That's quite right, Mr Chairman. That's exactly what you said. However, perhaps we can leave the argument there. I know one or two printers and I'm quite prepared to find out the cost of having the posters printed before the next meeting.

CHAIRMAN: Fine. Thank you, Mr Staines. I think that's an excellent idea.

MISS JAMES: I would like to second that.

CHAIRMAN: Thank you, Miss James.

MRS SMITH: Mr Chairman, before we leave this matter, may I say that I would like it put on record that I'm against the idea. I still think it should be left to the Chairman.

CHAIRMAN: Thank you, Mrs Smith. Your opposition has been noted. Now, is there anything else on the question of the posters?

MISS JAMES: Yes, Mr Chairman. Some weeks ago I was asked if I could design a poster and I've brought it along with me. Perhaps you'd all care to look at it.

CHAIRMAN: Ah, yes. I like it.

MR STAINES: So do I. Well done, Miss James. Nice and striking.

MRS SMITH: Striking?! If you'll excuse my saying so, it's far too – what's the word? – 'modern', far too 'jazzy' for my liking. As a member of this concert committee, I will take no responsibility for it.

CHAIRMAN: Surely, Mrs Smith, it's not too bold. We've got to try to attract the young people to our concerts . . .

Minutes of the meeting

Moving on to the matter of the posters for the next concert, the Chairman apologised for not having been able to do anything. He assured the meeting, however, that he would do so very soon. On being pressed further by Mrs Smith, the Chairman emphatically denied saying the same thing at the last meeting, and he respectfully reminded Mrs Smith that he had only promised to make enquiries.

Mr Staines agreed with the Chairman, he urged the committee to leave the matter there and offered to find out the costs of having the posters printed himself in time for the next meeting. The Chairman expressed his agreement and was supported by Miss James, although it was noted that Mrs Smith opposed the idea.

Miss James then showed the committee her design for the poster which she had been asked to draft. There was some disagreement about it however, since, while the Chairman and Mr Staines approved of the design, Mrs Smith dismissed it as too 'modern', too 'jazzy', and flatly refused to take any responsibility for it. The Chairman tried to placate her, pointing out that they had to try to attract the young people . . .

3 Now read this short verbatim transcript of a press interview with a film star who has just landed at the airport. Then write a brief newspaper report, giving the article a suitable headline.

REPORTER: How long do you intend to stay, Miss Strong?

MISS STRONG: It all depends.

REPORTER: What exactly are your plans? Is it true you're here to make a film with James Corn?

MISS STRONG: Yes.

REPORTER: Is there any truth in the rumour that you and your husband have recently separated?

MISS STRONG: No, certainly not. And that's all. Thank you.

C Vocabulary: common collocations with verbs *make*, *come to*, *express* and *give*

C1 We tend to use the expressions below when we do not wish to report in great detail what people said, in other words when we simply want to *describe* what happened, or what people did through speech, as opposed to *reporting* their speech.
Cast your eye over them, and then suggest utterances that might be described using the expressions, e.g.

> *I'll do it. Honestly.* (= He/She made a promise.)
> *Don't forget to come.* (= He/She gave them a reminder.)

(The corresponding verbs given in brackets are those we might use when actually reporting.)

to make a suggestion	(*suggest*)	to make an application (for)	(*apply*)
to make an accusation	(*accuse*)	to make an arrangement (to do)	(*arrange*)
to make a request	(*request*)	to make an attempt (to do)	(*attempt*)
to make a confession	(*confess*)	to make a comment (on/about)	(*comment*)
to make/take a decision	(*decide*)	to make a choice (between)	(*choose*)
to make an apology/one's apologies	(*apologise*)	to make a complaint (about)	(*complain*)
to make a promise	(*promise*)	to make a comparison (between)	(*compare*)
to make/put forward a proposal	(*propose*)	to make an inquiry (about)	(*inquire*)
to make a recommendation	(*recommend*)	to make (a) reference (to)	(*refer*)

to come to an agreement	(*agree*)		
to come to a conclusion	(*conclude*)	to give something some thought/consideration	(*think about/consider*)
to come to a decision	(*decide*)	to give someone advice	(*advise*)
to express admiration (for)	(*admire*)	to give someone an order	(*order*)
to express an opinion (about/of)	(*think*)	to give someone a reminder	(*remind*)
to express (dis)approval (of)	(*(dis)approve*)	to give someone a warning	(*warn*)
to express sympathy (for/with)	(*sympathise*)	to give someone permission	(*permit*)
to express thanks (for)	(*thank*)		

C2 What did the following people do? Use expressions from the lists above. (Remember to describe what the person did, not what he or she said.)

Example: 'You should see a dentist,' she said to him.
You say or write: She gave him some advice. *or* She made a suggestion. *or* She expressed an opinion.

1 'If you do that again,' she said to the boy, 'you'll be in trouble!'
2 'I'm thinking about it,' he said.
3 'I've decided,' she said. 'I know exactly what to do.'
4 'You're all doing a splendid job,' he told them.
5 'I admit I'm guilty,' the defendant said.
6 'So we'll meet here the same time next week,' said Bob. 'Yes,' said John.
7 'I'm terribly sorry, but if you'll excuse me, I must go now,' I said.
8 'I think that looks dreadful,' she said.
9 'Of course you can stay out till 10 o'clock,' he told his son.
10 'I'll have that green one,' she said finally. 'You can put the others away.'
11 'We'd like to thank you very much for inviting us to the conference,' he said.
12 'I was sorry to hear you didn't get the job,' she said.

D Socialising: telling others what you've read or heard

D1 Look at this dialogue and notice how we report news items or stories we've read or heard:

A: Did you hear about the burglars who rang for the police themselves?

B: No. Why did they do that?

A: Well, according to a report on the news yesterday, these two burglars went into a local factory – presumably to rob the safe – and the first thing they did was to take the phone off the hook.

B: That sounds a bit stupid.

A: Yes. Well, they told the police they did it to stop anyone phoning while they were there. What they didn't know was that it was connected via a direct line to the police station in out-of-work hours, and the moment anyone picked it up, the police (down at the police station) could hear everything that was said.

B: I don't believe it!

A: True! The police listened in to everything the burglars said and just went down and arrested them when they came out!

D2 Read this article through twice silently. By all means smile or chuckle to yourself, but *don't* discuss it with another student. When you've read it, cover it.

Burglar's peg-leg alibi

A MAN charged in a Glasgow court with knifing a neighbour at a party pleaded: 'My false teeth must have cut his hand. They were knocked out of my mouth when somebody punched me.'

A far-fetched excuse? Magistrates have heard worse.

A Frenchman accused of stealing a horse from a stable near Paris said he sold it to a farmer to save racegoers from losing their money on it.

When a burglar was caught robbing a restaurant in San Francisco, America, he told the policeman he'd stumbled against the window, broken it, and went in to leave his name and address so the repair bill could be sent to him. He just happened to be looking in the cash register for a pencil.

In Ontario, Canada, a burglar arrested with housebreaking tools said he needed them to mend his peg leg. And a woman in Dallas, Texas, said she put rat poison in her husband's beer in an attempt to stop him drinking.

A man, aged 88, driving a scooter without a licence in Durban, South Africa, said he hadn't applied for one because he thought he had to be accompanied by his parents.

D3 Keep the article covered and, in pairs, retell the 'cases' to each other using these cartoons as prompts. Embellish the stories if you want to. Begin each one like this:

A: *Did you hear/read about the man/woman who . . .?*

B: *No. What happened?*

A: *Well, apparently/it seems . . .*

E Exercises for homework

E1 Read this extract from a cross-examination in court. Then write a
one-paragraph report of the essential points using the 'starters' and
phrases suggested on the right.

PROSECUTION:	Now, Mr Mullins, Police Constable Hart told the court that he arrested you as you were climbing out of the window of the Social Club.	*When he was reminded . . .*
DEFENDANT:	Yes, that's right. But it wasn't what you think.	*. . . admitted . . .but denied . . .*
PROSECUTION:	Well, perhaps you'd explain to the court what you were doing climbing out of the window of the Social Club at two o'clock in the morning.	*On being asked . . .*
DEFENDANT:	Well, you see, I run a cleaning service . . .	*. . .explained . . .*
PROSECUTION:	A cleaning service?	
DEFENDANT:	Yes, for offices, clubs and so on.	
PROSECUTION:	I see. Go on.	
DEFENDANT:	Well, I'd gone in and cleaned the Social Club when it closed at eleven that night. And I'd locked up and gone home.	*He told the court . . .*
PROSECUTION:	Yes?	*Urged to continue, . . .*
DEFENDANT:	But I was just going to bed when I remembered that I'd left my jacket at the Club. So I went back to get it, and had to break in through a window because I didn't have a key to the door. I was climbing back out when the police constable turned up . . .	*. . .said . . .* *He finished by saying . . .*

E2 Write one-sentence reports of these brief exchanges, using the verbs given.

Example: 'Can you say anything about the discussions, sir?' the
reporter asked the Minister. 'No, I'm afraid I can't,' the
Minister said.
(*ask / decline*) or (*reply / refuse*)

You write: (When) asked if he could comment on the discussions,
the Minister declined to say anything.

or: Replying to a question about the discussions, the
Minister refused to say anything.

1 'You said you'd look after the finances, didn't you?' Bill said to John.
'I certainly did not,' replied John. 'I said nothing of the kind.'
(*comment / emphatically deny*)

2 'You must agree the job's got to be done as soon as possible,' said Sue.
'Oh, definitely,' said Mr Toms, 'But I'm certainly not going to do it!'
(*agree / flatly refuse*)

3 'Where were you on the night of the murder?' the policeman
asked Tom. 'Were you anywhere near the house?' 'You know I
was,' said Tom. 'But I had nothing to do with it.'
(*question / admit / declare*)

4 'What do you think of the plans for the new theatre?' 'What do I
think of them?' the Mayor said. 'I think they're totally ridiculous!'
(*comment / dismiss*)

5 'Do you hope to make an arrest soon, Inspector?' the reporter asked.
'I can't say,' the Inspector said, 'but I will give another press
conference tomorrow.'
(*ask / refuse / but promise*)

E3 The following is an extract from a novel. The scene takes place in a jury room. Having heard the case, the jury of 12 people have been sent out to decide whether the defendants are guilty or not guilty. Imagine you have been asked to write a script of this scene for a film version of the novel. Read the extract carefully, then write out a script of what the people actually said — or what you think they said. (You might also add brief stage directions.)

As the jurors filed into the oak-panelled room, no one said anything. One or two coughed, and there was a sigh or two: that's all. Gradually they each chose one of the chairs arranged around the long oak table and sat down. One or two of the women looked at their nails, one or two of the men chewed theirs; others sat in various poses, some leaning back, some with elbows on the table. Hardly anyone dared look at the others. For a while there was an embarrassed silence, punctuated by the occasional shuffling of feet.

It wasn't until one of the women coughed and made a proposal to the effect that they should appoint a foreman, as the judge had instructed, that they began to look around, and at one another. An elderly gentleman at the other end of the table agreed with the woman and suggested that since she had spoken first, she might act as foreman. She protested, but the nods and murmurs of approval around the table set the seal on it. She therefore accepted, but with some reservation for, as she admitted, she had never done anything like this before.

Responsibility, albeit enforced, often brings out the latent confidence in those not accustomed to it, and it did with Rose Chalmers. She glanced around the table and was somewhat surprised, and a little pleased, to see eleven expectant faces looking at her. She decided to take the plunge, and immediately suggested that they should each say what they thought about the case they had listened to for the past five days. Had Jeremy Hay, the pop singer, murdered his wife with the help of his girlfriend, Marilyn Asher? That's what they had been accused of. Had he perhaps murdered her and not told Marilyn? Had Marilyn done it, and Jeremy been the accessory? Or had Jeremy's wife actually taken her own life, as the Defence had suggested, and circumstantial evidence had pointed to Jeremy and Marilyn as 'murderers'?

Throughout, there was the odd comment of agreement or disagreement, approval and disapproval of one or other of the possibilities. It seemed that there would be no easy agreement among the twelve, especially when one or two of the men expressed the view that they thought Marilyn was 'a real beauty' and that they'd commit murder for her any day! and at least one woman thought Jeremy was 'her idea of heaven'!

Then one gentleman, who had until then remained silent, coughed politely and for a minute or so argued quite forcibly that both defendants were, in his opinion, guilty of murder as charged. He was then joined by one of the women jurors who agreed with him and pointed out to the others that the alibis of Jeremy and Marilyn were 'almost too good to be true'. This, however, did not gain general approval, as they were reminded by a young male juror of the mental state of Jeremy's wife.

It was going to be a long session . . .

E4 Referring to the case of Mrs Johns on pages 158–159, write a brief newspaper article (no more than 200 words) giving the relevant facts and the outcome of the court case. (The verdict will of course be the one your group came to in discussion in exercise **A3** on page 159.) Give your article an appropriate headline (e.g. 'Woman Guilty of Shoplifting', 'Acquittal of Woman Accused of Shoplifting', etc.).

A1 What are your reactions to these photographs?
What aspects of man's use or abuse of animals do they reflect?

Organised cock fighting

Death on the ice

Killed in the name of fashion

A2   Below are four extracts from a newspaper article on animal experiments. Work in threes. Read paragraph **1** together, then read one piece each – **2**, **3** or **4**. Afterwards summarise what you have read for the other two. Which of the three arguments sounds nearest to your own personal views?

1

MORE THAN four million animal experiments are carried out annually in Britain. Two facts are fundamental to the debate about them. First: without animal experiments much medical and biological research would grind to a halt. Second: some experiments do cause suffering.

2

Huge areas of medical research would be impossible if all animal experiments were banned. Most research on the nature of, and cures for, cancer would be impossible. Work on organ transplantation and other forms of experimental surgery would cease. Above all there would be no new drugs.

'The last 20 years or so,' says Sir William Paton, professor of pharmacology at Oxford and former chairman of the Research Defence Society, 'have seen the development of polio vaccines, drugs for high blood pressure, anti-depressants, and so on. Without animal experiments we would have had none of these.'

3

Brigid Brophy the novelist, a campaigner for total abolition of animal experiments, faces this issue squarely. 'The loss that might result is a loss humanity would have to bear,' she says. We would not, she points out, experiment on 10 children to find a cure for a disease that would save the lives of a thousand. 'If we abandoned experiments on other animals we might have to bear more losses of that kind. But I think the scientists could come up with alternatives.'

But how many people would accept the death of a single child if animal experiments could save it?

4

'The question is not, Can they reason? nor Can they

A cat immobilised for the implantation of electrodes into the brain

talk? but, Can they suffer?'

The arguments can be extremely uncomfortable: 'People will always defend animal experimentation on the grounds that animals are not rational, thinking creatures. Well, neither is a severely retarded person. The same people will then say that if you were to experiment on a retarded person it would be upsetting for their families. So why shouldn't we use, for instance, a severely retarded child who is also an orphan? The human model will always serve our purposes better than an animal. If you don't accept this, then logically you should not accept experiments on non-human animals.'

A3   Discussion

In groups of four or five, list and discuss the many ways man uses animals, such as:
1. for sport: horse-racing, fishing, . . .
2. for experiments: medical research, cosmetics, . . .
3. for food: meat, milk, . . .
4. as pets: dogs, birds, . . .
5. for clothes: fur, wool, . . .
6. for assorted products: ivory, oil, . . .
7. for work: bullocks, horses, . . .

What would be the consequences if we were forbidden by law to use or abuse animals in all of the ways you mentioned?

B Reading and role play

B1 In threes, read this newspaper article about a recent Animal Liberation Group attack on a pig farm, helping each other as far as possible to understand the meaning of new words.

Animal lib raid brings havoc to pig farm

IT was a quiet Sunday morning when farmer Mr John Walsh heard a strange noise coming from the area of his pig sheds. He went to investigate – and found his farm invaded by members of an 'animal liberation front'.

Cars and minibuses were parked all round the yard. Some 20 people sat on the roof of one of his sheds.

Others were climbing his food bins and running around the yard shouting and carrying banners.

Mr Walsh heard a scream and saw his wife trying to prevent a car leaving the farm. It was nudging her backwards down the lane.

He hurled a brick, hitting the car's side.

Then the farmer returned to his yard. And with even more people on his roof and others frightening the pigs in his sheds, he fetched his gun and fired two shots into the air.

Soon afterwards police arrived at the farm at Sharnbrook, Bedfordshire. They took the names and addresses of many of the protesters and told them to go.

But the protesters, who say they are opposed to animal cruelty, left a trail of trouble.

A terrified pedigree boar worth £800 had a heart attack and died.

Sows panicked and trod on their piglets. Fifteen died.

More than a fifth of the piglets born that day were stillborn.

And the roofs of Mr Walsh's buildings suffered £3,000 worth of damage.

But after all that only one person has been reported for criminal damage – Mr Walsh himself, for throwing a brick at a car.

Mr Walsh said: 'These people came in from the surrounding fields and sat on a sow-house which houses 200 pregnant females. As a result we have had mass abortions.

'They were running in and out of the sheds, flashing cameras. It frightened the animals to death.

'About six people seemed to be in charge and some told my workmen that they had intended to turn all my animals out into a wood. But we foiled their attempts.'

Mr Walsh keeps 800 breeding sows, 40 boars, and an average of 3,000 baby pigs on his farm.

He insists his methods are not cruel and thinks he was singled out for attack because when advertising for workmen in farm journals he uses the description 'intensive rearing farm'.

B2 After much persuasion, a radio station managed to get Mr Walsh and a leader of the assault together for a studio discussion. Act it out in threes: one of you is the interviewer, skilfully handling a delicate situation, another is Mr Walsh, showing controlled anger towards the third of you, an unrepentant militant.

C Communicative grammar: variations on conditional sentences

C1 Variations on sentences with *if*

Look carefully at these four sentences, then express them using more standard conditional patterns.

a 'If this *should happen* again, no doubt Mr Walsh will be ready.'
b 'If I *were ever to be* in Mr Walsh's position, I wouldn't fire in the air.'
c '*If it weren't for* this kind of protest, farmers would think they could do what they liked.'
d '*If it hadn't been for* Mr Walsh's courage, untold damage could have been done.'

These four comments were made by three different people:
1 Sally, an active, often militant campaigner for animal rights;
2 Tom, someone who is extremely angered by people like Sally;
3 Anne, someone with no strong views on the subject.
Who do you think made which comment? Who spoke twice? Give reasons.

C2 Study these three conditional forms with their initial inversion. Then again say which of the three people you think said which of the three sentences.

  a '*Should* this organisation one day *get* its way, (= If this organisation gets/were to get its way,) animals will/would have about the same rights as humans.'

  b '*Were* there *to be* a referendum on the issue, (= If there was/were to be a referendum,) the result would probably be quite close.'

  c '*Had* the Animal Liberation movement *existed* 50 years ago, (= If the Animal Liberation movement had existed 50 years ago,) millions of animals' lives would have been saved.'

C3 Replacements for *if*

Notice the alternatives we have for *if* in the following sentences and again decide which of the three people (in **C1**) were responsible for these comments.

  a 'I'm not opposed to protest occasionally, *providing/provided (that)* the law isn't broken.'

  b 'Millions of animals will die or be tortured *unless* we meet violence with violence.'

  c '*Suppose/Supposing* you were a caged animal, would you want petitions signed on your behalf, or would you want to be let out?'

  d '*In the (unlikely) event of* these experiments being stopped, medical science would be set back several years at a stroke.'

  e 'I don't really object to animals being killed for our purposes, *as long as/so long as* it's done with the minimum of suffering.'

  f '*But for* (= If it weren't for/hadn't been for) these experiments, thousands of human beings would already have died and thousands more would die in years to come.'

  g 'The protests will stop *on condition that* the butchery stops, too.'

A note on *unless*

'You won't pass the exam unless you work hard / if you don't work hard.'
'Oh he would pass the exam, unless he went to sleep / provided he didn't go to sleep.'

Although *unless* is doing a different job in these two sentences, both can be transformed: '*The only way* you will pass the exam is if you work hard' and '*The only way/reason* he would not pass the exam is if he went to sleep.' If such a transformation is not possible, (e.g. with: 'If I don't finish, I'll tell you' and 'It wouldn't matter if he didn't come') then *unless* should not be used. (*Unless* is not simply *if not!*) *Unless* also popularly introduces an afterthought, with the italicised phrases below:
'We'll do a test, unless *of course/for any reason/by any chance* you'd prefer not to.'

C4 To activate the above points, rewrite the sentences given below using the prompt words which follow each of them.

1 He'd have won the race but for that burst tyre. (*If that tyre . . .*)
2 I'd be very grateful if you'd give him my regards; that's if you see him, of course. (*Should . . .*)
3 You'd see a big swing to the left if there was a general election this year. (*Were . . .*)
4 I wouldn't have stood a chance of passing without your help. (*If it . . .*)
5 His presence would have ensured a more organised meeting. (*Had . . .*)
6 The only thing that might prevent us being there on time is a breakdown. (. . ., *provided that . . .*)
7 Given the choice, how many hours a day would you work? (*Supposing . . .*)
8 The weather is the only thing that stops me being completely happy here. (*If it . . .*)
9 If arrested, don't say anything you think might incriminate you. (*Should . . .*)
10 If you should by any chance get lost, just telephone us. (*In the unlikely event . . .*)

D Read and discuss

In small groups read together this extract from a Declaration of Animal Rights.
After reading each Article, discuss
- to what extent it has already been generally accepted.
- whether it is reasonable and practical to put it into practice.
- what would have to be done for it to be fully implemented.
- what consequences that implementation would have.

Universal declaration of animal rights

ARTICLE 1
All animals are born free and have the same rights to life.

ARTICLE 2
1. Every animal has the right to respect.
2. Man, as an animal species, may not exterminate other animals or violate the above-mentioned right by exploiting them; he has a duty to put his knowledge at the service of animals.
3. Every animal has the right to the attention, care and protection of Man.

ARTICLE 3
1. No animal shall be subjected either to maltreatment or to acts of cruelty.
2. Where the killing of an animal is necessary, it shall be instantaneous, painless and not cause distress.

ARTICLE 4
1. Every animal of a wild species has the right to live freely in its own natural land, air or aquatic environment and to reproduce.
2. Any deprivation of liberty, even for educational purposes, is contrary to this right.

ARTICLE 5
1. Every animal of a species traditionally living in association with Man has the right to live and grow at the rate and in the conditions of life and liberty proper to that species.
2. Any change in this rate or these conditions made by Man for commercial ends is contrary to this right.

ARTICLE 6
1. Every animal which Man chooses for a companion has the right to a lifespan corresponding to its natural one.
2 To abandon an animal is a cruel and degrading act.

ARTICLE 7
Every working animal has the right to a reasonable limitation of its working hours and work intensity and to restorative nourishment and rest.

ARTICLE 8
1. Experimentation on animals, whether medical, scientific, commercial or of any other nature, that involves physical or psychological suffering is incompatible with the animals' rights.
2. Substitute techniques should be utilised and developed.

ARTICLE 9
When animals are reared for food, they should be fed, housed, transported and slaughtered without any anxiety or pain being caused to them.

ARTICLE 10
1. No animal shall be used for human entertainment.
2. Animal exhibitions and entertainments involving animals are incompatible with animal dignity.

E Listening

 E1 You are going to hear Mrs Weston, a passionate believer in animal rights. Consider these questions as you listen.
1 What exactly did Mrs Weston do at a recent circus? Why?
2 How does she refute:
   a the suggestion that conditions for circus animals are not really so bad?
   b the accusation that she is depriving children of pleasure and education?

 E2 Listen again, then try to contextualise these phrases from the interview.
When were they said, why, or in response to what?
1 the cats
2 too soon to say
3 keeping our fingers crossed
4 an unqualified 'yes'
5 endangered species
6 doing normal things

F Functions: expressing criticism and regret, and comparing reality and appearance

F1 Study these eight critical sentences, arranged according to their directness.

Why (on earth) do you waste it like this?
You spend it as if it was water!   *You really should spend a lot less.*
It's time you tried to economise.   *I wish you wouldn't just throw it away.*
You might try and cut down a little.   *You could (always) cut out a few things.*
I'd rather/ I'd sooner you didn't spend quite so much.

Work out a variety of things you might say, using these structures, to someone who:
1 is always interfering in your affairs.
2 drives the car you share like a madman.
3 doesn't bother to control or train his enormous sheepdog.

F2 Now consider these eight criticisms, commenting on a past circumstance or event.

Why(ever) didn't you tell me before?   *It was as if I hadn't existed!*
You should have informed me sooner.   *I wish you'd got in touch with me earlier.*
You might have tried to contact me.   *You could (at least) have rung me.*
I'd sooner you had let me know in advance.
I'd rather you hadn't kept me in the dark.

Using these structures, think of all the ways you might criticise,
1 the person who was an hour late picking you up – in jeans! – to take you – by bus! – to a restaurant where, having no reservation, you had to wait ages for a table, at which you were eventually served one of the worst meals you have ever had!
2 a parent who, a long time ago, installed you in a private boarding school at the age of eight, sent you abroad for your holidays, bought you ridiculously expensive presents, clothes etc., and visited you once a year.

F3 Notes on *I wish* and *as if*

1 After *I wish/Don't you wish . . .?*, the tense of the verb is conventionally as it would be in an 'unreal' if-clause.
I wish we had more time. (We haven't!)
I wish I was/were coming with you. (I'm not!)
I wish you didn't have to go. (You do!)

I wish+ would indicates some future change in the status quo, however unlikely, is desirable. Compare: *I wish you spoke English. / I wish you would speak English.* The first suggests you can't/don't speak the language, the second that you can but for some reason won't.
Note: *I wish I would . . .* will never be natural.

Make sentences from these prompts.
a I wish / not rain / at the moment
b I wish / this rain / stop; / want/ go out
c I wish / this rain / come / last month
d I wish / not rain / so much / here

2 If, after *as if*, you are expressing a realistic, plausible idea, the tense sequence is 'normal'; for example:
It looks as if it's going to rain.
If the idea is unreal or very unlikely, recall unreal if-clauses:
This room looks as if a bomb had hit it.

Find a verb to complete these sentences:
a In spite of everything you say, it sounds as if you ( ) a good time last night.
b This homework looks as if a spider ( ) it.
c No, thank you. I remember you dance as if you ( ) two left feet.
d She works as if her life ( ) on the result.
e Sit down. Relax. You look as if you ( ) a hard day.
f You're eating as if you (never) a knife and fork before!

G Vocabulary

G1 Look carefully at this strange-looking creature for a while and at the vocabulary items listed on the right. Then test each other in pairs on the various parts of the creature.

tail	mane
hind legs	trunk
stripes	horn
spots	whiskers
fur	beak
scales	shell
wing	tentacles
hoof/hooves	tusk
paw	pouch
claw	fins
hump	feelers/antennae

G2 Look at the picture of the hedgehog and its dictionary definition on the right, and then look at the way it might well be described in everyday conversation, below.

hedgehog: small spiny nocturnal pig-snouted insectivorous mammal of genus Erinaceus

'Well, it's a smallish sort of animal, with lots of prickles, quite sharp enough to prick your skin, and it's got a face like a rat, and when it feels threatened or thinks it's in danger, it rolls itself into a little ball, that's it's kind of defence; yes, and you often see them by the side of the road, 'cause they seem to get caught by cars in the road quite a lot; don't know what they eat.'

In groups of three or four, describe an animal to each other, without giving its name (if you know it!), and see if eventually you can help each other to find out what it's called.

G3 A team quiz

1 Which of these hasn't got a shell?
  a a snail **b** a tortoise **c** a turtle **d** a crab **e** an octopus
2 Which of these insects doesn't sting?
  a an ant **b** a wasp **c** a bee **d** a ladybird **e** a scorpion
3 Which of these creatures will never bite you?
  a a mosquito **b** a flea **c** a butterfly **d** a bat **e** a snake
4 Which of these has spots rather than stripes?
  a a leopard **b** a tiger **c** a zebra **d** a skunk
5 Which of these hasn't got horns?
  a a rhino(ceros) **b** a bull **c** a goat **d** a reindeer **e** a camel
6 Which of these is not a mammal?
  a a porpoise **b** a dolphin **c** a shark **d** a whale **e** an otter
7 Which of these birds can fly?
  a a penguin **b** an emu **c** an ostrich **d** a goose **e** a kiwi
8 Which of these has most legs?
  a a beetle **b** a worm **c** a piranha fish **d** a spider **e** a centipede

9 Which of these animals is not extinct?

    a a mammoth   **b** a dinosaur   **c** a buffalo   **d** a pterodactyl   **e** a dodo

10 Which of these is not a mythical creature?

    a a dragon   **b** a unicorn   **c** a chameleon   **d** a mermaid   **e** a centaur

Give one example of each of the following:

11 a nocturnal animal **12** a marsupial **13** an animal that hibernates **14** an animal with a hump
15 an amphibian **16** a rodent **17** a species of vermin **18** a wading bird **19** a carnivorous
animal **20** a bird of prey

Still in teams, compose ten further questions for the other groups to answer.

H Exercises for homework

H1 Find one suitable word for each of the blanks in this text.

I agreed to it coming on (1) that the children fed and looked after it. (2) I known that in fact I (3) be left to deal with the monster single-handed, I would have put my foot down and (4) no. Everyone loves it, except me; no one feeds it, except me. (5) for my ridiculous sense of duty, the thing would have (6) to death long ago. And yet, (7) there to be a popularity poll among the females in the house, the creature (8) win hands down. It refuses point-blank to be picked up, (9) it is by one of the children. Me it scratches, kicks and eyes threateningly, as if it (10) my deep-seated dislike of it. It never actually attacks me. In a way, I would rather it (11). Then I (12) have an excuse for hastening its departure. Each night, as I chase it panting round the garden back into its cage, I desperately (13) it would (14) a hole in the fence. But it appears to appreciate the home comforts we offer. If it (15) not (16) its vandalism, we would have a pleasant show of daffodils and tulips at this time of the year. Our garden is brown. In the unlikely (17) of our ever (18) another one, I shall insist on a smaller version of the beast. Incidentally, (19) anyone reading this feel the desire to take on a black and white male rabbit, aged $3\frac{1}{2}$, please contact me on this number at any time, as (20) as it is after children's going-to-bed time: . . .

H2 Write a summary of the views expressed in this Unit by the book and your class. Entitle it 'Animals in the Eighties'.

Paragraph 1:
the uses, reasonable and unreasonable, we put animals to.
Paragraph 2:
the Animal Rights movement – what supporters would like to see happen and how they try to achieve their aims.
Paragraph 3:
the effects on our lives if the ideas of Animal Liberation were fully implemented.

Activity 6 (see Teacher's Guide Unit 20)

'You've joined a new gang darling? That's nice – and what does the Animal Liberation League do?'

Answers

Unit 7, page 63

This photo, taken at a pop concert, puts the faces on p 63 in their real context. They are faces of adoration and ecstasy.

Unit 13, page 115

Abbreviations Crossword Puzzle: Solution

¹U	S	²S	R		³M		⁴G	⁵P
S		R		⁶J	P			V
A		N			⁷E	⁸E	C	
				⁹B		S		
¹⁰P	¹¹C		¹²F	B	I		¹³P	S
	I			C				
¹⁴R	A	C			¹⁵P		¹⁶U	
I			¹⁷T	B		T		F
¹⁸P	M		V		¹⁹N	A	T	O

174

Listening comprehension texts

Introductory Unit

TUTOR:	Introductory Unit: 'English: varieties and register'.
	Look at page 10, section **D1**. You're going to hear part of a talk about varieties of English and register. Listen and answer the question. Ready?
LECTURER:	Um, one aspect of language which is often ignored is to do with tact and being tentative. Politeness of course is um very closely tied to being tactful or diplomatic. And in English, British English, that is – er we tend to use a lot of tactful language, mainly to avoid causing embarrassment, offence or . . . or distress. The fact that many foreign learners of English – even though they may speak the language apparently very well or very fluently – the fact that they sometimes cause offence or embarrassment goes to show that they haven't learned appropriate tactful language. Now many English people would prefer to say, for example, 'He passed away (or passed on) last week' instead of the common core, but rather blunt sentence 'He died last week'. In other words, to be tactful, they use what's called a euphemism: 'pass away' in place of 'die'. And in the same way, a woman might be heard to ask for the 'little girls' room' simply to avoid using the word 'toilet' or 'lavatory'.
	But tact is also sometimes shown in the structure a speaker chooses to use. An extreme case is the person who, er, while sitting in a room with friends or relatives, says 'Can you feel a draught coming from somewhere?' – knowing full well that someone's forgotten to close a door or a window. At least one of the other people in the room should take this as a tactful criticism and a request, and go and close the offending door or window.
	And in fact, in order to get along better with people that we live with, um or that we work with, we often tend to make requests, er orders, suggestions and so on as tentative and as polite as we can. And the more formal the situation, if you like, the more tentative we become. For example, 'Post this letter for me on your way home, will you?' can be made to sound more tactful by saying 'Could you possibly post this letter for me on your way home?', and even more tentative and tactful by saying something like 'I don't suppose you'd be good enough to post this letter for me on your way home, would you?'
	So the moral of the lesson is: if you don't want to sound blunt or impolite, and if you don't want to give offence or cause embarrassment or distress of any kind to the person you're talking to, learn to use tactful and tentative forms in your English.
TUTOR:	Now rewind the tape and listen to the talk again for exercise **D2**.
	And that's the end of the Introductory Unit.

Unit 1

TUTOR:	Unit 1. 'Oh, to see ourselves as others see us!'
	Look at page 16, section **B1**, exercise 3, and listen.
WOMAN:	John? It *is* John, isn't it?
MAN:	Well, well! Mary! Fancy meeting you here! I haven't seen you for, oh, what? . . .
WOMAN:	Oh – must be nearly ten years!
MAN:	Mm! Doesn't time fly! Anyway, what are you doing here? Are you living here now, or . . .?
WOMAN:	No, we're down here on holiday. And you?
MAN:	Yes, we're on holiday, too. Where are you staying, by the way?
WOMAN:	At 'The Seaview Hotel'.

Listening comprehension texts

MAN:	Oh, are you? That's not far from our hotel. We're staying at 'The Seagull'. It's quite good, and we're beginning to relax. I've had a very busy year.
WOMAN:	Oh, what are you doing now? I mean, where are you working?
MAN:	Oh, I still work for the same firm.
WOMAN:	And where are you living? In the same house in Manchester?
MAN:	No, we moved about six years ago. But we still live not far from my work. What about you?
WOMAN:	Oh. Well, we moved to London about three months ago because um Bob got a new job, and we're living in a small flat while we try to find a house, but er . . .
MAN:	Yes, it's difficult to find somewhere nowadays, isn't it?
WOMAN:	Anyway, it would be nice to get together again, wouldn't it, um with the families?
MAN:	Yes.
WOMAN:	Do you go out to eat most evenings, or do you eat in the hotel?
MAN:	Oh, we always go out.
WOMAN:	Well, what are you doing on Friday night? Perhaps we could all go out for a meal.
MAN:	Er we're not doing anything particular, I don't think.
WOMAN:	Well, look, I'll have a word with Bob, and we'll ring you at 'The Seagull' and make an arrangement. We're getting to know quite a few nice little restaurants here.
MAN:	Oh, good. We're still finding our way around.
WOMAN:	Well, I must be going. I said I'd meet the children down on the beach.
MAN:	And I've got to do some shopping. We'll expect a call from you then? Or leave a message at Reception.
WOMAN:	Fine. We'll see you Friday, all being well.
MAN:	Yes. And it really is nice to see you again after all this time.
WOMAN:	Yeah. Bye!
MAN:	Bye!
TUTOR:	Now rewind the tape, listen again and make notes.
TUTOR:	Unit 1. Look at page 18, section **D1**, exercise 2. Listen to these two people discussing their banks and the people who work in them.
HE:	I tell you, I'm really fed up with the people in my bank.
SHE:	Why's that?
HE:	Well, they're such a suspicious lot!
SHE:	Suspicious?
HE:	Mmm. Yes, they're always asking me to wait while they go and check that I've got some money in my account; things like that.
SHE:	But that's their job, isn't it?
HE:	Oh, I suppose so, but I mean, one or two of them even ask me for means of identification sometimes, and I've been banking there for nearly two years.
SHE:	Better safe than sorry.
HE:	Mmm, but surely they don't have to be so cold and unfriendly about it. There's this one woman, she's always giving me this sickly, condescending smile, as if it was *her* money I was asking for. And never a word more than is necessary. Really officious, they are.
SHE:	I sometimes wish my bank was a bit more businesslike, like that.
HE:	Oh, they're efficient, I'll give them that.
SHE:	Whenever I go into mine, the cashiers are either fooling around, laughing and joking amongst themselves, or keeping whole queues of people waiting by chatting to the customer at the front about their holidays or . . . And they're so unprofessional. You know, some of the statements I've received from them have been handwritten, would you believe it? And they can't do the simplest

	calculation without making a mistake; can't rely on them for anything.
HE:	Oh, I'd like it if the people in mine were a bit more human, sort of informal and relaxed . . .
SHE:	Well, informality's one thing, but . . . well, for instance, one or two of them *will* call me *Miss* White – it's things like that that really annoy me: carelessness, lack of respect for the customer. There's no excuse for that sort of thing.
HE:	Well, but as you say, at least they're happy and . . .
SHE:	Oh, they're always very cheerful . . . which is something, I suppose.
HE:	Well, it's a lot. At least it doesn't sound like a cemetery, which is what mine is like.
SHE:	Which bank are you with, anyway?
HE:	The Moneywise, for my sins. And you?
SHE:	The Hightown Bank. I've got to go down there now in fact to cash a cheque before I get back to . . .
TUTOR:	And that's the end of Unit 1.

Unit 2

TUTOR:	Unit 2. Attitudes and interests. Look at page 26, section **C1**. Sheila, an 18-year-old schoolgirl, has just taken her 'A' levels, the advanced level exams that pupils take in Britain in order to go on to further education. She's being interviewed on a local radio programme.
INTERVIEWER:	You've just left school, haven't you, Sheila?
SHEILA:	Yes, I finished last Friday.
INTERVIEWER:	You sound relieved.
SHEILA:	Well, yes, I don't mind admitting that I am. I enjoyed school, but I did object to having to go in every day once we'd done all our exams.
INTERVIEWER:	Well, what are you going to do now? Have you made any plans?
SHEILA:	Yes, I intend to go to university. That'll be in September. But it all depends on my 'A' level results.
INTERVIEWER:	You mean, getting into university actually depends on your passing your 'A' level subjects, does it?
SHEILA:	Oh, yes.
INTERVIEWER:	And what did you take at 'A' level?
SHEILA:	French, German and Spanish.
INTERVIEWER:	So I presume you're planning to study languages or linguistics, are you?
SHEILA:	Well, yes . . . although taking subjects at 'A' level doesn't always mean people go on doing the same thing at university.
INTERVIEWER:	No?
SHEILA:	Actually, I've always been interested in doing foreign languages, as you can see, and I'm hoping to do Oriental Studies.
INTERVIEWER:	Are you? That's interesting. That's Japanese and Chinese, is it?
SHEILA:	Mostly Japanese on the course I'm going to take.
INTERVIEWER:	But I would have thought that you would have gone on with one of the languages you took at 'A' level.
SHEILA:	Yes. My parents can't understand that, either. The reason is that I didn't really feel like doing more and more French or German literature – and a lot of university language courses are still like that. And to be honest, I've really had enough of doing prose translations.
INTERVIEWER:	I see. But can you go to university and study a language like Japanese without knowing anything about it?

Listening comprehension texts

SHEILA:	Oh, yes.
INTERVIEWER:	I didn't know that. But what about the future, after university? What do you want to do?
SHEILA:	Well, firstly, I'm interested in getting a degree – and that takes three or four years, remember.
INTERVIEWER:	Work all the time? No student politics, or anything?
SHEILA:	Well, certainly no student politics. That's not my cup of tea! But I don't think I shall work *all* the time, either. I hope to study hard and enjoy myself. Then after that, well, let's hope I can get a job using the language. Japan's beginning to do more and more trade with the West, and we'll need translators and interpreters . . .
INTERVIEWER:	But right now it's just a question of waiting for your results and killing time till September, I presume.
SHEILA:	Not quite 'killing time'. I've got a holiday job in a local hotel. But I really can't wait to get to university. It'll be the first time I've lived away from home and I'm looking forward to it.
TUTOR:	And that's the end of Unit 2.

Unit 3

TUTOR:	Unit 3. Unemployment and redundancy.
	Look at page 30, section **A2**, exercise 1, and listen.
	Anne's 18 and has been unemployed since she left school. She's being interviewed on the same radio programme series as Sheila in Unit 2. This week's programme is devoted to the attitudes of young people towards work and unemployment.
MAN:	Can you in all honesty say you've tried everything? To get a job, I mean.
ANNE:	I think so. I don't know. It seems you can't get a job without experience, and you can't get experience without a job. That's it, in a nutshell.
MAN:	But there are job opportunities schemes now, aren't there, set up by the government. In theory, you get the necessary experience . . .
ANNE:	I know. I know what you're going to say. But in practice, you just work for less money and do all the dirty jobs, the messy work no one else would do. Actually it's just putting things off for a year – at the end of it, the situation's still the same.
MAN:	But you've got some qualifications, haven't you? Some exam passes?
ANNE:	I've got four 'O' levels . . .
MAN:	In which subjects?
ANNE:	Er, biology, cookery – I mean, domestic science – English literature – that's a laugh – and oh, maths.
MAN:	That's a start.
ANNE:	A start!
MAN:	Well, what sort of job did you have your eye on?
ANNE:	With that lot? I used to dream of something involving travel, money, a bit of glamour, fashion perhaps, or something in tourism.
MAN:	And you had no success?
ANNE:	No. It seemed knowing a bit of Shakespeare and the difference between your tibia and your fibula didn't impress them that much.
MAN:	Have you considered secretarial work?
ANNE:	I haven't got shorthand and only a little typing. Anyway, I thought the day of the secretary was past.
MAN:	Something with children, then?
ANNE:	Out of the question! I can't stand kids! – You know, I even tried for a cleaning job

in one of the big hotels in town – two, in fact. They both said they had a – let me think – a 'fully-trained, highly competent staff'. That's how they put it. In other words, 'Get lost!'

MAN: Do you blame the school?

ANNE: My school? No. Yes. I don't know. That last year was horrific. A nightmare. I mean, generally the teachers were a bit out of touch, you know. But towards the end, you really got the feeling they were treating us like oh I don't know, like sheep. And we had the feeling too we were becoming statistics – for some Government figures.

MAN: What, you mean you um . . .

ANNE: Well yes, I mean, you'd look round the class and know that seven or eight out of ten would end up in the dole queue. – It's no wonder you get violence and trouble in a situation – in circumstances like that.

MAN: No. Er, what do you do for money now?

ANNE: I get my standard unemployment benefit – or rather, social security benefit. And I do a bit of baby-sitting on the side, for extra pocket money.

MAN: And how are things at home? You still live at home, don't you?

ANNE: Yes. Oh, I get lectures from Dad, lots of sighs and the odd outburst. It's not very pleasant. At least Mum gives me some sympathy . . .

MAN: What about in yourself? How do you feel?

ANNE: Guilty, in a way, I suppose. Yeah, a sort of guilt. And anger occasionally.

MAN: Against what? The system? Or . . .?

ANNE: I don't know what against. – Every now and then I feel real optimism. For a while. When I've written off for a job and think I've got a chance. Till the letter comes. Or doesn't come. Some of them don't even bother to write at all. That's really annoying – and frustrating.

MAN: Hm.

ANNE: My Dad says I 'lack ambition'. His words, not mine. 'I've got no drive', as he puts it.

MAN: Is he right?

ANNE: Yes, probably.

MAN: What *are* your ambitions?

ANNE: What, immediate or in the future?

MAN: Both.

ANNE: I really don't know. . . . There's always marriage, I suppose. . . . As a last resort.

TUTOR: Now rewind the tape, listen again and do exercise 2.

TUTOR: Unit 3.
Look at page 31, section **A4**, exercise 1, and listen.
Until recently Terry had a very good, seemingly safe position inside what appeared to be a successful company. Then came the axe of redundancy.

ROY: Terry, I wonder if you could tell me first just a little about yourself and and the work you do normally.

TERRY: OK. I'm 38 years old and I've been involved in the electronics industry since 1968, when I left college and went into the merchant navy. And in the last ten years I've worked in sales and marketing of high-technology electronic products.

ROY: So what training did you have for that originally?

TERRY: So . . . OK. I went to um two technical colleges, one in Southampton and one in Bournemouth, and I spent something like five years at college. And I've also had training on particular courses run by marketing improvement companies who show you how to sell the equipment, how to relate to people. And then also technical training on the products that we needed to sell.

ROY: But you are now, I'm – am I right? – unemployed?

TERRY: I'm now unemployed, yes.

Listening comprehension texts

ROY: Um, you've been made redundant, I gather. When were you made redundant and how, or perhaps I should say, why were you made redundant?

TERRY: OK. I was made redundant in October last year, four months ago (ROY: Uha.) – The . . . ma-main reason why I was made redundant was because the company did not achieve the sales it had forecast, and the bank could not stand an overdraft for the the long period of time that they saw coming in the future.

ROY: Did it come as a surprise to you, being made redundant? Or were you warned some time ahead?

TERRY: No. It was an absolute shock. I'd been in the States for six months, doing market and engineering research in the Silicon Valley in California.

ROY: Yeah.

TERRY: I was a Director of the company, and was effectively responsible for all of the sales and marketing operations of that company.

ROY: What was your – if you can remember – what was your very first reaction to being made redundant, because 'redundant' sounds such a final word. I mean, it it actually means 'not needed because there is no work'. What was it – what was your initial reaction?

TERRY: One of complete and utter puzzlement of why it should happen to me. Um . . .

ROY: How did you express that? Or didn't you?

TERRY: I didn't express it in any way. The the reasons why I was made redundant were perfectly clear. Um the company could not continue to exist and it was either make myself and a number of other people redundant or close the company. And obviously the choice was to make a number of people redundant and hopefully save the rest of the company.

ROY: How many redundancies were there, Terry?

TERRY: There were eight people altogether out of a total workforce of 35.

ROY: How do you feel now after, how many months is it?

TERRY: It's four and a half months now.

ROY: Four and a half months. How do you feel now?

TERRY: A little different than then. I've we've come to terms with the fact that I no longer work.

ROY: That's you and your family, you mean?

TERRY: That's my family as well. We've now got to the stage where we realise that a job of work is not just the money that comes in at the end of the day, and all jobs, if you were to pay somebody £50,000 (ROY: Mm) um, the job itself, if that was sitting in a room looking at a blank wall, (ROY: Mm) really wouldn't be worth doing, for that kind of money. There has to be a whole package for a job, which is not just the money, which is the interest in it and what the family that you're trying to support get out of that job as well. If there was a job advertised for a shop assistant (ROY: Yes.) and I could go down and have an interview and take that job, then it would certainly solve my problem in the immediate term (ROY: Well, . . .) of a certain amount of income (ROY: Sure.) which everybody says is the problem. (ROY: Yes.) However, if I have got a certain level of skills and a certain level of knowledge, and my particular interest is in the export of products from the UK into Western Europe, (ROY: Yes.) um then somebody else, who has not got those skills, could also do the shop assistant's job.

ROY: And a final question. If you, going on from what you've said about the way you feel about work and the sort of job that you'd really like, if you didn't really have to find another job, in other words, if you didn't really *have* to earn a living, (TERRY: Yes.) er to keep you and your family, would you still want to work?

TERRY: In essence, I would still want to do something constructive, whether you classify that as work is another thing.

TUTOR: Now rewind the tape, listen again and do exercise 2.

180

Listening comprehension texts

TUTOR:	Unit 3. Look at page 33, section **C3**. Listen to this excerpt from a comedy sketch, in which a man describes the onset of his addiction to television. Notice the way he uses the phrases listed, especially those in your column. Ready?
MAN:	Well, at first I was very strict with myself about what I watched, carefully selective and so on. I suppose at the beginning I wasn't watching more than an hour, hour and a half a day. But then when I got a colour set, it all changed. In a matter of weeks, I was watching breakfast programmes, lunchtime chat shows, and even some of the sport in the afternoons. All at once, my whole way of life seemed to change. In no time at all, I was – how do you say? – 'hooked' on just about all the soap operas, English and American. Then things just went from bad to worse. I mean – in in time I got set a set for nearly every room, and soon I was able to watch, shave and eat a boiled egg simultaneously. It seems now in in next to no time I was being warned about being absent from work; and then in due course, I got the three written warnings, of course, and and finally the sack. At the moment I'm having treatment down at the hospital, which perhaps will help, but in the past, I used to be quite an active person, you know, squash, tennis, that sort of thing. Now I rarely leave the house. I don't know what will happen in the future. At present I'm trying to limit myself to six hours' viewing a day, trying to cut out things like 'News in Welsh' and 'Play Group for the Under Fives'. It's just about proving possible, but it is a strain. I'm hopeful in the short term the treatment will have some effect; whether it'll work in the long run, I I just don't know. I suppose in the end it's just a question of willpower.
TUTOR:	If you wish to listen again, rewind the tape.
TUTOR:	Unit 3. Look at page 35, section **E3**. You're going to hear four colleagues arguing about the pros and cons of the 'new national service' described on page 35, **E1**. Listen, and as you do so, tick the phrases they use from the lists in **E2**.
GUY:	. . . for young people instead of being on the dole to er do something useful for the community.
ROGER: GUY:	Oh, I heard about that on the radio. (GUY: Mm.) It's just rub – it's stupid, I think. Why?
ROGER:	Well, it's just disguising unemployment, isn't it?
GUY:	Well, I mean, they're paying, the Government's paying money to these people for doing nothing. Why don't they . . . I mean, surely it it makes sense to to pay them for doing something?
ROGER:	It doesn't solve the basic problem, . . . as far as I can see.
GUY:	Not in the very long term, but sur – but but don't you see that for a year or two at least, it would give these people something useful to do with their lives. Then maybe that would lead on to other things.
ROGER:	Yes, . . .
JILL:	But who says it's something useful? Are they going to be found useful jobs to do? (ROGER: Yes.) Aren't you overlooking the fact that some of these kids have had no training whatsoever and they're being paid to do something to keep them off the streets?
ROGER:	Yes, but I I . . .
GUY:	That's true, I suppose. But that, that, that in itself is is something, isn't it? Er to . . . even if they're not fully prepared for this sort of work. I mean, at least they're doing something (ROGER: Yes, but . . .) more useful than . . .

Listening comprehension texts

ROGER: Are you going . . .? Are you telling me er that they they don't know that all they're doing is simply filling in two years because they can't get a job?

GUY: Well, that that may be true, but, I mean, look at it from the other point of view as well: that er the the community would benefit from what they're doing. (ROGER: Yes.) I mean, it would help things like the the environment. They could they could clean up our cities. They they could do a lot, I would have thought. Er, . . . (ROGER: Yes, but . . .) Don't you think so, Roy?

ROY: Yeah, I agree with er with you; it's um . . . I think they could be very helpful to the community.

ROGER: That, that's absolutely true, I'm sure they could, in in a sense. But they'd know very well that they were being exploited really; cheap labour! (JILL: Yes, I . . .) (GUY: But, but . . .) Purely cheap labour. They're not producing any wealth.

GUY: What, what point are you making? That just for these people it would be a bad thing er, worse than what they feel at present about being unemployed?

ROGER: I I think it . . . I think it's . . . I . . . As far as I can see, it's er, it's just er it it's it's it's sleight of hand. Er, economic sleight of hand.

ROY: ⎧ Oh, come on. Come on. What do you mean, economic sleight . . .
GUY: ⎨ That's nonsense.
ROY: ⎩ . . . of hand?

ROGER: And their problem is that these people haven't got any jobs, so they just say, 'All right, we'll get them to work for for low money . . . (ROY: I think there's . . .) . . . doing doing doing things er just to to er try to er', I was going to say, 'kid them along, that they've got, they've got a useful function in society'. I mean, basically they they they they haven't solved the problem of er creating jobs that really make money . . . for people.

ROY: But I'm . . .

JILL: Yeah, but it's it's . . . It depends on what you mean by 'a job'. Are they going to be trained or are they just going to be sent into a factory to do a a job that anyone can do, whether they're 50 or 15.

GUY: I think both of you, you seem to be forgetting that it does work in other countries. I mean, it's been proved that it it can work.

JILL: ⎧ I don't think it will work here. We've got too many . . .
ROGER: ⎨ No, I . . .
JILL: ⎩ . . . unemployed.

ROGER: I I don't think, I I don't think . . . I I think it's yet to be proved . . .

TUTOR: And that's the end of Unit 3.

Unit 4

TUTOR: Unit 4. Quality before Quantity. Look at page 41, section **B4**.
Look at what you thought the objects on page 40 were worth and listen to the auctioneer selling them. After each sale, comment on how close or hopeless your guesses were, using the structures in the box.

AUCTIONEER: . . . sold to the gentleman at the back for £200. Thank you. And moving on to lot B – a pair of superb 13-inch solid brass candlesticks – do I hear fifty pounds? Forty pounds? Thirty? I have thirty pounds. Any advance on thirty? I hear forty pounds. Any advance on forty pounds? Fifty? Er, do I hear sixty? In in splendid condition. Do I hear sixty pounds? Thank you, sir. Sixty pounds. Can I say seventy? Seventy. Do I hear eighty? Eighty. Thank you. Any advance on eighty? Ninety. Thank you, madam. Ninety pounds. Going at ninety pounds for the first time . . . going . . . gone. Sold to the lady in the blue and red floral hat for ninety pounds! . . .

. . . And now, lot C, a set of fine amber cut-glass German champagne glasses . . . Can I have an opening bid of fifty pounds? Do I hear forty? Can I say thirty? Thank you. Thirty pounds I'm bid for these . . . Forty. I have forty pounds. Do I hear fifty? Fifty pounds for this beautiful set any home would be proud of. Thank you. Can I say sixty? I have sixty pounds. Sixty pounds. Going at sixty pounds. Sixty pounds, for the second time. Gone. Sold to the gentleman with the beard for sixty pounds!

. . . And now one of the most prized lots for auction here today. Lot D. This Victorian rosewood, chiming grandfather clock – superb workmanship, an exquisite piece. Can I start the bidding at two hundred and fifty pounds? Two hundred? I have a bid of two hundred. Two hundred pounds. Any advance on 200? Can I say 250? I have 250. Thank you, madam. Do I hear 300? 300? I have 300 pounds. 350. I hear 350 pounds. Any advance on . . . 400. Thank you. Can I say 450? I have 450. 450 pounds. Any advance on 450 pounds? 500 pounds. Thank you, sir. 500 pounds. Going at 500 pounds, for the first time. I have 550 pounds. 550 pounds. Do I hear 600? Going at 550 pounds for the first time . . . a second time . . . Sold to the gentlemen in the brown tweed suit for 550 pounds. . . .

And the next lot in your catalogue, lot E, is a magnificent Beckstein upright piano . . .

TUTOR:

Unit 4.
Look at page 42, section **D1** and listen.
Here's an enthusiastic theatregoer who can't stop talking about a performance of Shakespeare's *Othello* that he's just seen.

MAN:

. . . you know, as soon as he came on, I mean, you could feel that something was going to happen, you know what I mean? Incredible! He sort of took your breath away. Must be the best thing he's ever done. Well, he never put a foot wrong, did he? . . . To tell the truth, I mean to say, personally, I've never thought that much of him before, but but this! Oh, it really did something to you. Amazing. Out of this world! At least, that's how I felt about it. I don't know what you think. I mean, you take all the different moods, being proud and then all weak and so on, and then, you know, the bit where he killed her . . . where he actually . . . Oh, great. Honestly, he knocked me out!

TUTOR:

Now you are going to hear a professional theatre critic phoning through to her newspaper office, dictating the review she wants the paper to publish. She's been to the same performance of *Othello*.

CRITIC:

. . . new paragraph. There was the distinct impression . . . right from his first entrance . . . that we were witnessing a great artist . . . in full command of his art. Full stop. It was a performance . . . that even he can rarely have equalled . . . comma . . . perhaps never bettered. Full stop. (Mm. That's nice.) New paragraph. With immaculate timing . . . and an infinite variety of expression . . . and movement . . . comma . . . he took us . . . mercilessly . . . through the whole range of human emotion . . . As (Oh. Sorry.) . . . Full stop. As Othello's . . . early pride . . . and thunderous authority . . give way to unworthy suspicions . . . and doubts . . . comma . . . he displayed . . . a remarkable mastery of technique . . . second to none. Full stop. The horror at his murder . . . and the resignation at his suicide . . . left the audience visibly moved. Full stop. I think that's about a hundred and fifty. OK?

TUTOR:

Now rewind the tape for the critic's report, listen and do exercise **D3**.

Listening comprehension texts

TUTOR:	Unit 4. Look at page 43, section **E**. Listen to the first of four short dialogues, as two friends talk about a shop that one of them is off to spend some money in. Look at **E1**.
GIRL:	What is it, a big store, is it?
MAN:	Well, not exactly, no, not that big.
GIRL:	Not a department store, like C and A?
MAN:	Oh no, nowhere near as big as that.
GIRL:	Oh.
MAN:	And they don't sell anything like as many things as . . .
GIRL:	What *do* they sell?
MAN:	Well, er men's and women's clothes mainly, but quite exclusive stuff – far better than most of the places round here: nice suede jackets, velvet trousers, some lovely pure-silk blouses you'd love . . .
GIRL:	It sounds more like a boutique.
MAN:	Well, it is, but er it's quite a lot bigger than the normal-sized boutique . . . and they've got a wider range of things. They sell some pretty expensive jewellery – 18-carat gold bracelets, that sort of thing, fantastic diamond necklaces, good quality Swiss watches. And they've also got a nice little leather department, where you . . .
GIRL:	Where is it then exactly? . . .
TUTOR:	**E2**. Listen to the same man in the shirt department of that shop. He's getting help from an assistant.
MAN:	Excuse me.
ASSISTANT:	Yes, sir?
MAN:	I've been looking at these shirts over here, but I see they're all 'regular fit'. . . . You haven't got any tighter-fitting ones, have you?
ASSISTANT:	Yes, we have actually. Over here there's our slim-fit range. I expect that's what you're looking for, is it?
MAN:	Oh yes. Yes. Yes, thank you. Oh, er . . . Mmm. All the er. . . the collars here are wide, aren't they? D-Do you sell any with um narrower collars?
ASSISTANT:	Just a few, down here, sir. Striped ones here, and er the plain ones on the other side.
MAN:	Ah yes. Yes. Er . . . Mm . . . Oh. Have you got this one in a in a darker shade of blue . . . and still with the white stripes?
ASSISTANT:	No, I'm sorry, sir. They don't do anything darker than this sky-blue one.
MAN:	Oh. Oh well, I'll take this one, then, if I may.
ASSISTANT:	Yes, of course. Er, do you know what size you are?
TUTOR:	**E3**. Our hero is now at a police station describing the luggage which has been stolen from his hotel room. Listen to his conversation with a local police sergeant.
POLICE:	All right, can you give me a clear description, then, of what this luggage looked like.
MAN:	What, the the bags themselves?
POLICE:	To begin with, yes.
MAN:	Well, the most important one was a large suitcase – it was a sort of browny green, a sort of olive green . . .
POLICE:	What, this sort of colour?
MAN:	Yes, but a bit darker than that, and not so bright. . . . And I think it had a brown plastic handle and a couple of green straps – green plastic straps – going round it, sort of inch-thick straps with metal buckles, you know.
POLICE:	Mmm.

MAN:	And the bag was about as big as this, with a zip going all along one side, but open at the top. And it had a few stick-on labels stuck on the side.
POLICE:	Something like that one over there, was it?
MAN:	Well, yes, similar.
POLICE:	So that's the lot, then, is it?
MAN:	Well, in fact my umbrella is also missing – it was a brand-new er grey and white striped one with an imitation ivory handle . . . quite a . . .
POLICE:	I see. Right, well, if you'd like to sign this statement here . . .
TUTOR:	The man goes on to give the sergeant a description of a suspicious-looking individual seen near his room around the time of the theft. Look at **E4** and listen.
POLICE:	What did he look like, then, this man?
MAN:	Well, he was er . . .
POLICE:	Tall, was he?
MAN:	Well, he was about your height . . . and your build roughly . . . perhaps a bit taller – certainly above average height – and slightly broader round the shoulders . . . quite stocky.
POLICE:	Mmm.
MAN:	And he had quite long brown curly hair . . .
POLICE:	No beard or moustache?
MAN:	Er no, but he was rather unshaven . . . and he was wearing a pair of gold-rimmed glasses . . .
POLICE:	What about his clothes?
MAN:	Er, well, I couldn't see much. He had a a long grey raincoat . . .
POLICE:	How long? Knee-length? Below the knee?
MAN:	Er, nearly to the ground, I think it was.
POLICE:	How old would you say he was?
MAN:	About my age. Late thirties . . . early forties, something like that.
POLICE:	I see.
TUTOR:	And that's the end of Unit 4.

Unit 5

TUTOR:	Unit 5. One man's vision of the future. Look at page 50, section **C1**, and listen. What you're going to hear is part of a sketch from a satirical stage revue. The sketch portrays the kind of interview you might hear on radio or see on television in a current affairs programme.
PRESENTER:	Good evening – and welcome again to 'It's Your World', the weekly programme in which we peer, on your behalf, into the murky depths of politics, ask searching questions on your behalf, listen to politicians babbling away in answer to our questions, so that in the end we can give you – no answers at all. The main question this evening: Is Big Brother Watching You? And to answer this question we have in the studio Mr Charles Noone, head of a large Civil Service Department.
NOONE:	Good evening.
PRESENTER:	Mr Noone, there are rumours that the Government has information on every one of us – computerised information. And what's more, that any civil servant, just by pressing a button, can look up what house I live in, what doctor or dentist I go to, how much I pay in tax, the last time I was stopped by the police for speeding – in

Listening comprehension texts

	fact, all the details of my life. Is this the beginning of a 'Big Brother' state? We've asked you to the studio as the man who wields the power, since the computerised information I've been talking about is said to be in your department.
NOONE:	Well, I am extremely pleased to have been invited to appear on the programme this evening, since it is one to which I regularly listen. Consequently, when I perused my secretary's note which informed me of the producer's invitation for me to appear, I was, not surprisingly, overjoyed. Similarly, when I received written confirmation, I . . .
PRESENTER:	Excuse me, Mr Noone. Could you perhaps answer the question?
NOONE:	I do beg your pardon. What was the question again?
PRESENTER:	Have you got, back in your department, computerised information on each and every one of us? Is Big Brother in fact Watching Us?
NOONE:	I think the answer to that, to be frank and honest, and without beating about the bush, is er yes, er and no. Similarly, one could say, no, er and yes.
PRESENTER:	So you admit that Big Brother is Watching Us.
NOONE:	Let's be quite clear about this. *Someone* knows the house in which you live, *someone* knows the doctor and dentist whom you visit, *someone* knows the occasion on which you were last stopped by the police for speeding – er – thus it is theoretically possible to assemble all this information at one time, er in one place, er . . . Nonetheless, there is no reason to assume that this has already been done, er that it is being done, or that it will be done. Moreover, there are safeguards to prevent anyone saying that this has already been done, that it is being done, or that it will be done.
PRESENTER:	In the same way, and by the same argument then, we don't know whether we're being watched or not. Is that what you're saying?
NOONE:	No. (PRESENTER: Oh.) There is no reason to assume that this has already been done, that it is being done, or that it will be done. I repeat, there is no reason to assume that this has already been done, that it is being done, or that it will be done.
PRESENTER:	So what you're saying is . . .?
NOONE:	This is XY546723. Query regarding computerisation of personal citizen information. There is no reason to assume that this has already been done, that it is being done, or that it will be done. I repeat: there is no reason to assume that this has already been done, that it is being done, or that it will be done . . .
TUTOR:	Now rewind the tape, listen and do exercise **C2**.
	And that's the end of Unit 5.

Unit 6

TUTOR:	Unit 6. Early Days. Look at page 59, Section **E1**.
	Listen to the way these people interact at a party. Notice the way they start the conversations and then keep them going.
SUE:	They tell me you speak Italian. Is that right?
TOM:	Sorry?
SUE:	I gather you know a bit of Italian.
TOM:	Oh, well, a bit, yeah, not that much, but, well . . .
SUE:	How d'you manage that, then?
TOM:	Well, a few years ago I I was redundant, you know, out of a job, and (SUE: Mm.) sort of looking around what to do and saw an advert for a job in Italy. (SUE: Oh.) So I went out with them, a company called ABC er I don't know if you've ever heard of them.
SUE:	I don't think so.

186

TOM:	Well anyway, they needed someone to go out there very quickly.
SUE:	To Italy?
TOM:	Yeah. Er, the chap who'd been working for them apparently had let them down rather suddenly, so, well, they asked me to go.
SUE:	Mm! Lucky you!
TOM:	Yeah, well, I'd been looking around for something different, well, anything really. (SUE: Yeah.) And er well sort of picked up the language um . . .
SUE.	I suppose you learnt it as you went along.
TOM:	Yeah, while I was out there, yeah.
SUE:	Ah.
MIKE:	I hear you went to Southampton University. Is that right?
DICK:	Yes, I did, actually. Seems a long time ago now.
MIKE:	Mm, I suppose so, but er how long ago was it, in fact?
DICK:	Oh, well, er, about '71. I think I graduated in 1971.
MIKE:	'71? How funny!
DICK:	Why?
MIKE:	Well, that's the year my brother er left.
DICK:	Really?
MIKE:	Yes, he was there um . . .
DICK:	Oh, that's a coincidence.
MIKE:	Yeah. I don't suppose you remember someone with um by the name of Harris, do you?
DICK:	Um, Harris? Um. No.
MIKE:	Yes. Donald Harris?
DICK:	No, I don't think so. You don't happen to know what department he was in, do you?
MIKE:	Um. Oh, dear, I should know. Um, no, I I really can't remember. Isn't that terrible?
MARY:	How come you know Jane's sister so well?
ANNA:	What, Gwen?
MARY:	Mm.
ANNA:	Oh, it's a long story.
MARY:	Oh?
ANNA:	Yes, I've um well I've known her on and off for er ooh for about twelve years
MARY:	Really? Long time.
ANNA:	Yeah, or more. Um. No yeah, er, more like fifteen, I think, yeah. (MARY: Mm.) Mm, yeah, it it goes back to to when Jane and I were at school together.
MARY:	Oh, yeah? Mm.
ANNA:	Mm, well I don't know if you know, but we um we shared a room for our last two terms there.
MARY:	Oh, no. I didn't know that at all.
ANNA:	Yes. Well, well one weekend well, we weren't doing anything special and um well she invited me back to her place. (MARY: Mm.) You know, for the for the weekend.
MARY:	Oh, you got on well together, then?
ANNA:	Oh yes. Well, well I mean, we'd been living in the same room for nearly a year, (MARY: Mm.) and um d'you know, she she'd never even told me she had a sister.
MARY:	How strange!
ANNA:	Yeah, well . . . Anyway, when we arrived, well just happened to be the week when when, you know, the family was . . .
TUTOR:	If you need to listen to the conversations again, rewind the tape.

Listening comprehension texts

Unit 7

TUTOR:	Unit 7. 'It's written all over your face – or is it?' Look at the photos on page 63 and listen. You're going to hear part of a radio programme called 'The Book Programme'. Listen and do exercise 2.
CHAIRMAN:	. . . following that review of the latest biography of George Orwell, on to our 'fun spot' for this week. We're giving each of our panellists in the studio five numbered photographs of young ladies' faces . . .
MARCIA:	What's this?
DEREK:	She's quite beautiful.
RAY:	I thought this was 'The Book Programme', not 'Photographer's World'!
CHAIRMAN:	. . . as you can hear, they're causing some comment. If you'll allow me, panel, please, for the benefit of yourselves and our listeners, I should explain that we've taken these photos from a book published some years ago. The book is called *The Human Face*. It was written by John Liggett and published by Constable. Some of you may have seen it when it was . . .
DEREK:	Yes, I do remember seeing it, but it was some years ago.
CHAIRMAN:	Well, Derek, if you remember the photos, please say nothing.
DEREK:	No, they don't look familiar.
CHAIRMAN:	Good. Well, what I want you all to do is to describe the photos briefly and then say what emotions you think are being expressed. Marcia?
MARCIA:	Well, the first one shows a girl just staring at the camera – or at something. I suppose she could be day-dreaming . . . Or perhaps that's an expression of fascination. I don't know. It's interesting that we can all recognise facial expressions like crying with pain, or scowling in anger, or the difference between a genuine smile and a smirk – but it's not always that easy, is it?
CHAIRMAN:	Ray, you wanted to say something.
RAY:	Yes, Marcia's right. I agree, it's difficult. The second photo shows a girl with eyes almost closed and the knuckles of both hands held up to her chin. I wonder if she's just about to burst into tears, or whether she could be sighing in ecstasy. It's very difficult to tell . . .
DEREK:	Yes. I mean – the girl in the third photo looks as though she's laughing at a joke – she certainly looks very happy: her mouth, eyes and cheeks tell you that – but you often can't really judge people's emotions just from the expression on their face. You need to know what's going on round the person, you need to know the context: where the person is, what other people are doing, what's just happened or what's just about to happen, and so on. I'm always amazed at how hotel receptionists and air hostesses manage to smile all the time . . .
MARCIA:	To quote Hamlet, 'A man may smile and smile, and be a villain'. Or at least I think it was Hamlet.
DEREK:	Yes, it was. But they do, don't they?
RAY:	Yes, yes but we all know it's a simulated smile, a a facial expression that we, the public, expect to see, regardless of what they might be thinking.
CHAIRMAN:	Er, may I interrupt a moment, please, and bring you back to the straight and narrow . . .
MARCIA:	Of course, dear, you always do. That's your job here.
CHAIRMAN:	Thank you, Marcia. You're too kind. What about the last two photos, Ray?
RAY:	Well, I'm not sure whether the girl in the fourth photo is laughing or crying – or doing both. But I'm pretty sure the girl in the fifth picture – the the girl with the long blond hair – is screaming.
MARCIA:	I agree. But the question is: is she screaming with terror? –
DEREK:	Or pleasure?
CHAIRMAN:	Yes, that's the puzzle, isn't it? The author devotes a whole chapter to the subject

of how well or how badly we judge people's emotions from their faces. But to put you out of your misery. I can tell you now that . . .

TUTOR: Now pause the tape until after you have discussed questions 2a, b and c.

TUTOR: Now listen to the end of the 'fun spot' of the programme and do exercise 3.

CHAIRMAN: . . . The author devotes a whole chapter to the subject of how well or how badly we judge people's emotions from their faces. But to put you out of your misery, I can tell you now that all these girls were in the same place at the same time and were expressing very similar emotions, as you'll see if you look at page 174. They were photographed at a pop concert and all are quite clearly faces of adoration and ecstasy.

MARCIA: Well now our questions are answered . . .

DEREK: We didn't do too badly, did we?

MARCIA: No, I don't think we did. What I was going to say was: can you give us the title of the book again, please? It sounds like an ideal birthday present for someone.

CHAIRMAN: Yes, it does, and I can certainly recommend it. A fascinating book. The title again: *The Human Face*. Author: John Liggett. Published by Constable . . .

Unit 8

TUTOR: Unit 8. 'So that's how it's done!'
Look at page 74, section **D1**, and listen.
You're going to hear part of a commentary which describes some of the processes during the manufacture of pottery. The commentary is linked to the six slides below, but the slides are not in the correct order. Your task is to listen carefully and put the slides A–F in the correct order according to the commentary. Ready?

SPEAKER: . . . and the plates are left to dry out slowly.

(One.) The dried pottery – cups, plates, saucers, jugs and so on – is now ready for finishing. After the sharp edges have been scraped off with a scalpel, any surface defects are smoothed over with a sponge by the people you see working in this section of the pottery known as the 'fettling' department.

(Two.) Here, any casting marks are removed by smoothing the article with a sponge and water. This is what the woman is doing here. 'Casting marks' are those marks or ridges which may have been left on the article when it was 'cast' in a mould. This hand-finishing also involves inspection, and any pottery not up to standard is rejected at this stage of production.

(Three.) The finished, unfired pottery is then brought into this warm drying room where more of the water in the clay evaporates. It's then much paler in colour. This slide shows coffee pots, vases, flower pots and Poole dolphins drying. Poole Pottery is famous for its dolphins, which you can see on the middle two shelves. The girl is inspecting a plant pot holder.

(Four.) Now ready for its first firing, the pottery is taken to this tunnel kiln. (A 'kiln' is the name given to an oven in which pottery is fired or baked.) A long, quite low fire brick structure, the biscuit kiln is fitted with rails on which trolleys travel down the tunnel, as you can see in this slide. Only the centre section of the kiln is heated by gas.

(Five.) The kiln trolleys are carefully stacked with pottery. They enter the kiln at one end: as one trolley goes in, another discharges at the other end.

Listening comprehension texts

As the pottery progresses in stages down the tunnel, it heats up, until it is at its maximum temperature in the centre furnace section, after which it gradually cools as it reaches the exit.

(Six.) After spending 29 hours in the tunnel kiln, the pottery is allowed to cool off. It's now at what is called the 'biscuit' stage - strong, unglazed and porous – like the layers of dishes, flower pots and other articles you see stacked on *this* trolley. The firing temperature depends of course on the ingredients of the earthenware mix, but it will be a carefully regulated temperature of over 1,000° Centigrade.

TUTOR:
Now check your answers. Then rewind the tape, listen again and make notes for **D2**. Ready?
And that's the end of Unit 8.

Unit 9

TUTOR:
Unit 9.
Look at page 82, section **C1**. While the others are reading the article, listen to this radio news item. It's about the same man. Ready?

NEWSREADER:
. . . And finally tonight, the heartwarming story of Leo, the tramp, who lost his home today, when two British Telecom employees came and . . . took it away. It was only a two-man job because Leo's home for the past five and a half months has been an out-of-order South London telephone kiosk. Rastafarian Leo, of Jamaican origin and thought to be in his early fifties, last night spent his first night for a long time away from home. He was in fact in police cells at Clapham. And this morning, while he was in court on one drunk and disorderly charge and one of misusing public property, the men from Telecom swooped.
But Leo has more friends than perhaps he had imagined. By lunchtime, neighbours had rallied round and collected clothes, food and cash totalling over £100. And this afternoon, just before closing time, Leo went off to the local Lloyds bank to open his first ever account. When asked how he felt about being homeless, he said, 'People are very kind. Now it's a lovely sunny day, and I just want to walk.' And with that he headed off smiling to a hostel – temporary lodgings, he assured us, until he can find accommodation that's more like what he's used to.

TUTOR:
Look at page 82, section **C3**. While the others are reading the article, listen to this radio news item. It's about the same man. Ready?

NEWSREADER:
. . . It seems that trouble is brewing up there in East Anglia over a small pine-wood hut, not much bigger than an ordinary garden shed. The hut, owned by Mr Michael Mease, a retired builder and widower, is now a tiny island in a piece of Northamptonshire that belongs to a large property development company. The company has succeeded in buying up all the land in the area except the offending hut – home for Mr Mease since the mid-sixties. He said last night: 'I'm too old to move. I'm 60 next month.' He added that he had set his heart on retiring in his four-by-three-metre home, and nobody was going to take it away from him.
A spokesman for the development company warned that if Mr Mease continued to hold out, they would be forced to take legal action to have him removed. He claimed that an extremely generous offer had been made, pointing out that he, Mr Mease, would be making a 3,000 per cent profit if he took it up. When asked if another higher offer might be forthcoming, the spokesman declined to comment. And a final word from Mr Mease. He told our reporter: 'I suppose I could afford to

live in a poky little flat in some ghastly tower block, but I've got everything I want here. It's healthy. I'm happy. I'm staying.'

TUTOR:	Unit 9. Look at page 82, section **D1**. You're going to hear a woman telling a friend about an experience she had. Listen and then answer the question. Ready?
WOMAN:	Yes, well I went along to one optician . . .
FRIEND:	Yes?
WOMAN:	. . . and he tested my eyes, and he said that I was slightly long-sighted . . .
FRIEND:	Oh, really?
WOMAN:	. . . and advised me to start wearing glasses for reading.
FRIEND:	Oh, dear!
WOMAN:	But I didn't like the sound of that, so I got a second opinion, and the second chap told me I was quite seriously short-sighted.
FRIEND:	How strange!
WOMAN:	So anyway, well in despair, I found a third one who said she thought I had perfect eyesight and would probably never ever need to wear glasses.
FRIEND:	Incredible!
TUTOR:	If you wish to listen again, rewind the tape. And that's the end of Unit 9.

Unit 10

TUTOR:	Unit 10. 'It takes all sorts . . .' Look at page 88, section **B1**. You're going to hear a conversation with Mrs Kaye who's talking about her particular fear.
GUY:	Er because I gather from er our earlier conversations that basically you're afraid of trees. Am I right?
MRS KAYE:	Not afraid.
GUY:	No?
MRS KAYE:	Petrified!
GUY:	Petrified? Er can I sort of a ask you wh what it is about trees that worries you? That frightens you?
MRS KAYE:	I just don't like them.
GUY:	Mm. I mean, how how bad is this? I mean, if you had to walk – shall we say a kilometre? – at night through a a an avenue with trees on either side, would that be possible?
MRS KAYE:	I wouldn't ever be in that situation. I cannot stand trees.
GUY:	You couldn't walk alone through a a tree-lined avenue?
MRS KAYE:	No. I can't even walk through a forest on a nice sunny day.
GUY:	I see. You were telling me earlier that er there was a chance of you moving house, I think. Er, . . .
MRS KAYE:	That's right.
GUY:	From your your present house.
MRS KAYE:	Yes.
GUY:	Er and there was some problem about it being surrounded by trees er, am I right?
MRS KAYE:	Yes, it was. We were looking at several houses, (GUY: Mm.) and we('ve?) liked the details when we read them of this particular house; but when we got there, it was at the end of a long lane and it was totally surrounded by trees. We stopped the car, (GUY: Mm.) and I wouldn't even get out of the car. My husband went to

look at the house and said, 'Oh, it's perfect; you won't mind about the trees'.

GUY: He liked it?

MRS KAYE: Oh, he loved it.

GUY: Mm.

MRS KAYE: And it was. It was an ideal house. But there was no way I could live among trees. I did once.

GUY: But don't you think if you had gone there to live, you would have got used to it? Perhaps you would've . . .

MRS KAYE: No. No, oh no. Never. It's not that kind of a fear. It's a very very deep-seated fear.

GUY: Mm.

MRS KAYE: If I'm out for an afternoon, and we're forced to go near some trees – in a car it's not too bad, because I feel safe, but if we have to get out and walk near trees – I get a horrible sensation that they're going to close in on me. I feel trapped. I just want to run.

GUY: Mm. What about your own garden? Have you got any trees at all in your garden?

MRS KAYE: Two. But they're at the end of the garden. (GUY: Yes.) I don't need to go near those.

GUY: You wouldn't have those nearer the house?

MRS KAYE: No, I wouldn't. I couldn't. I couldn't live in a house with a tree near a window.

GUY: And does this apply to to all trees? Evergreen trees? Deciduous, er . . .

MRS KAYE: Hedges are all right, but . . .

GUY: Hedges?

MRS KAYE: Hedges are fine. But it's just trees. I don't know what it is about them. They give me a sense of impending doom, of evil. I always look at a tree and feel that it's evil.

GUY: If you went into a room that had a a rubber plant or something like that, would that worry you?

MRS KAYE: Oh, that's . . . No, that's totally different.

GUY: That would be all right?

MRS KAYE: Oh yes, they're friendly. But trees are definitely not friendly.

TUTOR: If you wish to listen to the interview again, rewind the tape.

Unit 11

TUTOR: Unit 11. 'Did I ever tell you about . . .?' Look at page 94, section **A1**. You're going to hear Alan telling some friends a couple of jokes involving Americans in Europe. Look at the cartoons and listen.

ALAN: There's one about a . . . Did I tell you about the American farmer?

ROY: An American farmer? No.

ALAN: Yeah, no, there's this American farmer, see, and he's visiting England, and er he's visiting this English farmer in Devon, and showing him round, like, and says: 'What the hell is that over there?' And he says er 'That', he says, 'That's, that's a sheep!' He says: 'That's a sheep?' he says, 'My God!' he says, 'In America, we got mice that are bigger than that!' He says, 'Well, sorry', he says. 'That's, that's a sheep. That's, that's what it is!' So they go on a bit further and he says: 'What, what's that over there?' He said: 'Er, oh that's one of my cows, that is.' He said: 'A cow?' He said, 'For God's sake, we got dogs in America bigger than that.' So they go round a bit further and they arrive back at the farmhouse and he says, he says: 'Is, is that it? You know, that, that's your farm?' He says: 'Yes.' He says: 'We've seen it all?' He says: 'Yeah, yeah.' so er . . . 'Good God', he says er, 'My farm in America', he says, 'takes me all day to drive round it in a car!' And the little man said, 'Yeah', he said, 'I used to have a car like that.'

Listening comprehension texts

ALAN:	Another one about an American; he bought a vineyard, you see, in or in the South of France. And er this guy was visiting him; he said: 'You like to try some of my wine?' So he said: 'Oh yes, be very nice.' So he said: 'Hey, try this; this is my red wine!' So he start(ed?) drinking. 'Oh' He said: 'What's the matter?' He said, 'Well, it's, it's not very nice, is it?' He said: 'Well, it's it's my my red wine', he says, 'I grow it here, you know.' Says, 'Tr, try the white wine.' So he gives him a glass of white wine, and he 'Oh dear, dear, dear, this . . .' 'What, what's wrong?' he says. 'Well, it's, it's horrible, it's, it's too sharp, it's acid,' you know. He said. 'OK, OK,' he says, 'But you don't realise, my own wine this. I produced this', he says, 'Try the rosé.' Gives him a glass of rosé. Drinks it down. 'Oh, oh my God' he said, 'Oh, it's that's the worst of them all', he said. 'Look', he says, 'I don't think you understand', he says. 'You see out there? You see those fields?' he says. 'That's where this wine comes from', he says. 'I make it myself', he says. 'I I it comes from those fields out there.' The man says, 'Mm. Doesn't travel, does it?'
TUTOR:	If you wish to hear the jokes again, rewind the tape.
TUTOR:	Unit 11. Look at page 94, section **A2**. You're going to hear two friends talking about a new play. Listen, then see if you can complete the unfinished sentences on page 94.
GORDON:	Yeah. No, I went to the theatre last night.
NICOLETTE:	Mm. What did you see?
GORDON:	I went to see this play called *The Hired Man*. Have you heard of it?
NICOLETTE:	Wait a minute. Yeah. I think so. Melvyn Bragg?
GORDON:	Yeah. That's It's based on his novel. That's right.
NICOLETTE:	That's right . . . Isn't it his family? His own grandparents? Something like that?
GORDON:	Well, it's based loosely on his own family life. (NICOLETTE: Yeah.) It's a big family saga and it it starts at the end of the last century and goes up to about 1930. (NICOLETTE: Mm.) And the hero (NICOLETTE: Yeah.) is this man called John, who is the hired man of the title, and that means that he works on the land, and he has to go every day to see if there's any work. And of course he doesn't work every day. So when he's gets married and has a child, he um he can't afford to live that sort of life, so he goes to work in the coalmines.
NICOLETTE:	Oh, no! So you've got the agriculture as w – the pits as well.
GORDON:	That's right. (NICOLETTE: I see!) And of course his wife doesn't want to work mm want him to work in the mine, but of course he needs to. He needs the money. (NICOLETTE: Yeah.) Then it goes right through to the First World War. He's got a son and and a daughter by now, and the son –
NICOLETTE:	Is he in the war? Does he go in the war?
GORDON:	Well, he, Yes, he yeah goes into the war. And his son, who's seventeen, who works down the mine as well – (NICOLETTE: Oh.) He lies about his age. He goes to the war and he gets killed (NICOLETTE: Oh, gosh!) And then it eventually the wife dies and the the man decides he wants to go back and work on the land and so he becomes a hired man once again, once he hasn't got these responsibilities.
NICOLETTE:	I see. And is there any . . . Is um I mean – Hang on! It's musical, isn't it? Are(n't?) there songs? Yeah.
GORDON:	That's right. That's what makes it very interesting. It's a musical and there's this this marvellous um almost folk music in it, and it's er (NICOLETTE: Yeah.) so they sing as well as talk, the characters. And it's all very English.
NICOLETTE:	Mm. It sounds rather good actually.
GORDON:	Yes, you must go and see it.
NICOLETTE:	Yeah. Think I might.
TUTOR:	If you wish to listen again, rewind the tape.

Listening comprehension texts

TUTOR:
Unit 11. Now look at page 95, section **A3**.
You're going to hear someone describing a frightening experience he had some years ago. As you listen, look at the picture on page 95 and note down any differences or discrepancies you see between the picture and what you hear. Ready?

RON:
It was a lovely sunny day in Brighton in October, and I'd done some sailing during the summer in a an identical boat – so I thought I'd go out for a sail. So I hired the boat, rigged it, took it down to the the sea, jumped in and sailed off. And it was it was lovely. I had a lovely sail for about an hour. And there are two piers in Brighton, and I just sailed between the two piers. And I was just about to make the last turn to come into the shore to to give the boat back when all of a sudden the wind caught me in a way which I still can't don't understand – and anyway the the long and the short of it was, the next thing I/that happened, I capsized. I was in the water, feeling rather silly, because I was just about to go into the shore. So I – I've been in boats that have capsized before – so I tried to right it, and I couldn't get it up. I don't know why um b partly because I was on my own, I think. And um I made a couple of attempts, and on the second attempt the boat came right over on top of me so that I was actually trapped underneath the boat underneath the water. So there I am, stuck under a boat, very close to one of the piers, which is all encrusted in barnacles and looks very rough and not the sort of thing to go in to. I I'm swimming about underneath the boat, trying to get out. I finally come out of the boat, all tangled up in the ropes, and look up, and there are people on the pier laughing at me. So I think to myself 'Right. Well, I'm going to make a good show of this. I'll get this boat upright again.' So I had another go and failed miserably again. So I'm stuck there with the boat, getting nearer and nearer to the pier, thinking 'Any minute I'm going to be smashed up against the pier.' The shore was a long way away and I thought er this is just the point where I give in. So I signalled up to the people on the um on the pier for help, and fortunately they interpreted it as help, not just a sort of a friendly wave. And um they –

PETER
'There's a man down there waving!'

RON:
Yes, that's right. So er they did at least do something about it, and the inshore rescue boat came to rescue me and I was whisked out of the water – the boat was rescued as well – um whisked away in an ambulance to the hospital and dried out, suffering from cold and exposure.

PETER
But nothing more drastic.

RON:
Nothing more drastic than that, but it was very frightening to be in the water with a boat on top of you/me(?).

TUTOR
If you wish to listen again, rewind the tape.

TUTOR:
Unit 11. Look at page 95, section **A4**.
You're going to hear a bored young man twiddling the dials of his radio in search of some music. Instead of music, all he finds is a number of stations broadcasting sports commentaries. Look at page 95, then listen to try and find out which sports are being covered in the snatches you hear.

. . . So Liliana Pravda coming up for her third and final attempt; quite a fast approach, she takes off. Yes, she's over, clear, the bar's still shaking, but that counts as a clearance – and at a championship record height . . .

. . . Now, with Ferrari disqualified for two false starts, lane six will be empty, as they settle again on their blocks, eyes all fixed on the distant tape, . . . set . . .

. . . Jankovic to Mankovic, through to Stankovic, over the half-way line, he beats Zeissmann, knocks the ball into the penalty area, it's headed away by

Schlummbrunner, but only as far as Smirnoff. Smirnoff crosses to the near post, Bankovic is there, he's onside. No, he's brought down by Hummeldinger! Penalty! No, no, foul! Yes, no, yes, the referee's awarded an indirect free-kick for obstruction. And the crowd don't like it! . . .

. . . Schnaptikov moves across the circle like a caged animal, the right arm straightens and shoots out; Schnaptikov's left hopping on one leg like an overgrown ballet-dancer. Oh. He's got the red flag; now he won't like that – his third no-throw in a row. . . .

. . . She serves, Miss Hooper can't get to it, that's it. Miss Cupido rushes to the net, that's it. She wins 6–2, 6–0, in one of the most one-sided finals we've seen in the whole . . .

. . . here he goes, perfect take-off, there's a tremendous series of movements in mid-air, hitting the water completely vertical. He can expect good marks for that one, certainly enough to keep him in the overall lead . . .

TUTOR:	If you wish to listen again, rewind the tape.
TUTOR:	Unit 11. Now look at page 99, section **E**. You're going to hear different people speaking short sentences to you. You have to consider a suitable response. Choose from within each group of responses on page 99 and indicate by writing 1b or 2d or 3a which response fits which utterance. Look first at Group One. Group One.
GIRL:	Do you think he'll take the exam again, now that he's failed?
MAN:	What do you feel like doing tonight?
BOY:	My landlady wouldn't let me in when I arrived home at four o'clock in the morning.
MOTHER:	There was a pound note inside that paper bag you threw into the dustbin.
TUTOR:	Group Two.
NURSE.	Would you mind taking off your shirt for a moment?
GIRL:	Do you think it's going to snow today?
BOY:	If no one else wants this last biscuit, can I have it?
GIRL:	She's getting married again in the autumn, you know.
TUTOR:	Group Three.
MOTHER:	Our little Johnny didn't throw his dinner on the floor tonight, dear.
BOY:	How many inhabitants has Los Angeles got?
GIRL:	I think there's some blood on your shoe.
BOY:	I shall be glad when this exam is over.
TUTOR:	Group Four
MAN:	Where do you expect to be this time next year?
GIRL:	I felt like giving in my notice when my boss was rude to me like that.
WOMAN:	It seems I know your future employer – a woman called Smythe – we were best friends at school.
WOMAN:	Don't you bother about the washing up; I'll do it myself later.
TUTOR:	Group Five
MAN:	Could anyone here lend me ten pounds for a few days?
WOMAN:	I think it's going to be a nice day, isn't it?
MAN:	Do you mind if I invite your fiancée to spend the weekend with me in Paris?
MAN:	She got really furious when I told her she was more like a man than a woman.

Listening comprehension texts

TUTOR:	Group Six
MAN:	Which day would you rather we went, Saturday or Sunday?
WOMAN:	Have there been any accidents on this road this year?
MAN:	Look, I don't think I'm going to be able to repair that favourite vase of yours I broke.
BOY:	She slapped me when I told her she was old enough to be my mother.
TUTOR:	And that's the end of Unit 11.

Unit 12

TUTOR:	Unit 12. Old age and retirement. Look at page 105, section **B3**, exercise 2a. You're going to hear a conversation between a policeman and an elderly lady who was a witness to an attempted bank robbery. Listen and discuss the questions. Ready?
POLICEMAN:	Now, Mrs Smith, you said you saw everything that happened. Can you tell me about it?
MRS SMITH:	Yes. Well, as I said, I was standing outside the bank chatting to two friends of mine and I saw these two men go into the bank behind me.
POLICEMAN:	And what were they wearing?
MRS SMITH:	I can't remember, but Mrs Powell said she caught sight of a young man wearing dirty jeans.
POLICEMAN:	But Mrs Powell didn't actually see the two men go into the bank, did she?
MRS SMITH:	No, but then her back was turned. She only glanced round to see what I was looking at.
POLICEMAN:	I see. And what happened then?
MRS SMITH:	Well, then I heard a man shout 'Shut up!' – I'm sure it came from the bank – and we all heard a woman scream.
POLICEMAN:	Well, we'll check that. And then what?
MRS SMITH:	Well, we all looked towards the bank er and I felt someone rush past me. He nearly knocked me off my feet.
POLICEMAN:	'He'? You're sure it was a man?
MRS SMITH:	Well, I wasn't at that moment, but then I looked up and caught a glimpse of a young man running in and out of the crowd on the pavement.
POLICEMAN:	I see.
MRS SMITH:	And we all heard people shouting. Oh, and then we all heard the bank alarm go off. It was a terrible din.
POLICEMAN:	Just one thing before I go through it all again and take a statement from you: you said there were two men. Were they together?
MRS SMITH:	Well, I don't know now. I saw them both go towards the door of the bank but the other one was well-dressed, I seem to remember, so I don't know if he went in or not. I didn't actually *see* him go in, to be perfectly honest.
POLICEMAN:	Well, you've been very helpful. Now I'm afraid I shall have to ask you to go through it all again for a statement . . .
TUTOR:	Exercise 2b. Now rewind the tape, listen and take notes.

Listening comprehension texts

Unit 13

TUTOR:	Unit 13. Opinion poll. Look at page 114, section **D1**. You're going to hear a woman being interviewed in the street for an opinion poll. As you listen, look at the extracts from the questionnaire and tick the appropriate boxes according to what the woman says. Ready?
INTERVIEWER:	. . . so I'll put you down there as a 'Don't know'. Fine. Now on to the next question. Six. I'm going to read out things that some people worry about these days, and I'd like you to tell me from this card to what extent, if at all, you've worried about each one in the last 2–3 weeks. All right?
WOMAN:	Yes.
INTERVIEWER:	Well, going through them: first – not having enough money.
WOMAN:	Worried about it in the last 2–3 weeks?
INTERVIEWER:	Yes.
WOMAN:	Oh, quite a lot.
INTERVIEWER:	Uhuh. The education of your children.
WOMAN:	No. Well, we haven't got any children.
INTERVIEWER:	I see. Next – unemployment of yourself or members of your family.
WOMAN:	Er, no, not at all. My husband and I have both got good jobs.
INTERVIEWER:	Fine. Er, nuclear war, or world war.
WOMAN:	Oh, I don't know. I I don't think about it a lot.
INTERVIEWER:	I see. How about your health or your family's health?
WOMAN:	Oh, well, yes. I'm slightly worried about my husband's health at the moment.
INTERVIEWER:	I see. What about relations with your neighbours?
WOMAN:	Oh, yes, we've had a quite a lot of worry to do with neighbours over the past few weeks.
INTERVIEWER:	Mmm. Er – children doesn't apply. (WOMAN: No.) Um, relations with your husband?
WOMAN:	No. No worries at all.
INTERVIEWER:	What about work? Do you worry about how things are going at work?
WOMAN:	No, never. No, I said we've both got good jobs.
INTERVIEWER:	Fine. How about growing old?
WOMAN:	Oh, don't have time to worry.
INTERVIEWER:	Good. Er, do you worry about vandalism or crime in this area?
WOMAN:	Oh, yes. A great deal. We both do.
INTERVIEWER:	And lastly, in this question, do you worry about your housing conditions?
WOMAN:	Oh, just a little, yes.
INTERVIEWER:	Mm. Now there's a further question which I must ask you . . .
INTERVIEWER:	And now to question 8. I'm going to read out a list of things which can affect how happy people are. From this card I'd like you to tell me how happy or unhappy you are with each one. First, the district you live in.
WOMAN:	Oh, um reasonably happy.
INTERVIEWER:	The education you received?
WOMAN:	Well it wasn't very good, I'm afraid, but it could have been a lot worse.
INTERVIEWER:	I see. How about your family life?
WOMAN:	Oh, I'm very happy with my family life.
INTERVIEWER:	Uhuh. And your health?
WOMAN:	Oh, I'm in excellent health
INTERVIEWER:	Good. Your housing conditions?
WOMAN:	Well, as I told you earlier, I'm a little worried about that right at the moment.
INTERVIEWER:	So you're not very happy?
WOMAN:	No.

Listening comprehension texts

INTERVIEWER:	What about your job?
WOMAN:	Oh, both my husband and I are very happy with our jobs.
INTERVIEWER:	Good. Are you happy with your marriage?
WOMAN:	Of course. Extremely.
INTERVIEWER:	How happy are you with the way you use your spare time?
WOMAN:	Oh, mmm – reasonably so. I could do more in my spare time, I suppose, but . . .
INTERVIEWER:	I see. Well, and lastly, how about your standard of living?
WOMAN:	Oh, very happy.
INTERVIEWER:	Good. That's the end of that section, but . . .
TUTOR:	And that's the end of Unit 13.

Unit 14

TUTOR:	Unit 14. Attitudes to the handicapped. Look at page 123, section **D**. Roger, a teacher and writer who suffers from multiple sclerosis and who spends much of his life in a wheelchair, is having a conversation with Guy. Listen to four excerpts from their conversation, beginning with this, Excerpt One. Look at the questions on page 123, then listen. Excerpt One.
GUY:	The actual comment 'Let's move Roger to a better position' (ROGER: Position, yes.) suggests that people may sometimes talk about you as if you were not there. I mean, that happens to all of us, but does it happen (ROGER: That, that that that's right.) particularly to you? Er . . .
ROGER:	Well. Er no, no, it doesn't happen so much to me as it does to some people. But (GUY: Mm.) um because I think one of the things you have to do, the most important things, one of the most important things is to to er to communicate very clearly to people very soon when they meet you that you're not a blithering idiot. (GUY: Mm.) You're not er just because you're so stupid you can't walk, it doesn't mean to say you're so stupid you can't talk. I mean, so so, I can do that. I'm articulate. And I can indicate to people – put them at their ease. But, and they tend to talk to me, not er across me. (GUY: Mm.) Though people do say (it) to my wife: 'How is Roger today?' And I'm sitting there. Yes, that's (GUY: While you're present?) right. I mean, it's um and you feel like saying um 'Would you tell your friend that I'm fine,' you know. You know, you sort of pass messages (GUY: Yeah. Yes, yes.) like this.
TUTOR:	Roger goes on to give an example of people trying to help a disabled person. Look at the questions for Excerpt Two, then listen. Excerpt Two.
ROGER:	There's another thing, er people try and help you, I mean, they say typically on a train, you you get out of the wheelchair to get on the carriage get into the carriage (GUY: Mm.) and you put out your arm to grab the handle and at this point the – cause the porter wants to help, and he doesn't know how, he grabs your arm, which is ironic 'cause it's the only bit that's working properly, and he immobilises it totally, you know. (GUY: Yes.) You're just about to reach out for the the the handrail or or whatever, and suddenly this thing blocks your arm and you can't reach, and you, you know, you have to say very quickly, you have to say: 'Leave me alone!' And they think: well, you know, this guy's not very friendly. But you've got to communicate these things in an instant, because if they don't, you've fallen over. (GUY: Yes.) And then they don't know how to pick you up, or something (GUY: Yes.) you know. They they are just er so sometimes you've got to appear very rude, you know. 'Leave that alone!' (GUY: Mm.) 'No, I can manage, . . .

TUTOR:	In the third excerpt, Guy refers to the yachtsman, Mike Spring, about whom you read on page 122. Look at the questions for Excerpt Three on page 123, then listen. Excerpt Three.
GUY:	Er, we were reading earlier about a a yachtsman who who'd er gone off to the Azores (ROGER: Yes.), I think it was, to almost prove his point, prove that he he could er behave and take part in hobbies as as any able-bodied person. Er, do you you feel there's a part of that instinct in you to er . . .?
ROGER:	Yes. Yes. I'm not going to . . . I'm not going to leap into a yacht and sail from here to to um the South Pole and back, but er what I do feel is: I I I like to um, er, well, I still work, and this is the way I show I'm normal. Because people say to you: 'D'you work?' (GUY: Mm.) as though, you know, that was, that was a (GUY: Yes.) logical impossibility. (GUY: Yes.) I mean, it's just people make all sorts of assumptions about you. It's like seeing um, . . . but every time they see somebody in a wheelchair, they think, well, they they are incapable of economic independence. (GUY: Yes.) A lot of them are, but not all of them.
TUTOR:	In the fourth and last excerpt, Roger is asked about his own personal frustrations and regrets. Look at the questions for Excerpt Four, then listen. Excerpt Four.
GUY:	What in in the course of your life now do you feel most frustrating? What would you like to to be able to do that you are prevented (ROGER: Er.) from doing because of your disability?
ROGER:	Well, I I to do things without an effort. I mean, I'm not in pain, but just to get up and stroll out of the room would be great, you know. And um just not have to er sort of if you decide to go away somewhere, to enquire, you know: Are there any steps and (GUY: Mm.) you know, and just really figure out everything in advance. I mean, it also costs you a lot of money to be disabled. I mean, I went to Switzerland last year for a three-week holiday; it cost me a fortune. 'Cause I can't go on a package tour, (GUY: No.) 'cause the hotels would be unsuitable. I mean, and we had to take the car because er for various reasons you can't hire a car with hand controls. You it it it you can in America, and you can now in Britain but, I mean, I didn't know how to hire one in in in Switzerland, so so that costs money. (GUY: Mm.) You know, you're doing everything privately. But um, you know, it's it's um I I I . . . what would I? . . . Well, I just you know, just like, I feel, when I'm sitting down, I feel normal, but it would be nice just to be able to stroll out of the room and er tear downstairs like I used to (GUY: Mm.) without ha- holding onto the banisters, just just run down, you know. 'Cause inside me there's the same guy.
TUTOR:	And that's the end of Unit 14.

Unit 15

TUTOR:	Unit 15. 'The Play's The Thing . . .' Look at page 126, section **A3**, exercise 1. You've read the synopsis of the play so far in the programme on page 127. Now you're going to hear part of a rehearsal by an amateur dramatic society of a section of Act III. Listen and then answer the questions. Ready?
PRODUCER:	OK. Um, let's hold it there for a moment. Er, very nice so far. The general pace of the thing is good. Just one or two points, though. Um Mary – Now, I think your Lady Bracknell can afford to be even more haughty – um, let me think, yeah, perhaps more plummy and aristocratic, you know. Remember, you're the sort of, how can I put it, you're the 'interrogator' here. Perhaps more severe, um, judicial

Listening comprehension texts

even? And Lorna – now your Miss Prism here – she's, what can I say, devastated to see Lady Bracknell. And then a sort of relief comes seems to come through as she um tells this story she's kept secret for twenty-eight years. By the way, the voice, I think, was just right. Er all of you, the aristocratic bit – fine. And Jack – well – nothing to say, really. It's fine. Now, let's try it again from where Miss Prism comes in with 'I was told you expected me in the vestry' – and and let's keep the tension as the story comes out, OK? Oh, I know what I was going to say – oh, no, it doesn't matter. All right, Lorna, when you're ready.

MISS PRISM:	I was told you expected me in the vestry, dear Canon. I have been waiting for you there for an hour and three-quarters.
LADY BRACKNELL:	Prism! Come here, Prism! Prism! Where is that baby? Twenty-eight years ago, Prism, you left Lord Bracknell's house, Number 104, Upper Grosvenor Square, in charge of a perambulator that contained a baby of the male sex. You never returned. A few weeks later, through the elaborate investigations of the Metropolitan police, the perambulator was discovered at midnight standing by itself in a remote corner of Bayswater. It contained the manuscript of a three-volume novel of more than usually revolting sentimentality. But the baby was not there. Prism! Where is that baby?
MISS PRISM:	Lady Bracknell, I admit with shame that I do not know. I only wish I did. The plain facts of the case are these. On the morning of the day you mention, a day that is for ever branded on my memory, I prepared as usual to take the baby out in its perambulator. I had also with me a somewhat old, but capacious handbag in which I had intended to place the manuscript of a work of fiction that I had written during my few unoccupied hours. In a moment of mental abstraction, for which I can never forgive myself, I deposited the manuscript in the bassinette and placed the baby in the handbag.
JACK:	But where did you deposit the handbag?
MISS PRISM:	Do not ask me, Mr Worthing.
JACK:	Miss Prism, this is a matter of no small importance to me. I insist on knowing where you deposited the handbag that contained that infant.
MISS PRISM:	I left it in the cloakroom of one of the larger railway stations in London.
JACK:	What railway station?
MISS PRISM:	Victoria. The Brighton line.
JACK:	I must retire to my room for a moment. Gwendolen, wait here for me.
GWENDOLEN:	If you are not too long, I will wait here for you all my life.
CHASUBLE:	What do you think this means, Lady Bracknell?
PRODUCER:	OK. Good, it's going well. Now can we just jump the next few lines to where Gwendolen says 'This suspense is terrible'? – in other words, to where Jack comes back in again? OK Gwendolen – when you're ready.
GWENDOLEN:	This suspense is terrible. I hope it will last.
JACK:	Is this the handbag, Miss Prism? Examine it carefully before you speak. The happiness of more than one life depends on your answer.
MISS PRISM:	It seems to be mine. Yes, here is the injury it received through the upsetting of a Gower Street omnibus in younger and happier days. Here is the stain on the lining caused by the explosion of a temperance beverage, an incident that occurred at Leamington. Ah. And here, on the lock, are my initials. I had forgotten that in an extravagant mood I had had them placed there. The bag is undoubtedly mine. I am delighted to have it so unexpectedly restored to me. It has been a great inconvenience being without it all these years.
JACK:	Miss Prism, more is restored to you than this handbag. I was the baby you placed in it.
MISS PRISM:	You?

JACK:	Yes . . . Mother!
MISS PRISM:	Mr Worthing. I am unmarried!
JACK:	Unmarried! I do not deny that that is a serious blow. But after all, who has the right to cast a stone against one who has suffered? Cannot repentance wipe out an act of folly? Why should there be one law for men, and another for women? Mother, I forgive you.
MISS PRISM:	Mr Worthing, there is some error. There is the lady who can tell you who you really are.
JACK:	Lady Bracknell, I hate to seem inquisitive, but would you kindly inform me who I am?
LADY BRACKNELL:	I am afraid that the news I have to give you will not altogether please you. You are the son of my poor sister, Mrs Moncrieff, and consequently Algernon's elder brother.
JACK:	Algy's elder brother! Then I have a brother after all. I knew I had a brother! I always said I had a brother! Thethily – oh, sorry!
PRODUCER:	All right. All right. All right, Jack. Not to worry. It was going very well. So let's go straight on and pick it up from where you say 'Cecily – how could you have ever doubted me?' . . .
TUTOR:	Now rewind the tape, listen again and do exercise 2.
	And rewind the tape again for exercise 3.

Unit 16

TUTOR:	Unit 16. 'I've never been so embarrassed in all my life!' Look at page 139, section **D**. You're going to hear Guy and Roy telling personal experiences. Listen to both, look at section **D1** and answer the questions. Ready?
GUY:	. . . years ago, it was when or ooh I suppose I was just eighteen and I'd recently passed my driving test. Also recently I'd just met this girl. And er (ROY: Did you know about this, . . .?) I wanted to er impress her, naturally enough. Didn't have a car, but I could drive so er she spoke to the to her father and er asked if we could have the car for the afternoon – drive down to the sea. And er I can't remember what car it was, but it was pretty big, pretty nice, quite new, I think. And, only having passed the test a few months before, er I really didn't know much about er how to handle a car on the road. And during that afternoon I had two crashes. You wouldn't believe it, (but) it was absolutely true. Er the first one was, pulling in to get some petrol, I thought I'd judged the wall right, and and scraped the passenger door. As – shaken from this, I mean, she was a bit cross at this, but we we thought, you know, we could explain one accident, but then the – I think I was still shaken when I got to the actual place we were going to. Drove into the car park and this car waited for me to pull round into a parking space and I must have thought he was going to move, I think. And he didn't. And then very slowly I just drove into him. Absolutely awful! Er it it (ROY: What happened when you got back?) Well, er I think I had to explain myself. No, I think, that night she went and explained to her father what had happened. (ROY: Coward!) The driver of the car, I should say, he stalked out of the car, and he was getting on, and he said: 'That was the worst piece of driving I've seen in twenty years.' And I'm not surprised. Absolutely, I mean, straight ahead. I just drove into him, you know, thinking that he was going to move off, and he didn't.
ROY:	Yes, that that reminds me. When somebody mentioned um musicians and er and

and playing and so forth. Um I think it was th- one of the first jobs I ever did as a pianist. I was asked to go and join a drummer and a clarinettist – What a combination! – um at the Working Men's Club for a Saturday evening dance. And I'd nev- as I said, it was about the second time I'd ever played out and er we had to be there at, I don't know, to start at half past seven. So we walked in at er twenty past seven. There were all these people sitting around – anything from fifty up, you know, and all with their pints of beer and all waiting to for this Saturday evening dance, expecting a superb band. And er I'd never been there before, as I say. Th- We went in, I helped the drummer sort of get his kit out, and the clarinettist opened his case and we we got music out – we had music in those days – and I didn't even *try* the piano! Just sat down, opened the lid, put my music up, and er - and the er drummer sort of said gave me the nod, you know, to to start, and I put my hands down on the piano and there was not a sound! The thing was totally dead! All the hammers had gone on the piano! Absolutely dreadful!

TUTOR:

Now rewind the tape, listen again to each separately and make notes for section **D2**.

And that's the end of Unit 16.

Unit 17

TUTOR:

Unit 17. Emergency!
Look at page 147, section **D1**.
You're going to hear two people talking about two different kinds of emergency. The first is from a radio series called 'Drive'.
Listen and make notes. Ready?

INTERVIEWER:

So now we know what to do if a tyre bursts at high speed. But what do you do, for instance, if your windscreen shatters while you're driving along?

MAN:

Yes – a common enough occurrence. If it hasn't happened to you yet, there's every possibility that it will sooner or later – especially with all the grit on our roads. Well, er, the thing you don't do is to grip the steering wheel in a er vice-like grip in absolute panic! Er um the moment the windscreen shatters, you should begin to take your foot off the accelerator. Not completely off, of course, 'cause you might be in heavy traffic with another vehicle right behind you. But certainly slow down and keep going in the direction you've been driving. Some people *will* brake immediately. That's fatal and you should never do that. And you shouldn't swerve, either. Again, you could cause an accident like that. Um when you've slowed down a little, punch through the shattered windscreen – so that you can see where you're going. And then pull in and stop at the earliest opportunity.

INTERVIEWER:

Well, once you've punched through the windscreen, can't you drive on to the nearest garage? I mean, as long as you can see where you're going?

MAN:

Well, we don't think it's advisable. Far better to pull in to the side of the road, or into a lay-by, and clear out more of the glass to give yourself a better view.

INTERVIEWER:

And then drive on?

MAN:

Yes. But you should keep all the windows closed then. Otherwise you run the risk of the rest of the glass collapsing into the car – and all over you and any passengers – because of wind pressure.

INTERVIEWER:

Well, thank you, John. They're all useful tips, I hope you'll agree . . .

TUTOR:

Now listen to the second piece of emergency advice. This is from a 'Safety First' radio spot. Listen and make notes. Ready?

WOMAN:
Electricity is dangerous. It can paralyse, it can cause unconsciousness, it can kill. But accidents will happen. So how can you help if someone receives a paralysing electric shock? The first thing is not to electrocute yourself while helping. If you can, switch off the current, tear the plug out, or rip the cable free. But remember: if you can't do any of these things – or if you can't hook or push a live wire out of the way with a piece of wood or a plastic stick (not metal!) – you should move the victim away from the live wire or machine or whatever he got his shock from. And the way to do that is to make sure you insulate yourself by standing on rubber, a pile of books or newspapers, or wood – and then knock the victim free, again with a piece of wood or plastic. You should never touch the victim with your bare hands or with metal. (Otherwise there'll be *two* electric shock victims!) By the way, this procedure is only safe with ordinary household current: with high-voltage cables, for instance, do nothing until the electricity has been cut off. And stand well back.

And when you have freed the victim from the cause of the shock, you should keep him or her still until medical help can be called. Artificial respiration may be necessary, but leave the treatment of any burns to a doctor or nurse.

TUTOR:
And that's the end of Unit 17.

Unit 18

TUTOR:
Unit 18. 'You are kindly requested . . .'
Look at page 154, section **D1** and listen. Ready?

ANNOUNCER:
. . . And now for the local news, from Ken Barry.

NEWSREADER:
The Director of a local firm has expressed surprise that, unlike many other companies in the area, *his* firm can't get *enough* workers. In an interview, Mr Brian Wide, Director of Hightown Electronics, told us that they are legally required to employ a certain number of disabled people, and that, although they have advertised, they still have three jobs held open for disabled applicants. Further, despite constant advertising, workers are still badly needed for assembly-line work.

Two men who were caught stealing property from a bungalow in Broadtown late last night have appeared before the local Magistrates' Court today accused of breaking and entering.

A man who had been falsely accused of stealing ten pounds from his employer said in an interview today that money had always been left lying around the office. He admitted that he had been sorely tempted, but had never taken a penny. The man had taken his employer to court because he felt he had been unfairly dismissed. His appeal was upheld and he was awarded £500 damages.

There was an accident late yesterday afternoon between a car and a motorcycle at the junction between High Road and West Hill in which the motorcyclist was severely injured. Anyone who witnessed the accident or was in the vicinity at the time of the accident is asked to contact their local police station or ring Broadtown 7575753

The death was announced earlier today of Mr Alan Hope, a well-known local personality. He was greatly admired for his work with young people and youth organisations. He will be sadly missed by all concerned with youth welfare in the Broadtown area.

Listening comprehension texts

And now for the weather. The rest of the day will be fine, with some rain showers . . .

TUTOR: Now rewind the tape and listen to the news items again for sections **D2** and **D3**.

Unit 19

TUTOR:
Unit 19. Your verdict!
Look at page 158, section **A2**.
You're going to hear extracts from a court case.
Extract One. Listen.

POLICE CONSTABLE: I then asked the defendant if she would open her bag and take the things out – which she did.

PROSECUTION: And what were the articles in the bag?

PC: Oh. Er . . . there were six ladies' handkerchiefs – white – two pairs of men's socks – grey, medium size – a girl's kilt – ages nine to eleven – half a dozen eating apples, and a piece of cheese wrapped in cellophane. Oh, and and a 500-gram packet of coffee – ground coffee, that is.

PROSECUTION: And what did you do then?

PC: I asked her if she had bought these things in the shop. She said: 'I can't remember.' I then asked her if she had put them in her bag. She said she must have done or they wouldn't have been there. And when I asked her if she'd paid for them, she said: 'I don't know. I don't think so.'

PROSECUTION: What then?

PC: I asked her if she had a receipt for any of the goods. She said: 'Probably not.' Now the store detective had already told me that he had seen her put the articles in her bag. When I put this to her, she replied: 'Then he's probably right.'

PROSECUTION: I see.

PC: I should make it clear that these articles were from two different shops: Evans and Sons, and Simpson Brothers, where the defendant was apprehended. It seems that in neither shop did she pay for any of the articles.

PROSECUTION: And how did the defendant seem to you, Constable? Upset? Confused?

DEFENCE: Objection. This is asking the witness for his personal assessment.

JP: Objection overruled. You may answer, Constable.

PC: She seemed . . . er to accept that she had been caught. Resigned, in a way.

PROSECUTION: Did she say anything else?

PC: Well, I suggested to her that she had stolen the goods and had obviously had no intention of paying for them. She replied: 'That's not true. I don't know what came over me.' Er she became a little emotional at that moment.

PROSECUTION: I see. And then later, when you cautioned her, she . . .

TUTOR:
Look at page 159.
Extract Two. Listen.

PROSECUTION: Now according to Police Constable Hawkins, you said you couldn't remember putting the articles in your bag. Is this really true?

MRS JOHNS: I can't remember what I said to him. I I was upset. He said I was lying. I didn't like that. I don't think it's very nice to be called a liar. I'm not a liar. I don't tell lies. And I don't think it was very nice . . .

PROSECUTION: Quite. Mrs er Johns. Why did you choose to take from the two shops the articles it seems you did take?

MRS JOHNS: I don't know. I never normally buy my husband's socks. It was so stupid. And none of my grandchildren are aged nine to eleven. My daughter's children are er fifteen and . . . no, fourteen and . . .

204

PROSECUTION:	Yes, quite. So you would have no reason to want any of the articles found in your bag that afternoon.
MRS JOHNS:	No.
PROSECUTION:	You don't eat apples?
MRS JOHNS:	Pardon?
PROSECUTION:	I asked if you and your family ate apples.
MRS JOHNS:	Well, yes.
PROSECUTION:	But you just said there was nothing in the bag that you would want or normally buy.
MRS JOHNS:	I thought you meant . . .
PROSECUTION:	Yes?
MRS JOHNS:	I don't know.
PROSECUTION:	You don't know?
MRS JOHNS:	I er . . .
DEFENCE:	Objection. The prosecution is deliberately trying to confuse the defendant.
JP:	Sustained. Delete from the question about apples.
PROSECUTION:	Mrs Johns, did you have any money on you that afternoon?
MRS JOHNS:	Yes, about eight pounds, I think.
PROSECUTION:	In your purse?
MRS JOHNS:	Er yes.
PROSECUTION:	In your handbag?
MRS JOHNS:	Um yes. Why?
PROSECUTION:	Do you normally take a basket or trolley round a food store with you when you go shopping?
MRS JOHNS:	Yes.
PROSECUTION:	And did you on the afternoon in question?
MRS JOHNS:	No.
PROSECUTION:	Why not?
MRS JOHNS:	I don't know . . .
TUTOR:	Look at page 159. Extract Three. Listen.
DR JOHNSON:	Let me give you an analogy. I have today driven down from Gloucester – a distance of some one hundred miles . . .
PROSECUTION:	I hardly think this is relevant.
DR JOHNSON:	With respect I think it is. During my journey I passed probably over twenty sets of traffic lights. As I was driving, I was – shall we say? – er, preoccupied. I think it's conceivable, indeed quite possible, that I drove through one, maybe two red lights, without even . . .
PROSECUTION:	Possible, but unlikely.
DR JOHNSON:	Oh, very possible. Yet I am not a law-breaker. What I mean is: I believe Mrs Johns drove through two or three of her own red lights on the afternoon of the fifteenth, and may have been quite unaware of what she was doing.
PROSECUTION:	This is pure conjecture, of course. And we're not talking of momentary lapses here. This is not the absent-minded action of a second or two, is it? Mrs Johns, you will recall, suffered this – shall we say? – 'loss of awareness' long enough for her to half-fill her bag in Evans and Sons, cross the road, enter Simpson Brothers, and fill the rest of her bag there. Is it normal for the sort of lapse you're describing to continue for half an hour? Even an hour?
DR JOHNSON:	It can happen.
PROSECUTION:	But it would be rare?
DR JOHNSON:	It can happen.
PROSECUTION:	When did you er examine Mrs Johns?
DR JOHNSON:	She came to me on the morning of the eighteenth.

Listening comprehension texts

PROSECUTION:	Three days after the alleged crime.
DR JOHNSON:	Yes.
PROSECUTION:	And?
DR JOHNSON:	I found her an extremely disturbed woman – in an extremely disturbed frame of mind. The strain of tending a sick relative – her uncle, in fact since deceased – had left its mark on her . . .
PROSECUTION:	But enough to excuse her behaviour on the fifteenth?
DR JOHNSON:	You must understand that Mrs Johns is a very nervous and emotional woman. Six months spent virtually at the bedside of a dying man would affect the most balanced of us, let alone an extra-sensitive person like Mrs Johns. If I may say so, I cannot otherwise understand how a woman – with a husband on over twenty thousand pounds a year – would want to . . .
PROSECUTION:	With due respect, Dr Johnson, your failure to understand is not of great importance at the present time. If we may return to the facts of the case, what we really need to establish is . . .
TUTOR:	Look at page 159. Extract Four. Listen.
CHARACTER WITNESS:	She is the most understanding of people, who can never do enough for others. Apart from recently nursing her sick uncle, she's dedicated her life to the service of her er family, friends, and the community in general. This includes er considerable . . . a considerable amount of work for charity and er other good work. Mrs Johns belongs to that very special group of people who believe in half of the old saying 'Neither a borrower nor a lender be'. She's always quick to help, er to lend, to give, but she's never to my knowledge ever been in debt – in her life. Never had anything on HP. Never kept a credit card longer than it took her to tear it up and throw it away. This is the sort of woman Mrs Johns is: the sort of woman who'd walk back two miles to a shop if she discovered they'd undercharged her – rather than keep the money and return it on a later occasion. I remember her husband once telling me that he only wished his wife was just a bit more selfish sometimes. There really aren't enough people around like her nowadays . . .
TUTOR:	And that's the end of Unit 19.

Unit 20

TUTOR:	Unit. 20. Animal Rights. Look at page 170, section **E1**. Mrs Yvonne Weston describes herself as an 'animal activist'. Here she is talking about her attitude to circuses.
GUY:	. . . I gather you were one of the the group of people who er actually chained yourself – am I right? – to the the cages of the the animals (MRS W: Yes.) at the circus.
MRS WESTON:	Yes, that's right, we did. Yes, we had er there were about eight of us. We had chains round our waists and a padlock on them, and then in the interval, when they were setting up the enclosure which consists of large um bars for the cats to appear, (GUY: Mm.) we chained ourselves. Um, unfortunately, they had already been informed and they came out with their bolt-cutters and they released us; and the police hurried us out very quickly. They didn't want any um anything to be made of it.
GUY:	I see. Er, do you think this this latest er in a series of actions will be successful, that er er you will succeed in stopping the the circus er in the town.

MRS WESTON:	Um. Well, it's probably too soon to say, but we're certainly giving them a lot of aggravation. (GUY: Mm.) Um, so we're just keeping our fingers crossed.
GUY:	Do you really feel that animals would be better-off if they didn't er live in er the circuses with circus people?
MRS WESTON:	Well, yes; an unqualified 'yes', certainly. Um, I mean, if you were a tiger, for example, would you like to spend your whole life with five other Bengal tigers in a cage, hardly big enough to turn round, not being able to mate? Um, and deprived of any form of normal life? Um, . . .
GUY:	Mm. And you would be happy to see circuses continue, but without the animals, am I right? Er, . . .
MRS WESTON:	Absolutely. Yes, absolutely.
GUY:	Mm. And and do you feel similarly about zoos? Er, . . .
MRS WESTON:	Um, . . . Well, there are people who think that zoos can serve a purpose, um, breeding endangered species for example, um, an educational purpose; those two purposes. And there are a few zoos that do that um, but there are a lot that don't, and a lot that should be closed down today.
GUY:	You're you're a mother of two children, aren't you? Er, . . .
MRS WESTON:	That's right.
GUY:	Don't you think it would be rather sad, as far as the children are concerned, er, if they had no circuses, no zoos, if there was no contact er with any er er wild animals for the children of the country?
MRS WESTON:	Mm. Well, um, I think it's time that people realised that um animals have rights. Um and I think people are realising this. Um and I don't think I'm depriving or would be depriving children if there were no more circuses or no more zoos. Um and there are marvellous wildlife programmes on television. You get open zoo-parks like Marwell, where you can see animals in natural conditions, doing normal things. (GUY: Mm.) And in many zoos and in circuses certainly, they do very abnormal things. Um, so I don't think I would be d depriving children if zoos and circuses or bad zoos and circuses um were to be banned. No.
GUY:	Well, thank you very much.
MRS WESTON:	Not at all.
TUTOR:	Now rewind the tape, listen and do exercise **E2**.

And that's the end of Unit 20.

Acknowledgements

We are grateful to the following for permission to reproduce copyright illustrative material:

Associated Newspapers Group Limited for page 78, and the Mac cartoon on page 173; The Automobile Association for page 77; British Telecommunications plc for page 149; Mel Calman for the cartoon on page 37; Camera Press Limited for page 55 (top) photo by Joe Coomber; 'COI, Reproduced with permission of the Controller of Her Majesty's Stationery Office', for page 87 and 109; Bruce Coleman Limited for page 166 (bottom right); Cornish Photonews for page 122, photo by David Brenchley; Department of Transport for pages 76 and 125; Dominic Photography for pages 54 (bottom) and 126; Fotogram Stone for page 167 (top), photo by Corson; John Hillelson Agency Limited for page 64 (top), photo by Henri Cartier-Bresson/Magnum, and 64 (bottom left), photo by Jean-Paul Paireault/Magnum; London Express News and Features Services for the cartoon by Mike Atkinson on page 167 (bottom); Longman Photo Unit for pages 30, 31 (top), 70 (left and right), 71 (left and right), 74 and 92; Mary Evans Picture Library for page 131; Network Photographers for page 111, photo by Mike Abrahams; The Photo Source Limited for page 100; Picturepoint Limited for page 38; Popperfoto for page 92; The Post Office for page 118; Radio Times Magazine for page 46; Renray Group Limited for page 120; Rex Features Limited for page 103 (right) and 166 (top right); Bradley Smith for page 143; Heath cartoon from 'The Sunday Times of November 7th 1983 for page 34, David Montgomery/The Sunday Times Magazine for page 22, and The Sunday Times for pages 54 (top), photo by Paul Harris, 103 and 119; 'The Times' of August 5th 1983 for page 31 (bottom); Syndication International Limited for pages 55 (bottom), 64 (bottom right) and 166 (left); Weidenfeld and Nicolson Limited (by John Minnion) for page 140; Zefa Picture Library (UK) Limited for page 26.

The photographs on pages 62, 63 and 64 were taken from 'The Human Face' published by Constable Limited. We have been unable to trace the copyright holders and would be grateful for any information that would enable us to do so.

Our special thanks to Poole Pottery Limited for allowing us to take the photographs which appear on page 74.

We are grateful to the following for permission to reproduce copyright material:

Associated Newspapers Group plc for the articles 'Burglar's peg-leg alibi' Weekend Magazine No 4064, 'Karate Black Belt Gives Court Demonstration' p 3 Daily Mail 11/3/83, 'Nessie Surfaces Again' p 10 Daily Mail 9/8/83; B T Batsford Ltd for the 'Theatre Budget Sheet' p 62 Amateur Drama: production and management by Martyn Hepworth (1978); the editor, Bournemouth Evening Echo for the slightly adapted article 'A Look at Orwell's 1984 – from the perspective of a closing 1983' by Tim Walker p 6 Bournemouth Evening Echo 30/12/83; the author's agents & Lady Glenavy on behalf of the estate of the late Patrick Campbell for an extract from 'Tooking for a Lowel' pp 39–42 The P-P-Penguin Patrick Campbell (1965/7); Thomas Cook Ltd for extracts from Thomas Cook Holiday Brochures (1983/84); Andre Deutsch for an extract from pp 21–22 Boomerang: Australia Rediscovered by George Mikes (1968); Fodor's Travel Guides Ltd for an adapted extract pp 51–52 Fodor's GREAT BRITAIN 1983; International Association of Teachers of English as a Foreign Language for extracts from p 1–2 Seventeenth International Conference sheet IATEFL, Twickenham 5–8 April 1983; London Express News and Feature Services for the slightly adapted article 'Animal Lib Raid . . .' by Mark Elsdon-Dew p 5 Sunday Express 18/12/83; Market & Opinion Research International Ltd for questions 6 & 8 pp 3–4 North/South Poll May 1981, ref JN 6756 © MORI/The Sunday Times 1981; Marshal Cavendish Partworks Ltd for an extract from the article 'Aerosol spray can' p 28 How It Works © Marshall Cavendish Ltd 1974; The Observer News Service for an extract from the article 'And for our next trick . . .' by Judith Bull Observer Magazine 31/3/68; Office of Population Censuses & Surveys for a simplified version of table 15.6.2 from the article 'The Elderly at Home' by Audrey Hunt OPCS Social Survey Division, HMSO 1978; The author's agents on behalf of the estate of the late Sonia Brownell Orwell, Martin Secker & Warburg Ltd & Harcourt Brace Jovanovich Inc for an extract from pp 5–7 Nineteen Eighty-Four by George Orwell copyright 1949 by Harcourt Brace Jovanovich Inc, renewed 1977 by Sonia Brownell Orwell; Poole Pottery Ltd for a slightly adapted version of transcript from slide-sound show for Poole Pottery; The Post Office for extracts from International Year of the Disabled People Stamps Presentation Pack 1981; Punch Publications for extracts from 'nb' section p 56 Punch 4/4/84; the author, Ian Serraillier for his poem 'Prisoner and Judge' p 56 I'll Tell You a Tale © Ian Serraillier 1973, 1976; the author, David St George for his article 'Short sharp lecture in karate' p 5 The Guardian 11/3/83; Penguin Books Ltd & Gemini Smith Inc for slightly adapted extracts from pp 50, 51, 55, 58, 59 The Emergency Book: How To Handle An Emergency and Save a Life by Bradley Smith and Gus Stevens; Syndication International Ltd for the slightly adapted article 'Leo the Tramp' Daily Mirror 4/2/84, the articles 'Mick turns down £30,000 for a Little Wooden Hut' p 11 Daily Mirror 20/1/83 and 'Defenceless Japanese was Karate Expert: Black Belting for the Hotel Mugger' p 7 Daily Mirror 11/3/83; Times Newspapers Ltd for the articles 'A Degree of Conformity' by Brian Moynahan p 17–22 Sunday Times Magazine 1/8/82, 'Film-makers claim Nessie sightings' p 3 The Times 9/8/83, 'Nearly half of children aged 7 to 16 "have seen a video nasty"' by Richard Evans p 3 The Times 8/3/84, 'Disabled yachtsman triumphs' by Craig Seton p 1 The Times 30/8/83, 'Disabled sailor raises £20,000' p 1 The Times 17/9/83, 'Four of these tests would be banned in Britain' by Brian Silcock (slightly edited) and 'Animal Lib' by Peter Singer Sunday Times 20/3/83, 'Life doesn't end at 65' by Arthur Godfrey (slightly adapted) p 18 Sunday Times 5/12/82, 'Neighbours: What we think of the folk next door' by David Lipsey p 33 Sunday Times Review 12/12/82; Weidenfeld (Publishers) Ltd for an extract from the essay by James Herriot 'Vet & Author' p 71–74 Robert Morley's Second Book of Bricks (1981).

Illustrations by Gecko Ltd; pages 10, 27, 29, 37, 44, 45, 58, 59, 61, 69, 75, 83, 85, 99, 101, 105, 110, 114, 115, 142, 144, 146, 147 (top), 150, 151, 157, 161, 174; John Fraser, pages 18, 24, 46, 65, 94 (top), 104, 125 (btm), 147, 166; David Mostyn, pages 14, 94 (right), 103, 125 (top), 145; Fred Apps, pages 12, 86, 94 (left), 163; Martin Salisbury, pages 36, 78, 158, 159; Michael Ffolkes, pages 15, 20, 134; Per Dahlberg, pages 43, 91, 172; Ray Burrows, pages 40, 172; Lynn Breeze, page 54; Tony Kenyon, page 6; Pat Tourret, page 161; Michael Whittlesea, page 95.